You C[...]
The Dynam[...]
of Your Sun Sign
for Positive Personal
Change!

POWER ASTROLOGY takes you *beyond* sun sign character traits to show you how to achieve true inner peace—and a life of positive opportunities! In this ground-breaking practical guide, Robin MacNaughton shows you how to reach this higher level of experience, and how to:

- Enhance your positive sun sign traits through the unique gifts that each sign can call upon
- Avoid being controlled by fear or anxiety
- Know when and how to express your feelings so that *you* remain in control
- Tune in to your own best intuition
- Use simple, powerful meditation techniques to encourage positive thought patterns and attitudes that lead to success

With **POWER ASTROLOGY** you can unfold the amazing power within you! Just turn the page and begin . . .

POWER ASTROLOGY

ROBIN MACNAUGHTON

POCKET BOOKS

New York   London   Toronto   Sydney   Tokyo   Singapore

An *Original* Publication of POCKET BOOKS

POCKET BOOKS, a division of Simon & Schuster Inc.
1230 Avenue of the Americas, New York, NY 10020

ISBN: 0-671-67181-2

First Pocket Books printing February 1990

10 9 8 7 6

POCKET and colophon are registered trademarks of
Simon & Schuster Inc.

Printed in the U.S.A.

Acknowledgments

I would first like to thank Claire Zion for her great inspiring enthusiasm upon acquiring this project.

I wish to thank my editor, Sally Peters, for her excellent editorial job as well as for her deep understanding of the many complex factors that went into the making of this book.

I also wish to thank my exceptional agents, Lori Perkins and Barbara Lowenstein for their extraordinary competence, attention and care.

Contents

Contents

Introduction

POWER OF THE SUN SIGN

> *Everything we do, everything we are,*
> *rests on our personal power. If we have*
> *enough of it, one word uttered to us*
> *might be sufficient to change the*
> *course of our lives.*
>
> —Don Juan, in Carlos Castaneda's,
> *Tales of Power*

Power is something that everyone wants to feel within themselves. When we feel our own power, we feel more alive and have a greater sense of possibility. Personal power makes life more positive and situations more successful. It frees you from the self-imposed limitations that come about through fear and enables you to experience each moment more fully and with greater richness.

The powerful person is noticed, remembered, favored and rewarded. This person is both popular and privileged, and these characteristics imply a much higher quality of life than experienced by the average individual.

The *really* powerful person is one whose emotions are not easily triggered by ordinary frustrations and setbacks. This person has acquired enough inner peace and wisdom to be able to watch disturbing situations without being diminished by them. The *truly* powerful person maximizes experience and creates doorways of possibility in *every* situation. This person knows when to advance and when to withdraw, when to be emotionally dispassionate and how to express feelings in a masterful way. Most of all, this person has discovered a higher, wiser, more luminous part of him or herself that has its own intuitive voice which serves as an inner guide. No longer controlled by fear or anxiety, this person lives through the positive power of the highest aspect of him or herself.

This book will show you how to work and grow toward this elevated state of being through astrological psychological awareness and practical exercises designed for each Sun Sign.

Every Sun Sign has negative characteristics that hold a person back and positive strengths that must be developed for greater personal power. Certain signs are more instinctively powerful than others because of a tendency toward a particular way of thinking or behaving. There are also different levels of psychological functioning for each Sun Sign. These different levels create different levels of experience which, in turn, make life successful or problematic. So, in essence, the same day can be completely different when played out through these disparate headsets. And while we can't change our Sun Sign or the color of our character, we *can* change the *shade* of our character to become the best of what we already are.

The exercises, inspirations and meditations at the end of each section are very powerful, personally proven from years of work with a learned Buddhist master. Some Sun Sign exercises are longer and more complicated than others. But, that is not important. Each is thoughtfully designed for the unique problems and potentialities of the specific Sun Sign. However, all of the exercises must be practiced with discipline and consistency to be effective. This self-discipline and dedication is not easy; however, it is most worthwhile. After all, it is your life, and your life is very precious, regardless of the problems and emotional pain that may sometimes make you feel that it is not worth very much.

I wrote this book from the depths of my heart with the passionate desire that all of you who read it grow both more powerful through your unique light and more understanding and compassionate for others. With that in mind, on to the fascinating journey of the self, the mystery of which is far deeper than the mind's eye.

I

ARIES
(March 21–April 20)

Aries Nature

The Aries essence is the principle of acceleration personified. "Fast" is the word that governs all activities from falling in love to saving a hopeless situation. Ariens talk fast, think fast, move fast and have no patience for people who don't. Aries is the apotheosis of energy, and with a focused will, is equal to the most demanding task.

Ariens thrive on challenge and are born leaders, eager to break through old barriers to watch their ideas take hold. Their nature is fiery, dynamic and fiercely determined to have its own way, regardless. And because they can be such an audacious, impassioned, overwhelming force to handle, they get their own way more often than not.

Ask an Aries to perform a task, and consider it done. Ariens tend to move first and think later. And when they take off, those left behind can only stand back and stare.

5

This is a sign associated with courage, and among its members are the last vestiges of the truly heroic. Ariens are idealists, driven by their larger-than-life ambitions and sheer zest for life. They are the most positive people of the zodiac, exuberantly enthusiastic for all that pleases them and wildly impatient with all that doesn't.

A displeased Aries can be like a tornado: if caught standing in the path of either, there is no way to remain impervious. There may be disturbing sounds and things will start to fly, but it doesn't last long. An Arien explosion can be as quick as getting a hypodermic from your friendly doctor. Close your eyes tightly, and when you open them its over. With a breath of relief, you're looking into the beaming face of someone who's already moved on to another subject.

The secret to Aries temper tantrums is that they tend to be harmless steam valves. Yet most people don't know that and can't simply shrug it off and walk away. Negative Ariens know this and tend to take advantage.

A negative Arien can be a big bully, who in a bad mood will look to slaughter a little lamb. Among the less developed members of this sign, there is a cruelty that will come out around very weak people. In a miserable moment, this sort of Aries can say some shocking things. However, if courageously confronted after the fact, they have no problem apologizing for their wretched behavior. An endearing Aries quality is that they respect truth and will patiently listen if it is rationally presented. There is a disarming sort of innocence to even the most brutal members of this sign, an innocence that comes through in the capacity of trying to make the best of a bad situation. And after that moment, they want to move on, and not have, God forbid, the conversation repeated.

Aries is the first sign of the zodiac. Likewise, Ariens associate with only "the best" people and choose to take part in only "first class" functions. When immature, Ariens like to drop names and be seen in the company of significant people. Money, glamour, prestige and status are high priorities. Even more than that, though, they need to feel terribly significant in the midst of it all.

Ariens have strong ego needs and possess a desire to feel their own power, which can be very positive. However, when a childish, demanding ego interferes with the expression of a powerful individuality, there is a problem. Instead of a savant, we have a tyrant. Aries can be either and are very often both until they outgrow their need for show and tell.

This is the sign of great initiators; the idea people who know how to put their thoughts in motion and who may very well be ahead of their time. The psychologist Abraham Maslow is an excellent example of a great Aries mind. His pioneering work on peak experiences and human potential paved the way for psychologists working with people in terms of their power rather than their problems. Ahead of his time, Maslow focused on the personal power of extraordinary people and sorted out the characteristics that set them apart from the non-luminous members of the herd. In so doing, he was able to show scientifically that human beings are capable of a very high, inspired existence if they are able to operate from certain values. A classic Aries experience is to see beyond limitation, and in typical Aries fashion Maslow saw beyond the limits of his field and generated from it a vital psychology pertinent to the meaning of human life.

Ariens are highly generative and immensely positive in their approach to all they undertake. This attitude, combined with their extraordinary mental and physical energy, is most powerful. A classic Aries flaw is a lack of compassion for the weak and limited. Ariens are smart, ambitious and get what they want quickly. They are also self-centered and subjective and cannot understand why weak people allow themselves to be limited. Try explaining to Ariens a narrow-minded perspective and they will think about it, and come around and be very grateful. However, the next time they encounter a dull individual, impatience will once again prevail.

The Aries style is spontaneous and eager for new experience. A speeding bullet soaring through space doesn't bear any relationship to land. And thus it is with the Aries mind. Therefore, they can be both aggravating and inspirational. A childlike innocence causes them to cavort with the world on the freshest terms so that whatever their imagination captures, comes aflame. Ariens are also original, inventive and daring. Their joy and enthusiasm can bring the dead to life. Success is a *sine qua non* to their personality, which perceives possibility where failure prevails. Arrogant at times, yes. Bad at details too. Infinitely a child at heart dwelling in the glory of drama, they mythologize themselves and exalt their visions and momentary passions into peak experiences. Aries brings the breath of life to each undertaking. Exuberantly, they startle the gods who sigh and smile down upon the death-defying course of each new Aries challenge.

Aries Strengths

Ariens are like a light in a thick dark forest, a light which beams brightly into outer space. The Aries energy bursts forth freely, and is positive and dynamic, powerful and luminous with life.

Aries has the most magical way of minimizing problems and getting to the heart of the matter. Their thinking is streamlined and direct and their approach sharp, fast and focused. Because of this, Ariens know what they want and get it in record time.

There is extraordinary courage in this sign that springs from a vitality and confidence that sings of miracles. This is a sign that senses possibility in the improbable and that can create new conditions out of chaos. The Aries vision is progressive and expansive, and their approach enthusiastic and inspiring. They bring an incandescence to everything they care about. And as is usually the case, they tend to care about a lot of things.

To the Aries mind, life is a celebration of self. And the youthful eagerness that expresses this celebration encounters self in everything it thinks about. The immediate realm is an extension of self in the moment. And to that comes a spontaneous responsiveness that is positive, expansive and generative. Aries generate ideas, projects, people contacts, the totally improbable and always lots of excitement. Wordlessly, they plunge in and prepare for victory while others dillydally in the thinking stage. They can accomplish so much in so little time that it's understandable why these people are so impatient.

The positive attitude of Aries says action always knows its own reward. Ariens get what they want whenever they really want it, and from that is born a positive self-fulfilling prophecy. At times this self can be blinding—to itself and others. The emotion of the moment is more vital than peripheral considerations. And from this thrust comes the power to part crowds.

Aries exudes the spirit of *aliveness*. Ariens' snap and crackle wake up the world. This, along with a hair-trigger brain, is the source of their larger-than-life successes. Ariens are born leaders, living on the edge and loving it, making the most of every moment, consumed with energy and passion and happy to be alive.

Aries people tend to be exciting and dramatic, gravitating to the center spotlight and destined for matters of much importance. They can also be restless dreamers, fearless and fiercely convinced that their ideals will one day dawn upon the darkened world.

There is also a great deal of generosity in this nature that so enjoys sharing their ideas, toys, visions and bounties with select friends. Ariens are thrilled to help another get ahead and quick to lend a hand in crisis. Just as quick to pick up the check for a crowd of treasured companions, Ariens' largesse can be dramatic and far-reaching. The Aries mind thinks big, acts big and is big. Loathing pettiness, laziness, lies and disloyalty, Ariens go for the best in life.

This brings to mind an Aries boss I once had when I was a copywriter in a small advertising agency. Every day he charged through the door full of energy and ideas. Although he was the vice-president of the agency and the creative force behind all the wheels, it was not advertising or low-level power that invigorated him, but his utopian political ideals. In his heart, under all the surface snap-crackle, he was kind, generous and exquisitely compassionate. Yet he suffered because of this unusual brilliance and sensitivity.

Many years later I looked him up. At that time he owned his own agency, which was not doing particularly well. I sat through a meeting with a free-lance art director, and when he left, I looked at my friend and said, "You're not involved in this at all, are you?" He quickly answered "Nope!" and started talking about going to South America to become a revolutionary. At this time my friend was near sixty. "You're crazy!" I said to him. "What if you were killed?" He shrugged. "It's a good way to go," he said, "fighting for freedom." "But honestly, wouldn't you be scared?" I persisted. "Nope!" he said and started talking about transpersonal values. I was, as always, both galvanized and deeply moved by his words.

Evolved Ariens are interested in everything. The Aries mind is awake—thinking, pulsating, making connections and simultaneously discarding what is unimportant. Ariens are glorious sources of intelligence and wonder. Pure, undiluted spirit, they sparkle with a vision that dynamically sets the world afire. Breathless with possibility and impatient with suffering, Ariens will carve their own way and their will shall be done. *Affirmation* is the essential word of the Aries experience. When highly developed, Ariens are their own power and exude a luminosity that cannot be contained.

Aries Pitfalls

As one Aries man I once knew put it, "I'm a very spoiled person and the person who spoils me is me." An immature Aries can be like a kindergartner behind the steering wheel of a Cadillac. The windshield reads "Me, Myself and I." When out of focus, an Aries' nose is pressed up against the picture window of his own desires. And Ariens have a lot of desires.

An unevolved display of Arien behavior is one that is consummately self-centered and controlled by egomaniacal greed. The greed may be for compliments, attention, assurance, or plain old money and power, or all of the above. The more childish an Aries, the more obvious the size and nature of his or her appetites.

One strength this sign is missing is subtlety. And one way this deficiency comes through is with the kind of candor that can kill.

This is quite often mixed in with a touch of the boastful. "See what you could have if you were almost as smart as me?" says such an Aries proudly showing off his toys.

The unevolved Aries gains enemies like Donald Trump acquires buildings. Yet if forced to face the fruits of their self-deluded dreams of power and love, Ariens react with great shock and self-righteous outrage. Ariens' dreams are their condo in the clouds, and things like earth, and reality are far beneath them.

Self-aggrandizement can be an Aries addiction, especially when it comes to what the self owns and does. Often it seems that such Ariens own and do everything. "Just *please* shut up about it!" one is always tempted to shout at them. But few of us do, because the Aries energy takes up so much mental space that one can barely think, never mind speak coherently and with conviction. This sort of Aries can easily step on your feet and then scold you for being there.

In the mental space of the immature Aries, all of the sentences begin with I and end with me. In between, there's a lot of noisy chatter. An Aries I once knew taught himself to go to sleep when anyone else spoke for any length of time. Another Aries I once knew was so desperate for attention that he roamed around the room trying to seduce his girl friend's female dinner guests.

The Aries ego can be like the mouth of a voracious infant: after a while, one starts to feel sucked apart. It seems that in this sign there are only extremes. When Ariens are good, they are very good; when they are bad, they're horrid.

The most undeveloped of this sign have a sadistic streak that displays itself in ugly ways. This sort of Arien feels power from sabotaging the self-esteem of another person and will stoop very low in the process. One Aries

11

man I knew had the trick of hiring the most powerful men he could find from other companies just so that he could fire them. Little by little he had their furniture moved into the hall while he let them guess their future. This gave him the sense of superiority he needed.

Whatever the activity, immature Ariens have only one vision: themselves. From birth through love to death, this self-involvement is like a locomotive. And sad to say, this is a sign that often grows old without growing up. Power to this type means greedy gain at the cost of thousands or a highly significant few. Any Aries can win. However, to grow, gain dimension and achieve greatness, immature Ariens must suffer through their worst fears. Only then will they develop compassion and an ability to perceive the emptiness within everything it blindly grasps. Only then will they be able to look within for fulfillment. In the process their reflection may be lost, but a light will be found that will eradicate the deep anxiety and illuminate the way to peace and grace.

Power and Love: The Aries Woman

The Aries woman is on a quest to catch a rising star. Whether this is felt in the power of a moment, a person, a project or an affair of the heart, she wants to feel the rise and experience it as an extension of her own individuality. This aggressive, wildly energetic ball of fire believes her own dreams, ideals and fairy tales. She is a colorful person who is vital and alive.

However, when it comes to love, sadly, she must compromise. Despite her romantic desires, the world is not her castle. Before her very eyes, heroes turn into trolls and princes start to shrivel and give conspicuous frog croaks. In anger and abject disappointment, she looks away into herself. Many Aries women stay there and never marry. Others compromise or work hard to invent a suitable drama that will not disappoint them. A desire for connection is always there. Yet with age, her vision of romance changes and she is able to separate the person from the dream.

Aries

In the archetypal horoscope, the Aries–Libra polarity forms the relationship axis. Therefore, in life, the issue of relationship is a challenging one. Likewise it involves lessons which promote emotional growth. In the early years, Aries women find themselves pulled into certain relationships that have an all-or-nothing quality. In the moment of contact there is a sense of magic and inevitability that intensifies all experience. However, with the truth of time, these erstwhile mythic experiences come to require a great deal of sacrifice and sometimes a certain degree of sanity. They are, in fact, initiations of the self from which one can learn, change and grow into true personal power.

The Aries woman knows the value of her own individuality and expresses it freely. However, such freedom is often at odds with the demands of a relationship which requires certain sacrifices of time and attention. This ensures conflict. It is not uncommon, therefore, to see Aries women connected to weaker or highly liberated men who do not attempt to control them or demand that they leave themselves behind.

In everything she does, the Aries woman must play a dynamic role, and in the area of relationships, she has no problem being a breadwinner if she is mated with a man whom she respects. Such a man fires her passion and enthusiasm and cements her loyalty. On the other hand, attentions from any man whom she considers unworthy are met with chilling indifference, if not annoyance at the infringement on her time.

When completely and passionately committed, the Aries woman will not only give everything but will create anything for love. Aries women love the idea of being in love, because ideally they want all life's experiences to be electric. Grand love gives her a special something to look forward to. Even after the initial wine of the relationship has turned to water, the Aries woman will find a way to keep the motor running like a finely tuned Maserati. When totally taken, the Aries woman will want to spend every waking moment with her man.

However, Aries women are often undone by the all-

or-nothing syndrome. They don't want a balanced lifestyle because the idea of it is boring. Yet, balance will bring her back to herself in a regenerative way and at the same time allow her to extend herself lovingly as a full person who always has a rich personhood to come back to.

For the Aries woman to be powerful in love she must not get lost in romantic dreams that are based on psychological projections and lead, in time, to disillusionment. It is critically important for her to be aware of who she is and who the other person is, may be, and realistically *can* be. Romantic dreams are great fun, but they can also be very damaging. Realism, on the other hand, can help to make a situation creative, vital, deep and enduring. The Aries woman *can* have it all. She can have herself and the other person if she consciously decides that's what she wants. But she must first hold that as a value and take responsibility for her decision. Taking responsibility means that maybe things won't happen as quickly as she would like them. However, if she keeps her goal in mind she will eventually spark her own vision. And it is only a matter of time before her positivity puts her on a new, powerful course of love.

Power and Love: The Aries Man

As one Aries man so blithely put it, "Don't confuse me with the facts!" This is a man who is on a breathtaking quest for the ideal. And unless he is mature, this ideal does not have to do with character, Nobel prize–winning intelligence, or Albert Schweitzer–type contributions to the benefit of mankind. It has to do more with looks: a Dallas cheerleader with great legs, a *Playboy* bunny with big breasts, a Miss Denmark with ice-blue eyes, white-blond hair, Olympian height.

Subtlety tends to be lost on the Aries man, who is more comfortable with his clothes off and lying horizontal than sitting up discussing politics. Aries men like to get to the point—very quickly. And when it comes to women they resort to cliches and stereotypical visions. Aries men expect women to be women. Not stockbrokers, eye sur-

Aries

geons, or supreme court justices. If they *have* to be those things, then they had better look great with their clothes off. Shallow? Yes, when it comes to love and sex. It is no surprise that they tend to be lotharios.

The good news is that they are also masculine, enthusiastic, generous and not terribly smart about the psychology of sex. Therefore, it is easier to smile at them than fight with them, because willingly they will never give in.

Aries is not a sign that takes kindly to fidelity, since each new conquest is like an elixir of life. This is also a sign that can stay fourteen years old forever, while the list of women gets longer and longer. The Aries man will settle down only if he feels he's found his ideal or if he gives up and decides he'll never find it. However, his restlessness is not easy to live with. Unless it is channeled through work, athletics or riding his motorcycle through the living room, his compulsive behavior will lead him into yet another affair.

When immature, Aries men don't want anything from women except that they are sexual caricatures. Try discussing a little Nietzsche or sharing your favorite Mozart piano quartet and on will come the television. Come forth with your deepest feelings, thoughts, and fears, and instead of looking at the whites of someone's eyes, you will be reading the black-and-white print of a newspaper. On the other hand, put on a low-cut negligee, the newspaper will quickly crumble and everything will end up on the floor.

Aries men take great pride in being "real men." This they see as a source of power. Therefore, when it comes to physical pain or bothersome emotional feelings, they are above it all and want everybody else to be at the bottom.

Aries men usually don't deal with their feelings in any thoughtful, intelligent way. And they also are not terribly fond of listening. Likewise, their energy and charisma can be so overpowering that they don't have to compromise. They command, and that's the way they like it. Therefore, there is no getting around this issue: to get anywhere that has any emotional meaning, they have to grow up.

Unlike the other freedom-loving fire signs, Aries has a need for a partner with which to share experience. Therefore, that dashing lothario who acts as if he's just fallen in love for the first time, probably has a wife who's at home sleeping, and should she leave him, he would be shattered. Mr. Aries wants it all, and he often gets it.

Unless they are very old and no longer restless, Aries men usually do not know the power of mature love. Hot with life, they are determined to pursue it in every direction, without restriction. When faced with the challenge of commitment, *other* challenges suddenly become more attractive.

For many signs, this sort of lifestyle would seem shallow. However, for the Aries man it is his only learning experience. He is the first sign, the baby of the zodiac, and like all babies, he must learn through living the significance and mystery of experience and how its meaning changes through time.

Power and Work: Aries

Ariens are born leaders who have a very hard time following. Their drive and determination are boundless and bountiful. Therefore, in whatever they do, they have to be in the forefront. Their path has already been cut—straight to the top. And they will succeed despite all obstacles. However, they must feel the freedom to express their ideas without interference. An Aries under oppression is like a "pet" jaguar in a very small cage. Sooner or later, something has to break and it's usually the Aries' supercharged focus. No one can hold them down for long, nor would they really want to. An Aries who has lost incentive is not a pretty sight. Dull, apathetic and detached, their brain power works against them. Therefore, it is crucial that they feel their own power in their work.

During their upward climb, they are inspired by the challenge. They love having something to look forward to, and investing their energies in success multiplies them, regardless of the amount of time they put in. When the payoff comes, they're eager to move on to the next point. In the Arien scheme of things, something must always be happening or about to happen. Ariens can take crisis, devastation and disaster. However, they cannot bear a lengthy lull.

In this sign of superior brain power, courage and energy, patience is a weak point. It is this paucity of patience that can put them out of control. When impatient, Ariens can be restless, irritable, irascible and irrational. Without thinking, they can be sharp, insensitive and even scathing to anyone who gets in their way. Their sense of timing tends to be subjective and not necessarily realistic, constructive or compassionately conceived. And it is here that they can greatly benefit from using their own power wisely.

Ariens must practice expanding their perspectives so that they do not lose everything to their goals. They must stand back and take in the entire picture, which, during a waiting period, *does* include other people who have their own way of perceiving and performing. Ariens must also develop the ability to wait things out with dignity and maturity, and during this time must divert themselves with other meaningful activities. Ariens must recognize the fact that their immediate world is not contingent on the fulfillment of their immediate desires. Others have desires, too. When Ariens learn how to relax around the seeds that they have planted and watered, they will begin to develop an inner trust that can turn fortune their way. Excessive impatience is subversive to confidence. After a while, it starts to become like anxiety or worry and can destroy what they are trying to build.

The most powerful thinking is calm, confident and patient. This doesn't mean that Ariens will succeed in everything they strive for. But it does mean that the proper perspective will allow them to perceive possibility from another place.

To increase their power in the work place, they must be able to stop, shut the door and view the life of their undertakings from the side of the treadmill. They must listen to themselves as they address other people. They must ask themselves whether their behavior brings out the best in the people they're addressing. To go for the best in themselves and other people, they will get the best back. Sometimes that takes time, but to truly accomplish it takes power.

Powerful Aries Psychology

With freedom such as gods may give,
discover what it means to live!

—Goethe, *Faust*

Aries love larger-than-life experiences and loathe lulls. At times this impatient compulsion to see something happen can create limitations on your perspective. Try to make the most of *each* moment, even the little ones which may appear to be dead or dragging. Whether something is dead or "happening" is really a state of your own mind. Slow moments, can, in fact, be marvelously fertile periods for planning a project, or as a relaxing end in themselves. Try to benefit from all experience, whether or not it initially appears to be satisfying.

It is the Aries tendency to pass by quiet moments and quiet people in the feverish quest for what appears to be exciting and consuming. Learn how to switch the focus from yourself to another person, their joy, pain or pleasure. Seek them and draw them out. Make the experience of people an exciting exploration which you bring with you everywhere. When you get beyond yourself and are able to see into other realities and perspectives, and when you are able to take the time to *look,* you are opening doors in your life. You are extending your limits, and in the process you are creating possibility all around you.

On the other hand, when you allow restlessness to overtake you, you are narrowing your focus. You are diminishing it to a point. Consequently, that point is not an alive moment; it is not consciously experienced as something creative. *All* moments are creative. It is just a matter of your mind. When your mind is calm and focused, when it is compassionate, that is, able to empathetically merge into the experience of another, it is centered. And this is very powerful. All experience of life comes *not* from the object that is being experienced, but rather from the witness of your own mind. It is therefore possible to go through a circumstance of great external suffering with no pain, and likewise, to be given a circumstance of great pleasure and to feel only sorrow.

There are times in life when very negative circumstances may befall you that seem totally out of your control. However, in truth, these experiences are often endings to situations that you no longer need and that may be holding you back. It is the strength of the blind attachment that is causing you the pain. But this attachment exists only in your own mind. You formed it and you can decide what to do with it.

For instance, the relationship that ends may be because you have grown as much as you can with that person, and it is time to allow new experiences to enrich you. The financial disaster may be because you are using yourself in the wrong way, you are impoverishing yourself and must regenerate your entire way of thinking and being in order to grow.

In such situations, patience will allow you perspective and to see with greater depth and clarity. Time can be an important catalyst if you do not allow it to put you out of control.

If you make your mind center itself in the life that is you in *each* moment, you will not lose in *any* moment. You will grow. You will become multiplied by all the things that you are able to see, feel, hear and take into your heart, and you will experience greater power through being at one with all but being contained by none.

Maximizing Your Aries Power Potential

Your will and your drive are tremendous power factors in your personality. Your ability to demolish obstacles in your path is a doorway to all human possibility and a great inspiration to others. Your spirit is like a white light that leads the way. You must always remember this in your darker moments. You must remember your vast internal strength and your special talent for manifesting what you want most.

Along the way, there are always problems, conflicts, karmas and dramatic events that appear to dampen the flame that is your future. Should the dark times persist for too long, you lose your patience. Intense frustration interferes with your ability to think ahead with the exuberance that is so characteristic of your nature.

You can take advantage of these slow times by developing an inward-looking dimension to your personality. Go deep within yourself and divine the meaning of these times which are merely moments put in panoramic perspective. What have you been holding on to that you need to release? Have you been too impulsive at the wrong time? Is your sense of timing off because of your strong impatience? Have you put someone or something in the way of what you want to achieve? Has self-indulgent behavior dampened your fire and temporarily made you feel frightened and full of dread?

These are very normal feelings which fire signs fight intensely with both anxiety and guilt. Aries and Leos can easily burn up a planet with their brains. However, when intense frustrations persist, they start to feel like another person. And it's a person they don't like.

The undertaking described below will help to generate positivity during the more perfect moments as well as the problem times. It is called visualization and it is very powerful.

All the power we will ever need is within our own minds and visualization helps us to access that power. Your mind can do anything if you develop its power and direct it properly. Visualization has been used successfully not only to create positive circumstances, but also to eliminate negative ones like disease. For instance, much scientific documentation exists on the successful use of visualization to eradicate cancerous tumors. Even the rate of our heartbeat can be changed by our own thinking. However, what I *must* stress is that this works *only* with discipline and consistency. And that means working at it *every* day and preferably twice a day.

If you do it properly, visualization will bring you such rewards as greater intuitive ability, more self-confidence, greater emotional strength, greater creativity and the realization of your goals. And all it takes is practice and patience.

Begin by going alone into a room in which you feel comfortable. The object at this point is to relax. Therefore, this undertaking can be aided by playing soothing, recorded music that will insulate you from noises coming from outside the room.

Next, breathe deeply from your abdomen and concentrate on the rhythm of your breathing, in and out, like the steady ocean tide. Close your eyes and let each part of your body go limp and loose. All the cares of the world are behind you now as you communicate with your deepest self.

In your mind's eye, see before you the scene or image that you want to achieve. Keep in mind that if you are five-foot-two, you're never going to become five-nine, obviously. However, you may start to feel taller and begin to impress the world with the sort of personal power that certain tall people have. Visualization works for weight problems, problems with self-esteem and, as I have mentioned already, sickness. I have used it successfully for such mundane yet essential things as getting taxis in deserted parts of New York City. During one instance in which I was late for a lunch date with an editor, through intense concentration and visualization, I pictured a cab outside, sitting at the curb of a certain block, waiting for me. When I finally emerged from the building it was sitting exactly as I had pictured it, in an area where cabs never strayed. As I opened the door of the cab, I noticed that the driver was eating his lunch, which normally means that the driver is off-duty. I asked the driver if he would take me to midtown, and he said he would. Then he commented how strange it was that I found him, remarking that this was an area in which he never traveled. However, an out-of-the-blue impulse directed him down there to have his lunch. I smiled. Visualization was something I had used consistently as a member of a healing group. I even used more complicated forms of it to bring down fevers quite rapidly. Therefore I had confidence in it. And confidence is very important. If you sit restlessly a few times a week, picture your image and think to yourself that it will never work, it won't. It's that simple.

When you visualize your image, concentrate on detail, color, shape, smell. In short, concentrate on everything that will make it as graphically real to you as the last time you had a great dinner, or rode in a friend's brand new car. Whatever details you leave out will be left out when the visualization materializes. One woman I know pictured the man of her dreams, and in time, she met him. However, there was one very large problem: he was cheap. She had pictured him as being wealthy; however, she neglected to picture him as *also* generous. This is an essential point. Always take special care to include *all* the details.

One final note: when visualizing during a depression or negative mood, it will take longer for the visualization to take positive hold. This is for the obvious reason that in a negative frame of mind, you will be sharing your mental energies with the negativities that are consuming you. Even if you are not thinking of them consciously, they are still there exerting their own power. Therefore, it is important to compensate for this drawback by doing your visualizations more often, allowing them to become a powerful part of your life.

Patience is required for your progress—patience and diligence, which are not Aries' strength. However, your will, positivity and sheer belief in your own vision can carry you through to create greater power in your life. At this very moment, the future is waiting!

II

TAURUS
(April 21–May 21)

Taurus Nature

Taurus is archetypal earth, steady and enduring, solid as the ground beneath one's feet. By nature, Taureans are strong and basic, practical and uncomplicated in their approach to life.

In most families, it is the Taurus who is the Rock of Gibralter, the shoulder for all to lean on, the one who is unflappable in the midst of utter madness. Taureans sometimes suffer from being the caregiver in their families. Yet their poised, grounded, placid approach to problems makes them the likely candidate for such jobs.

Taureans are loyal and loving in pragmatic ways that promote positive feelings. Builders of bonds, nests and families, Taureans know instinctively how to make a house a home and can turn a dark corner into a cozy nook. Hospitable and gifted creators of culinary delights, Taureans entertain with a sensuous *savoir-faire* that makes dinner guests want to move in.

In earth-bound pleasures, Taureans have great taste. They come alive in luxury but can invent a sense of the

Sybaritic from merely Spartan surroundings and the most humble means. Sensitive to color, texture, form and taste, the typical Taurean personality can create from the simple trappings of life and can make something look substantial and seriously enjoyed.

Taurus is a material sign, concerned with what is tangible and taken with appearances that are pleasing to the eye. Taureans take great pleasure in their possessions, sometimes to the point of being owned *by* them. To many Taurean women, fur coats are not luxuries, they're necessities. Taurean women become the clothes they are wearing down to the texture, design and sense of style. Cher is a great example of the Taurean tendency to make style a sort of spiritual experience. Taurean women are strongly body-conscious and take great care in grooming and getting themselves in shape. Bianca Jagger once claimed to eat violets to maintain her perfect figure, while Barbra Streisand wears a diamond ring half the size of her hand as a sort of symbol of her material self.

Taureans have a way of consuming their own possessions, or preserving and cherishing them like objects of fine art. The sheer sensuous pleasure that a Taurean is capable of taking in life is something the more mental signs can learn from. However, like anything else, it is prone to excess and can pose its problems.

In the area of love, both sexes can reduce their partners to sensual or material objects. When the need for gratification snuffs out the subtle light of the inner spirit, refined qualities can become gross and sensitivity can be reduced to selfishness. Selfishness, on many levels, is the testing ground for the Taurean. Rigid in attitudes and shallow in perspective, Taureans tend to judge and condemn, punish and blindly bear grudges.

At the core of the Taurean experience is the heart. The Taurean heart either looks outward in loving warmth or turns inward and cuts itself off from others. A most wonderful Taurean quality is the ability to care and to do something constructive from emotions. At its best, Taurus can be as abundant as Nature itself, bestowing sunlight, food and physical beauty on the earth. However, Nature can also be a ravager, a power of death and a ruthless destroyer of possibility. Thus we have the Taurean tyrant such as Hitler, obdurately fixed in a vision and on a course of destruction.

The Taurean turned negative can be cold, brutal, violent and sadistic, the type of person to take a life simply to make an angry point. Bottled up and often displaced anger is a key problem of Taureans, who appear so serene and placid at first sight. Taureans do not deal with their deeper emotions well. They prefer to remain safely on the surface of life where reassuring routines lull them into a secure certitude that there is ground beneath their feet. Their own anger dissolves this grounding and plunges them into insecurity, where their demons can take control of their personality. Such Taureans, in a surprising flash, can become cruel and vicious, pull out a gun and shoot it, or take their own life.

Steady when it comes to others' instabilities, Taureans are terrified of their own darkness, so terrified that it often forces them further into the superficial trappings of the material world, which only offers emptiness in the face of emotional devastation and deep heartache. The first of the three earth signs and only the second of the twelve zodiacal signs, Taurus is something of a baby, fascinated by its own fingers and toes and blinded by the colors of its own crib. The sides of the Taurean's crib are the walls of daily life. However, there are walls defining all experience, and Taureans must grow and become free, not bound by their own compulsive limitations. The typical Taurean limitation is to be caught in a fixed pattern. The pathways out of these patterns, beyond the walls, out into the sunlit meadows, are only to be found within. The books of Taurean Shirley Maclaine explore this idea. However, each person must discover this freedom on his or her own. Techniques for personal expansion abound. Yet for Taurus, the most difficult part is the will. The will to grow is very weak in this sensuous and sedulous sign of emotional enertia, and the great temptation is to try to be with someone else to forget the inner self that feels incomplete. Wordsworth once wrote, "Life is a sleeping and a forgetting." This reminds me of Taurus, who must be shocked and forcibly awakened to perceive the true power and possibility of what can be.

Taurus Strengths

When pure of heart, Taurean warmth is a powerful force that is able to heal and generate love. The positive Taurean values love and expresses it naturally and freely. They bring that spirit to all involvements and attachments. The great guru Swami Muktananda was a Taurus. The blinding radiance that shone forth from his face was the power of his heart, pure and simple. Swami Muktananda represented the power of human possibility in its most exalted state, as did Buddha, born in the sign of Taurus, born to lead the way for others to discover compassion in their own hearts. Through the experience of its heart, Taurus is capable of great wisdom.

The evolved Taurean evokes beauty, pleasure, warmth and rich, heartfelt connections. Loving to share, they are giving and nurturing, kind and sincere. There is a fertile quality to the Taurean mind. Taureans' appreciation of the physical and sensual aspects of life is life-promoting. Taureans instinctively say "yes" to life by their capacity to enjoy material abundance. Likewise, their ability to generate it is a talent from which many other signs have a lot to learn.

Taureans often have more talent than they do ambition. Those who are not too frightened, blocked or lazy to use their talent can be found in the arts—from singing to acting, from painting to architecture and writing. And of course, there is the conservative world of finance in which Taureans reign supreme. When Taureans are determined to achieve a goal, they will do it regardless of obstacles. Taurean patience and persistence can build empires and make them flourish. It can wear down resistance through intestinal fortitude and the force of follow-through taken to the extreme. Taureans are stable and organized, responsible and able. Unshaken in the face of adversity, Taureans remain steadfast and unflappable, prudent in judgement and practical in the planning of their goals.

Loyal and thoroughly dependable, Taurus is a devoted friend during bad times. Generous and kind, they can be extremely giving in spirit, never expecting praise, reward or gratitude in return. The evolved Taurus is a positive person, open and trusting, cheerful and friendly, bringing out the best in others and seeking to also live through the best in themselves. This sort of Taurus values love and gives it freely to everything and everyone they take into his or her heart. They can also give love in a variety of ways, from the emotional, to the sensuous, to the purely material.

Taureans are born culinary masters and can make a meal a creative and resplendent extravaganza that is both attention-getting and utterly unforgettable. Taureans know instinctively how to entertain with great style and elegance and do it with such ease that it appears as if they were doing nothing at all.

Quiet understatement is the mark of the evolved Taurean personality. Humble and honest, Taureans are more interested in truth than in applause or in egotistical affirmations. Theirs is a solid, basic identity which is beyond the falsity of pride and the petty needs of flattery and fanfare. This sort of Taurus *does* what a lot of people talk about one day wanting to do. And there it is: an extraordinary creation, or a major accomplishment, while in the background, the person quietly admires another's dreams.

Taurean Pitfalls

Unevolved Taureans have a way of staying in the same place emotionally until they grow roots and the roots eventually grow immovable. Fixed, earth, Taurean minds are rigid and often narrow, bogged down by the banal and bound by their own emotional blindness. Selfish and insensitive to the feelings of others, the undeveloped Taurus nevertheless nurses her or his own slights and bears grudges interminably, capable of ruthlessly cutting another out of her or his life forever for one ill-chosen word.

Power Astrology

Undeveloped Taureans are materialistic, possessive, shallow and superficial, interested in self-gratification and uncaring of how they hurt themselves or anyone else to get it. Taurus is a sign that can place status and material reward way above and beyond human consideration, reducing other people to pawns or objects and playing power games to cultivate self-importance.

Taureans often covet power, the power of feeling terribly important because one knows the "right" person or because one thinks he or she is the "right" person or might become the "right" person to know. Along with that goes a lot of judgements that discard or fully deny a lot of nice people because they fail to meet superficial standards: great looks, lots of money, fame, formidably beautiful body, social position, polish, class, clout.

Undeveloped Taureans judge others from the outside as if the only human worth was how you look, whom you know and how much you get paid. Needless to say, communication does not get far before it hits a wall. However, the Taurean does not notice, because she or he is too emotionally dense to distinguish the simply shallow from the painfully bored and superficially polite. They also don't ask questions because they tend to be highly self-involved and preoccupied with the petty details of their own life.

Taurus is a sign that has to suffer a great deal in order to learn emotional basics that other signs are born with. Jealous, paranoid, suspicious, competitive, and often deeply resentful and full of rage, it looks for the darkness in a person. At the lowest, this sign represents the power of the purely destructive force of the human ego out of balance with what is pure and wholesome. Ugly and stupid, it is a power nonetheless. And one that is played out with arrogance and self-important ignorance on a daily basis in the Taurean realm of the material world.

Power and Love: The Taurus Woman

Her roots grounded in the eternal feminine, the Taurus woman is the old-fashioned "man's woman." Not complete unless she feels "filled in" with love, the Taurus woman exists to find an enduring, committed relationship.

Unfortunately, she does not understand men, and looks upon them in a literal sense, leaving little space for subtlety, complexity or emotional problems. Taurean women notoriously choose badly. And once they make their choice, they hold on with a calm endurance that defies logic, intelligence, and often sanity. Once they are solidly on the track, no amount of unkindness can get them off. Through storms of abuse and years of neglect, they will still find the energy to rationalize all wrong-doing, and what they cannot rationalize, they will do their best to deny. "He may look like a brute to you but I know in my heart he loves me" is the classic Taurean woman's posture. It is one that is so tightly constricted that it denies any potential for truth.

Taurean women often feel that they are going to die unless they are grounded in an ongoing relationship, regardless of the quality. Content with very little emotional nourishment and able to make do with what they have, they can hold on for a lifetime, never learning or looking very deeply into themselves.

It is impossible to influence the mind of this woman once she has sunk her teeth into the carpet and the pattern has taken hold. Impossibly stubborn, her thinking defies all attempts at intelligent communication. Enslaved by her own sense of stability, she remains fixed on her course, deaf and blind to any other way of being.

This brings to mind one Taurus woman who had a "relationship" with a man for seven years that was based on his dropping by her apartment for a Taurean-prepared meal and sex to be followed by his return to his office. This man, who made a lot of money on Wall Street, bought her one meal in seven years. And because of his busy, compromised work schedule, could not afford more free time than an hour or two away from the office. How-

31

ever, totally convinced that she was terribly important to him, she gave him a marriage ultimatum, only to see him quickly disappear. Later, through friends, she found out that "her man" had, in fact, been busy wining and dining various women. Someone finally asked Ms. Taurus what, in seven years, did she *think* he was doing? And she replied with total credulity, "Well he *told* me he had a lot of meetings."

On this subject of Taurean trust and belief, I must recount the "Shelf Story." A Taurus woman I once knew was married to a man who had emotional problems and who had consequently become impotent. However, being an Aries and having a large ego, he told her that he would not make love to her because she was a bad housekeeper. In point of fact, she was an excellent housekeeper and her house was spotless. One day a neighbor found her perched on top of a step ladder, dusting a shelf that was already polished. Asked by her neighbor what she was doing, the Taurean woman replied that her husband told her that only if she became a better housekeeper would her husband make love to her and that this was the only place in the house where she thought she might be able to find dust.

It must be said that neither of these Taurean women were stupid. But because the Taurus woman perceives through her needs, she often makes herself powerless in romantic situations. Fundamentally she is powerless because she places value on her attachment and not herself.

Taurean women become deeply attached remarkably easily. And they also have a lot of needs for both security and sex that they seek to satisfy at all cost. And quite often this cost is very high.

Until she comes to a place in her own evolution where she begins to value herself and her life as an individual, the Taurus woman will pay a very high price to remain powerless. Only when she gets beyond her primal urge to nest and begins to nurture herself, will she be capable of authentic feminine power: the power of love expressed from a place of wholeness instead of a needy vessel that demands to be filled.

Power and Love: The Taurus Man

A fool for a pretty face and a beautiful body, the Taurus man does not dig deeper. Nor is he carried away by a woman's character or brains. Unless he is very highly evolved, his desires revolve around security and creature comforts. However, what sets it all in motion is sex.

The Taurus man's nature is sensuous, earthy and uncomplicated. Once he digs his hole in the earth, he stays there. The Taurus man is possessive. However, this does not mean that he is incapable of straying. The Taurus man can be easily seduced by a beautiful body with an assertive approach. However, assuming that he is not so lucky, it is likely that he will be in the same situation year after year.

The Taurus man always marries and settles into the domestic scene with bliss. The classic Taurus man does not like to be alone. His consciousness centered in the conventions of the outer world, he is happy to carry on in his routines as long as there is a body waiting at home. Taurus men don't question. Nor do they tear their world apart looking for content.

Taurean men can be highly creative. They can also possess an intelligence that brings them a lot of money and power in the material world. However, within the context of their own relationships, they tend to be remarkably ignorant. Emotionally, they do not understand other people or their own inner makeup. Therefore, the quality that they bring to love is one that is complacently unconscious. Marriages can come and go, and over years, patterns repeat themselves, yet the Taurus man is still uncomprehending. He can be a Nobel Prize winner, yet ask him why he fell in love with someone else or why his wife left him, and innocent and baffled, he will reply he doesn't know. The Taurus man is not big on emotional understanding. Likewise, he never questions or probes. In essence, his sense of psychology is very basic. Black is black and white is white and beyond that, whatever something looks like is what it is. Intensely aware of color and shape, the Taurus man thinks, perceives and relates at face value. On this level, he can be an excellent provider who will offer both security and material support. However, as a person, he tends to be helpless when it comes to emotional intangibles. It is as if a part of his brain is dozing and the quality of communication is as articulate as a snore.

One highly intelligent Taurus man I know had his life totally shattered by his wife's repeated, blatant infidelities. Deeply angry, he blames her for his misery as if he were the most innocent victim. However, he cannot see how his completely self-absorbed ambition left her, an emotional water sign, with an empty, routinized, passionless life. Deeply saddened, obsessed and completely powerless, he can no longer live with her, yet he can't stop loving her. Caught in between, he is a victim of his own lack of awareness and insight.

Taurean men can suffer deeply without consciousness dawning and enlightening their lives. Fixed, earth, they rigidly hold on to blind emotional attitudes that support their foolish patterns and do not readily break, open up and grow. Because of this, of all the signs, Taurus tends to be the most emotionally powerless, perpetuating its own problems and in all its blindness, plodding on to prepare itself for more.

Power and Work: Taurus

When fixed in a chosen direction and highly motivated, the typical Taurean can outendure all competition, opposition and obstacles of every kind. However, the motivation has to spring from something that is highly valued.

A Taurean who is confused or who has to "find himself" is a Taurean who has to discover and experience his or her own values. So many popular astrology books equate Taurean ambition with the desire for money. However, fixed signs are never that simple and are always on a quest for meaning of some sort. Therefore, Taureans are motivated by money strictly in terms of what money *means* in their individual expression of life.

Taurus

Taureans value self-expression, and a firm financial foundation allows one to devote one's energies to that. It is not likely that one will ever hear a Taurean boasting of how much money she or he makes or maintains in various forms of securities. This is the dialogue of a daredevil Aries, an insecure Libra, a frightened control-crazed Scorpio or a Leo who doesn't feel that any of it is real. A Taurus, on the other hand, understands money. Taureans understand that in life money is something one should *never* have to worry about. Therefore, whatever they choose to do workwise, this is their basic premise.

Taureans are far more consciously concerned with power than with money, and this finds expression in many different facets of their lives. As the earthiest of the earth signs, Taurus is often overly status-conscious. This is tied to a deep desire to attain a measurable self-value. Taureans care what other people think. Therefore, they pay great attention to the details of their physical existence, such as how their bodies look, how their clothes look, how their homes and cars look, and how their children look. Taureans also seek to attain a positive self-value through their choice of friends as well as their work position. Therefore, work is often viewed as a means of establishing a sense of power in the world. And having power in the world is generally considered to be a high priority.

Taureans often possess "accomplishmentarian" philosophies or suffer inwardly from accomplishmentarian inadequacies. Therefore, the future of their work life becomes either an achievement of their essential values or a compensatory struggle for "true" reward. It must be mentioned here that the infamous Taurean Hitler was originally a highly driven, failed art student who was considered mediocre at best. Taurean fears of inferiority, judged in the most superficial and conventional terms, are characteristically played out in the career place. This forms, quite often, the basis of Taurean ambition, which brings in a strong sense of competition and a psychological need for material reward.

In the achievement of material power, Taureans seek

to snuff out that needy, vulnerable self, the earthly creatureliness and the anxiety about age, death and possible
aloneness. Only when mature do they realize that they
must still face the self, in one way or another—even if
only in the effort to flee it.

Powerful Taurus Psychology

> The circumference is the restricted, lit-
> erally circumscribed view of life, but
> from the centre it is possible to see in
> all directions with the minimum of
> effort and movement. The centre is the
> ultimate simplicity. . . . It is also the
> centre of power.
>
> —J. C. Cooper, Taoism

The nemesis of the Taurean mind is that it is controlled by
its own attachments. The need for attachments is powerful here and results in great weakness, deep emotional
insecurity and unhappiness.

Being fixed earth, the Taurean mind tends to be rigid,
inflexible and does not readily learn from experience.
Therefore, it perpetuates its own suffering by not seeing
the illusions to which it clings.

A fundamental problem in the Taurean thinking pattern is its tendency to look exclusively to externals for
satisfaction and fulfillment. Therefore, it is often lonely
and empty when left alone.

To become more powerful, you must become more
conscious of the subtleties of emotional and psychological situations. Quite spontaneously, Taurus often acts un-
thinkingly, from ignorance and compulsion, seeing
situations through the ego. This behavior forms patterns
which are repeated without consciousness or understanding. Consequently, negative situations arise that bring
suffering. When this occurs, the typical Taurean reaction
is to feel angry and victimized.

This lack of insight into cause and effect is the classic

36

Taurean stumbling block. It is like a block that is impossible to penetrate mentally. There is almost no way to get a typical Taurean to take responsibility for a bad situation which he or she has set in motion. Mentally, Taureans immediately turn off at the mere idea that it might have something to do with them. Likewise, they tend to bear grudges and reinforce negative behavior patterns by defensive attitudes.

It is important to understand that you can have all the money in the world, but you will never have power if you lack understanding and awareness. Without power and awareness, you will never be able to enjoy fully the experience of your own money. You must begin to hear and see yourself on the outside to understand how you cause conditions to arise. And you must begin to evaluate the dynamics of the entire situation if you are to arrive at the sort of truth that can liberate you.

When you rigidly say no to everything you don't wish to hear and remain closed to other points of view, you are cutting yourself off from exploring deeper aspects of your own psyche. Developing an introspective focus can be an exciting exploration that can actually change your life and bring it greater meaning. However, at the very least, you will come to have greater control over your own destiny, which includes the pattern of your relationships.

Look at your mental attachments. Look at them as if you were an opposing person. Are they self-protective? Are they defensive? Are they holding you back by making *you* hold back?

Confucious once said, "There is a great resemblance between the art of archery and the man of true breeding: when he misses the target, he looks for the cause in himself."

The powerful Taurean proceeds from this sort of understanding and builds further experience upon it. Deeply aware, and fully responsible, you can create your own circumstance and grow from it. Steadily gaining wisdom from your insights, you move forward, finding meaning in each new connection and experience. Untainted by fear and fully alive, you are free to be yourself. With time, this keeps changing and growing along with the sense of adventure and possibility that makes being on this earth a pleasure.

Maximizing Your Taurean Power Potential

To maximize your potential, you have to learn how to let go and free your mind of the clutter of emotional biases that are holding you back.

On its own, the typical Taurean mind operates from conditioning and does not question or probe beneath the surface of appearance. Quite often, there is no solid, substantial foundation for any of the habitual responses. The responses are often reactions that are limited, subjective emotional states. Consequently, the Taurean mind usually treads the circumference of the same circles, fixed in its course, never going deeper or gaining insight.

Taurean rigidity is its own form of death and likewise, it brings about a dead, mechanical quality of existence. The essence of life is that it is dynamic and ceaselessly changing. To impose a static frame on this is, ultimately, to bring about one's own pain. Taureans tend to cling blindly to the very things that bring about their own pain. Likewise, they cling blindly to the apparent security of the logical, material world where everything supposedly conforms to a set of prescribed standards. However, in truth, even the stock market has its mysterious fluctuations, the pattern and nature of which can only be speculated upon. The only true stability in this world is change, and the Taurean mind must learn to be more open to that change and to ride with it. In so doing, you must work on making your mind flexible and free, able to bend in *any* direction, open to differences, inquiring, perceptive, aware and interpretive.

When you open up your mind and become free to experience fully in the moment without inhibiting attitudes, your entire experience of life changes and becomes full of possibility. When that possibility *only* comes to define you as a person, you come to have great power and are capable in a thousand different moments of experiencing the subtlest of joys.

The mantra given below, called the Prajna Paramita mantra, opens the mind, magnifies the intuition and empowers you from within. Your illusions dissolve, your awareness is enhanced and you become able to deal with things more successfully through insight into their nature.

On a purely mundane level, extended, disciplined mantra recitation sharpens the mind, enhances the sense of well-being by stimulating endorphins in the brain, markedly reduces mental fatigue and restlessness, improves concentration and overall mental performance, and aids decision making. Many doctors, including Dr. Bernie Siegel, author of the bestselling *Love, Medicine and Miracles*, emphasize the importance of meditation for physical as well as mental maladies. However, mantra use is even more powerful and concentrated in its effects upon both the inner and the outer world.

The Prajna Paramita is an ancient Buddhist body of wisdom going back to the sixth century B.C. Originally it filled approximately eighty volumes. These eighty volumes have been distilled into one very powerful sutra or brief transcript. And the Heart Sutra has been distilled into one mantra. This ancient mantra, which carries the power of the original eighty volumes, is the most powerful mantra for profound transformation and empowerment. It is

gate gate paragate parasamgate bodhi svaha (pronounced gâ-tāy gâ-tāy *para-gâ-tāy* para-sâhm-gâ-tāy bō-dee svâ-hâ). It literally means, "Gone, gone, gone, safely passed to the other shore. So be it."

Gone are your illusions, which are mental encumbrances. The other shore is the shore of conscious awareness from which all powerful behavior proceeds. The safety is the power that arises from within that begins to manifest externally.

Recite this mantra aloud, vibrating the syllables carefully from your diaphragm every morning, in the still hours, upon awakening. Do it for *at least* twenty minutes.

Also do it mentally when you are tired, irritable, fearful, feeling emotionally out of sorts or out of control. It will calm your mind. It will give you answers you need to know intuitively. It will open up your head and allow you to see more with more depth. It will give you a deep feeling of compassion and understanding for other people. And it will give you courage during the darkest moments when you may feel confused, lost, or alone.

The more you recite this mantra, the deeper it penetrates your subconscious mind, and the stronger its power to help.

You do not have to believe anything for this mantra to work. All that you have to do is say it consistently in a disciplined manner and you will eventually experience positive change. This mantra is very powerful, and it is scientific. Doing it produces results. It changes your mind, polishes it. It makes it wise. In time, it frees it of self-imposed limitations. To thus change your mind is to change your life. And to thus change your life is to know true power.

III

GEMINI
(May 22–June 21)

Gemini Nature

"I think, therefore I am" is the classic Gemini code for carrying on with life. Geminis meet all of their problems "head" on and have a set of reasons for all of their motivations—including those that are purely emotional.

People born under this sign are smart and glib, social and superficially clever. Gemini is the sign of communication, and most Geminis can talk their way out of a maximum-security prison. Or, when the guileful trickster takes over, they can manipulate somebody else behind bars.

Master of the fast line, Geminis are comedians and copywriters, journalists and perceptive commentators on whatever is *au courant*. Easily bored and infinitely restless, they tend to leave a lot of unfinished projects in their path, along with erstwhile friends who become fatally displeasing.

43

Characteristically, Geminis are quixotic and not terribly dependable. The Gemini mind moves in its own concentric circles, and whatever slides over the idiosyncratic line will quickly be canceled out. Geminis use wit, charm and self-righteous reason to get their own way—and it usually works, regardless of the attending consequences.

Geminis tend to be self-involved and fear those who sabotage their sense of freedom. Seeking stimulation but having a strong sense of self-preservation, they will avoid anything that seriously threatens their ego base. Instinctively, they select and sort out what and who is most useful to their scheme of things. Quite often such discriminations are based on a desire for power.

The kind of power that so many Geminis need has to do with plain and simple ego assertion. There is a strong desire in the Gemini nature to feel superior and to impress others in obvious ways. Typical Geminis tend to get terribly caught up in the idea of having to be perceived in a light that is special and exceptionally favorable. Whether the specific image is "femme fatale," "sophisticated person in the know," "most competent in a specific area," or simply "smarter than everyone else," the self-consciousness is a strong controlling factor in their personality. Spontaneously, Geminis tend to perceive people in terms of image rather than deep, complicated wholes. Likewise, they seek to project an image they identify with. This image may be, and often is, false or subversive to the truth of the complexity of the personality. However, it serves as a sort of ballast which directs the focus. And it also feeds and protects them by making them feel important in a world that so increasingly places emphasis on externals.

The television actress Joan Collins is a Gemini, and it is so often implied that her public image is the image of her personal self. Yet underneath that cold, ruthless, power-oriented persona there is also an ability to love which may be the more authentic chord.

This issue of authenticity is difficult for Geminis because, as they see themselves, so they become. This can incite confusion and can insidiously bring about self-alienation. The energy that goes into having to uphold a self-created face can be toxic to the life of the rest of the personality. And needless to say, it does not promote growth. However, probing into the modus operandi of such a Gemini, one finds a large gap between thinking and being. The individual experiences this as a feeling of emptiness which she or he often needfully projects onto a partner. However, if love leads the way, it often brings individuals back to themselves through emotional disappointment. And it's as if life were saying, "You wanted to be this person to that person but that was not really you. It didn't work. Who are you?"

Quite often Geminis don't know who they are, and this can become a pervasive source of misery. However, this suffering, when consciously experienced, is the first step toward finding out. Geminis have to learn how to live through the truth of their unique essence, which is the trademark of their polar opposite, Sagittarius. There is such power available in being able to incorporate the characteristics of the polar opposite. In doing so, one stretches one's own narrow parameters that so often confine and define experience. In reaching past these boundaries, one reaches further into life and becomes freer to embrace many different possibilities. Ultimately, when there is true power, true authenticity, the personality does not have to consciously embrace any stamp or posture. The person just *is*, and is *fully* alive in the moment. That aliveness shines out, illuminating connections with other people and bringing meaning and richness to small moments.

It is a characteristic Gemini weakness to overemphasize the importance of intelligence, rather than penetrating into what intelligence *is*, how it functions, and how it is not *necessarily* a source of truth. When you come to a deep understanding of what an attachment is not, you can then obtain a much more profound insight as to what it actually is. Therefore, if Geminis could begin to look at their own minds from such a perspective, they would be able to realize, on a much deeper level, their own true identity.

There is great power in such a realization, for you are controlled by nothing, not even your own illusions. Our illusions are very costly in that they can keep us in an invisible prison where the bars are our own brains. The Gemini mind is highly susceptible to outside influences that, according to their own nature, fluctuate. Likewise, the Gemini mind fluctuates and feeds on the input. Therefore, it is important for this highly mental sign to become aware of the power of its perceptions and how their fallibility can form a situation that is ultimately self-destructive.

Both curious and inquisitive, Geminis should consciously develop the power of their own minds and make them a tool for going deeper. Truth and power have to do with depth and the kind of pure, free-flowing wisdom that comes from depth perception. This sign, so often associated with a split personality, must consciously work to become integrated. There is no power or freedom in fragmentation. In such personality splits, everything that's worth anything falls out through the holes. Scattered, fragmented or compromised, Geminis leak their own emotional life force through their mental complications. They need to slow down the chatter of the mind and allow their deeper intuitions to arise to resolve conflicts. To be happier, healthier and freer, Geminis must understand that intelligence is merely a filtering device designed to preserve its own filters. Within this experience, fears, biases and ideas concerning failure all come into play. When one is open to the fallibility of one's own thinking, when one is able to perceive mental attachments as nothing more than what they are, then one moves beyond the circle of limitation into experiences that have to do with learning. From such learning, it is then possible to develop an awareness that cuts through all illusion and creates an infinite, internal panorama with which life can ceaselessly be explored.

Gemini Strengths

At its best, the Gemini personality is like an iridescent bubble on a sunny summer afternoon. It is mirth and frolic, fun and fancy alongside a lot of light, amusing conversation.

Highly verbal and gregarious, Geminis have a gift for talking and taking advantage of the attention that their clever words attract. There is great power in their ability to generate an eager and receptive audience. Caught up in the moment, they lack self-consciousness and have the ability to get the most dolorous crowd to break into contagious laughter.

Popular and blessed with a fun-loving personality, Geminis move quickly through a variety of people and places, restless and stimulated by exchanges that spark their minds. Versatile and well-versed in an assortment of subjects, they have curious minds that take them in many directions. They are quick studies who love learning exciting, unusual subjects to which they bring the best of themselves. Usually well-read, they hold a high respect for knowledge and know how to show it off to their best advantage. They take great pride in their sense of understanding and quickly make the kind of mental connections that bring a quality of meaning to experience.

Geminis are highly observant and see far more than most intelligent people. They are in tune with the times and in step with the most *au courant* cultural happenings. Geminis have a special talent for spotting what is chic and tasteful yet understated. Their eye for detail determines their sense of beauty, quality and harmony and likewise gives them a flair for fashion, furnishings and fine jewelry.

Geminis can communicate fluently and through many mediums. They are instinctively alert to many possibilities and to seeing things from many perspectives. Their mutable nature allows them a multifaceted personality that often evokes excitement. Depending on circumstances they can charm, command or cavort from moment to moment, all the while giving the impression of being many different people.

When put to use and applied to some serious pursuit the Gemini mind is a master of its undertaking. Through thinking they can create an empire, a new language, an outlandish invention or a fiction that unfolds a significant truth. Being able to envision, connect and communicate with precision is a special power, a power that can awaken the minds of others and make those who are mentally limited imagine.

Gemini Pitfalls

Nervous, restless, capricious and compromised by desires coursing in several directions simultaneously, Geminis are typically capable of throwing a gala party to which they never show up. Immature Geminis can easily stand you up, arrive egregiously late or commit a rude, impulsive act and never call at all. Emotionally cold and selfish, they are centered in their own heads and caught up in whatever thought happens to be consuming them at the time.

Because the thinking process overrides their ability to feel, Geminis have to train their minds to work for them rather than against them. A powerful mind is a calm, focused, disciplined one. On the other hand, a mind that is out of control gets nowhere, and this is a Gemini pitfall which finds expression in many aspects of life.

Chronic sufferers of insomnia, many Geminis are overwrought thinkers. When caught in a conflict, they are unable to confront truthfully themselves and compassionately assess the effects of their behavior. The brilliant occultist, Aleister Crowley, did an exhaustive study of the charts of criminals, and discovered that the characteristic planet in most cases was Mercury (mental detachment), the ruler of Gemini.

To encounter this mental detachment is a chilling and shocking experience. When the immature Gemini decides that he or she no longer wants to hear a person, that person is mentally canceled out as if she or he never existed. And though Geminis form friendships with the sense of forever, when a serious conflict occurs that makes it not quite so much fun anymore, they kill it off and move on. There is a ruthlessness to this sort of behavior that makes it appear monstrous, partly because it often comes unexpectedly and is the result of a lot of solitary, self-righteous thinking, and partly because it has such a *fait accompli* effect.

This brings to mind one Gemini woman I knew who, upon moving in with her boyfriend, decided that he had problems that made her uncomfortable. She delivered the death verdict in the classical nonconfrontational Gemini manner: with the coldest and most deadly delivery, she uttered a vague, impersonal statement that indicated that "it" wasn't working. She never said *why* she thought that "it" wasn't working, just that it *wasn't* working and she was leaving.

Completely devastated, the man lost forty pounds. Nevertheless, he persisted in trying to find out the reasoning behind her ultimatum. He wrote her numerous letters in which he entreated her to give him some explanation. Finally ferreting out the truth, he explained his own position, and she, after some thought, accepted the explanation and moved back in.

Her lover had changed completely, she informed me with great satisfaction. I listened intently and said to her, "Is it that he *really* changed or was it your *idea* that changed?" Reluctantly, she admitted that it was her idea that had changed. I persisted. "Well, do you think that he was as bad as you originally thought or that maybe you were wrong somewhere in your thinking?" She admitted that she had been wrong and that she had acted on what she had *thought* she was seeing, which she now thought was a distorted view. "Are you frightened, is that why you were so impetuous?" I asked her. She admitted that she was frightened because she had made mistakes before. The result was that she finally saw that communication between *two* people, not merely herself with herself, was the only way to have a hope of any happy, healthy relationship.

Fear and ambivalence concerning commitment are classic Gemini problems. There is often an unattractive childishness in the behavior that is simultaneously tyrannical and lacking in personal responsibility.

"We're going to play the game *my* way or I'm going to beat you up with my toy" is how Gemini fear is often expressed. Anger, cutting off, insomnia and severe mental obsession are the avenues of this fear. The underlying cause is a weak ego which doesn't integrate the head and the heart. On the positive side, this is why Geminis have such remarkable acting ability: there is no true self and the fluid, changeable and mutable center enables them to become anyone or anything at all.

Immature Geminis very often pretend they are something they are not. Thus, here lies a subtle and complicated problem. There is a strong ego need in this sign, yet there is a very weak ego. The weak ego is masked by the fluency with which Geminis communicate, the extraordinary adaptability to situations and the remarkably quick time in which they can pick up cues from their environment. Gemini knows how to flow and how to appear to fit in. Yet under the surface, there is an anxiety and a gnawing emptiness that begs for something more. Being a dual sign and not an emotionally deep one, the elimination of this anxiety is going to be sought through the need for completion. In this sort of pain, Geminis blindly go to others to solve the problem, rather than going deeper into themselves to understand why, in the first place, they are alone.

In the attempt to sort out this problem, the Gemini will go over and over the details of his or her dilemma in the most repetitious and exhaustive manner. Hours pass, days pass, months pass, years pass and the story becomes more complicated, but nothing, in fact, changes. Gemini is the fool of the zodiac. It spends its time copying and criticizing other people and no time confronting and living through itself. The tricksters of the zodiac, Geminis fool themselves out of their own life through self-invented scripts and dialogues. Consequently, there is no authenticity, no sense of *now there is a rich person*. Scattering themselves or "spending" themselves on the surface, they fail to go deeper, into their own underworlds, where it is frightening, yet where lie the real rewards: emotional growth, depth and transformation.

Often, when Geminis do form relationships, they are symbiotic and dependent. I do not mean the emotional dependency of a water sign, but the tendency to use the relationship as a substitute for the self. The relationship can then become all-consuming. However, around middle age, when one has done all the experimentation and cannot successfully play at life anymore, issues of authenticity arise and demand to be heard.

The nature of the essential Gemini pitfall is paradox. The mind is at war with the emotions and the question is. where does one end and the other begin? Those Geminis who know the difference manage to get beyond themselves.

Power and Love: The Gemini Woman

In the first five minutes it may seem that the Gemini woman needs nothing but whatever she might be doing in the moment—and that is usually chatting merrily to as many people as possible. Because she goes with the flow, many find her difficult to read. Underneath the perfectly timed repartee, what is this woman really feeling? If she is typical of her sign, it is likely she doesn't know.

In the area of love and romance, she knows what she's *not* feeling and that is usually the excitement of being mindlessly swept away. When it comes to love, the Gemini woman has a hard time leaving her mind behind, and that is her basic problem. She also has a highly developed faculty for making a problem out of love. And that can become the focal point of her life.

If she is characteristic of Gemini, she is mentally in search of her lover's shortcomings. Likewise, she judges from criteria that are highly superficial. A Gemini woman can become infatuated with a man because he drives a Maserati. Or, she can become blind because he is witty, has a chauffeur, and chats with his stockbroker on the car phone. To the Gemini woman, looks count. If it's not the

51

face, then it's the family crest or the fact he *looks* smart and rich and runs his father's company.

The Gemini woman can turn love into a mental game where rewards rule the quality of her response. Or she can test and tear apart the apparent shortcomings of a person until that person decides to walk away. It is perhaps then that she will do a turnabout and find the missing person more attractive than she originally thought.

While it is true that much of love is a mystery, the Gemini woman turns it into a puzzle that is difficult to solve. But, of course, there are no solutions. Only shortcomings. Or the sort of made-in-heaven happiness that is the initial love scene of a grade B movie. Along the route, there is no convincing this woman that her version of reality may not be what is really taking place.

The Gemini woman is often more attached to her own ideas than to actual people. Because her ideas are so self-righteously important, it is not easy for her to admit that she's been wrong. She also likes to play head games and feel that she has the power to keep men guessing. However, in the end, the hardest game for her to play is growing up.

It is very common for these highly intelligent women to remain emotionally juvenile long into adulthood. Here we have the basic lesson of how the head can hurt the heart. It is a remarkably difficult task for the Gemini woman to operate from both perspectives. With her mind she manages to complicate her emotions beyond anything normally recognizable as feelings. This is because deep down, underneath all of the complications, she is either completely indifferent or very much afraid.

Gemini is a dual sign and one ruled by a mental planet. And it is here that we find the essence of the problem. The Mercurial influence makes her seek a mental ideal while the duality of the sign leads her to long for a soul mate to complete herself, or more to the point, fill in the blanks. Until she matures, the Gemini woman's quest for love is an allegory of her own selfhood played out from her head.

The experience of emotional involvement can bring a

powerful transformational experience, providing one possesses the ego strength to incur the risk. To attain great emotional power, there is always a heavy price to pay, and here it is the sacrifice of the Gemini woman's mental illusions. The more tightly the Gemini woman clings to these, the more they will hold her back, and the result is often a great deal of loneliness or shallowness which comes to define her existence.

By middle age, if these women continue in their mental patterns, they often feel doomed. Midlife crisis is a particularly difficult experience for Gemini, which strongly identifies with youthful ideals and which likewise suffers from subscribing to cultural stereotypes.

The challenge for the Gemini woman is wholeness. In order to attain this, there has to be, somewhere along the line, a loss of control. This loss of control is an experience which many Gemini women deeply fear, and rightfully so, since it evokes primordial chaos and contributes to a sense of lost selfhood. The Gemini woman finds herself through her ideas and thinking patterns, and should these be seriously threatened, a painful identity crisis could ensue. An intense romantic involvement often brings about this sort of crisis, and it is almost fascinating to watch this cool, competent, self-controlled woman crumble into a vulnerable, helpless little girl.

Marilyn Monroe was a Gemini, and the drama of her doomed life demonstrates the deep need for connection that consistently put her out of control. She was once quoted as saying that in the beginning she always thought men were interested in her and in the end realized that they were only interested in themselves. This one sentence demonstrates how she was a victim of her own false ideas and illusions, the pattern of which repeated itself with each new experience. However, had she been able to use the disillusionment, emotional pain and momentary madness, to see *her own mind,* and to come to an awareness through that of what she was really seeking, she could have gained power, and not have died a victim. Out of horrifying chaos *can* come rebirth—but only for the person not seeking to escape or deny themselves.

If the Gemini woman cannot face the truth of who she is and what her connections really mean, she will be weakened by the empty reasoning of her own mind. However, if she willfully directs her attention to living her life in a state of emotional honesty, despite the cost to her ego, she will eventually be able to bridge the gap within herself between her mind and her emotions. Only then will she be able to really love—without conflict, crisis, denial, or ambivalence. Only then will she fully express the total person of who she was meant to be. Only then, in the sharing of her *complete* self, will she know the power of her own womanhood. This power will expand her, deepen her and light the way like a vast, penetrating intuition.

Power and Love: The Gemini Man

You can always spot him by the twinkle in his eye. If he's not talking, he's darting glances in every direction and on the verge of saying something.

Emotionally, the Gemini man is very much like his natural chemical element: quicksilver. Now you see him, now you don't. Well, maybe you do, but he seems so different.

The Gemini man is a chameleon of sorts. He takes on the tenor of his surroundings. He is clever, glib and can talk his way out of *almost* any situation. However, where, exactly, is the person underneath all that noise? Aha! This is precisely the riddle of Gemini.

The Gemini man is a mind in motion. He is cerebral, cool, calculating and clever. I will never forget the comment of one male Gemini who confessed, "My entire childhood was one long thought." Many Gemini men live a lifetime on the brain plane, inordinately uncomfortable with their own feelings, preferring, by far, to immerse themselves in thinking.

Therefore, when it comes to the area of love, this is a man who has many lessons. And unfortunately, because he can be so slippery he does not readily learn. With remarkable deftness, he can change the conversation in record time. And when painfully confronted, will cut and run in his own unique way.

Unless he has a lot of earth in his chart, the Gemini man does not like to commit himself. Furthermore, commitment is something he tends not to think about until it assaults him from behind. To the typical Gemini, fidelity is foreign and confining. He wants to feel free to move about and chatter, banter, flirt or engage with whomever crosses his path. All the momentary grins and smiles aside, what initially appears to be so refreshing and friendly, is usually about as personal as paying your accountant at tax time.

The way to the Gemini man's heart is straight through his brain. His is a dual sign that seeks completion. Therefore, a mind as amusing, versatile and clever as his own will set his emotions moving. Whether it be the onslaught of love or the loss of it, Gemini has to be startled out of his self-centered patterns that preserve his modus operandi. And in order to be startled by any woman, there must be something in her that he would like to own.

This man needs fun to feel alive. He also needs to feel himself and watch it moving. Therefore, he is most moved by a woman who captures this sense of vitality. In this way, Mr. Gemini may be the least chauvinistic of men. He admires independence and individuality. He also has no need for a *Playboy* bunny, but instead needs a great friend where the sense of fun is never ending.

When Gemini thinks he's met his match, it is a match that might be taken seriously. However, this is not a situation for a security-oriented woman who needs lots of closeness and emotional reassurance. Rather, his entire being resonates to a restless, versatile, generative mind that makes him laugh, shares his ideas and ideally turns him on to new intellectual vistas, perspectives and pastimes.

Many Gemini men suffer from a Puer complex, that is, it takes them a very long time to grow up. Even in a black business suit, they can be tricksters, and pranksters, con artists and non-caring cavorters who dabble around for short periods of time without getting anything major done. They are also superficially very smart, often manipulative and have an astonishing knack for the sort of mind games that make something seem like what it is most definitely not.

Unless they have a lot of water in their chart, Gemini men have little tolerance for things called feelings and even less patience for prolonged emotional confrontations. The Gemini man wants the workings of his relationships to be like lighting a match. This is not necessarily bad in itself. However, at times his lack of emotional understanding is limiting. And he manages to mask this fact by being so clever, versatile and fast-moving.

His flexibility and fluidity are most definitely a strength. He does not stay angry long, nor does he dredge up the past, sulk or play punishing games.

However, as with all air signs, Mr. Gemini tends to confuse his thoughts with his feelings and project these onto the workings of a world of people. What he thinks people should be and feel, are not necessarily how they are. Therefore, as a person, greater power would come to him through greater understanding. And the avenue that provides the greatest opportunity is love.

Through taking the time to dwell on the differences between himself and his lover, he has the potential of moving beyond his own superficial state of reasoning into a place of depth awareness and compassion. First of all, he must come to understand the validity of those differences for that person. He should also spend some time observing how they work successfully in the complexity of that personality. Finally, he might want to take on some of the differences to see what they feel like.

By doing this he can begin to *feel* a person rather than possessing a static mental image of that person. The motivation can come from personal love. However, the growth and the understanding will extend to many people—people who at first glance look "funny," people whom he wants to label, people who have feelings the depth of which he doesn't understand.

In understanding other people with greater emotional

depth, he extends his own boundaries. He is capable of having more experiences, experiences that can be richer and vaster than his superficial logic could ever clearly define. In the process, he leaves behind the grinning, pointing adolescent who tolerates nothing outside of his own world. He becomes a person with perspectives who has a greater capacity to comprehend the emotional confines of his fellow man.

Love has a great potential for empowering the Gemini man—if he will let it. Its richness can make him wise and brilliant and able to extend himself in many different directions. The mind, then, has a different quality of thinking. It is stunning, insightful and deeply aware. Instead of projecting himself outwards, this sort of Gemini man has learned to take the world in, translate it, and incorporate it. In doing so, he communicates through what he hears with his heart. Love has brought its power to life, and it lights up Gemini minds and the minds of others who are so touched.

Power and Work: Gemini

Possessing many talents but having no singular identity, Geminis have to find themselves through work. And that is not always easy.

In general, Geminis do not like to compromise their values. Therefore, career considerations have less to do with making megabucks than with securing a sense of freedom and autonomy in an area that is stimulating but not confining. Idealistic, and sometimes rigid in outlook, Geminis are strongly guided by their beliefs rather than by the dream of a big bank account.

Commonly thought of as restless Peter Pan types, in actuality, Geminis are capable of remaining in one job for years, providing that the atmosphere works for them rather than against them. Security is far more important than would appear in this sign. Therefore, they can hold out for a lengthy period of time for the promotion that is down the road and the profit sharing and pension plan that will one day provide a measure of financial freedom.

Geminis tend to project competence rather than power in the work place, and when it comes to raises would rather avoid the confrontation. Never as confident as they appear, Geminis often lack conviction in their communication regarding salary and will allow stingy bullies to have the upper hand. This is an area they will be tempted to shun, since such heavy-handed battles wreak havoc with their nervous system and leave them sleepless at the very anticipation. Fueled by fear, reluctance and ambivalence, Geminis often settle into patterns that prevent the growth of their talents and abilities. Thinking things through until original opportunities cease to exist, they suffer from emotional inertia, confusion and poor timing.

Serious, persevering workers, Geminis are also often lacking in ambition concerning the big picture. Forever enthralled with the idea of being something rather than being blown away by actually doing it, they are often stymied by their own thought patterns. Only when they willfully push ahead, past their fears, consciously surrendering to the urgings of their own dreams and desires, will they come to experience their power in the realm of work. What usually interferes with this is a litany of rational excuses that prevents or delays the actual process. Geminis have to stretch beyond their worn out scripts and follow their own heart. From that central point, as from the center of the circle, lies all possibility. It is the place of balance between the head, the heart and the body—the place where all true power is born.

Powerful Gemini Psychology

The Sage . . . does not view things as apprehended by himself, subjectively, but transfers himself into the position of the thing viewed. This is called using the Light.

—Chuang-tsu

The Gemini experience is about formulating divisions in the mind. And it goes like this: This is good and that is

58

bad, I am right and you are wrong, this is the right way of doing it and that is the wrong way, this person is this way and that person is that way, this is spiritual because it obviously looks spiritual and that is behavior that is terrible because it doesn't look right. The mind of the conflicted Gemini can easily become a fomented inferno emitting gaseous wastes from churning thoughts. Geminis tend to make things more complicated by their inability to get beyond the surface appearance which often involves paradox. "I am what I perceive," says the Gemini, who takes great pride in the startling accuracy of these perceptions. However, they are not always accurate. They are very often *partially* true. And the danger of partial truth is that it's like being a doctor who knows a little medicine.

The weakness of the Gemini mind is that it never perceives *itself*. It doesn't penetrate into the *truth,* as for instance, what on the inside of my being is causing me to perceive the nature of that image on my mental screen. Is it my mental luminosity or is it a residue of anger, prejudice, jealousy, fear or resentment? Geminis never want to look at their feelings. They only want to associate with their thoughts, which will instruct them as to the next step. Consequently, consciously or unconsciously, those denied emotions come to have a very powerful effect on the mind.

The divisions that your mind mentally erects create emotional tension which can be highly contagious to others. But more important, those tensions are contagious to other aspects of your life as well. For instance, seeing your father with severity will affect your experience of men and likewise, viewing the mother as "distant" will dictate the pattern of all of your relationships.

These imprinted mental patterns projected outward on to emotional situations are so strong that they often come to dictate the experience itself, which inevitably has to do with some sort of communication breakdown. Too many of these breakdowns and your life will become a lonely, shallow, emotionally fragmented lie devoid of rich, generative connections.

The quality of emotional connections experienced in

your life is a metaphor of how connected you are within yourself. Therefore, the sorts of problems you have in relationships are the result of blocks within yourself. However, projected outward, lights flash on a mental board that read "COLD, WEAK, WITHOLDING, UN-TRUSTWORTHY, SELFISH, DISLOYAL, FASCINAT-ING, NEEDY." And the truth is that the people upon whom you impose these stamps may only *appear* to be those stamps. They may very well be some unheard of stamp that your experience is not prepared for. Or they may be many different stamps at once.

To empower your mind, you must connect it to your heart and let it have no stopping points. *Always* be able to go deeper—with your own judgements and with the feelings of others. Never assign yourself supreme authority at the expense of another person. *Always* be open and able to see in *any* direction. And above all, in your private life, renounce your judgements and your need to twist things into place. Each person in life, no matter how limited they may appear, is unique. Each person has the potential of becoming a miracle unto themselves. Look very deep and you might begin to believe in miracles. Go even deeper and you might even be able to become one.

Maximizing Your Gemini Power Potential

Your mind is your doorway to possibility. Or it can be your gateway to hell. What lies between these two states, is the experience of freedom.

In order to experience freedom, you must know your own mind. You must watch your opinions and beliefs and know yourself. In general, Geminis do not know themselves. They know their beliefs, their opinions, their likes and dislikes and their impressions of other people. However, they do not know the truth from where all of this arises.

The cacaphony of the mind interferes with the Gemini experience of truth. These thoughts become impowered by ego, and new illusions spring up. However, to be truly powerful, the mind must be free from illusion. It must be clear, penetrating, not attached to ego beliefs. It must be aware. Being smart, clever and observant of what others do is not being aware. Being aware is being aware of one's own mind and the games it plays on itself.

The following discipline is called Vipassana meditation. It can be done as sitting meditation, walking meditation or in your day-to-day activities. It is a powerful Buddhist technique and, with practice, cuts away all the fat and flab of false ideas. It strengthens and deepens the mind, potentially making it a powerful prism of awareness. It diminishes the false sense of duality and transforms the mind into a brilliant, hard, diamondlike vehicle that cuts through illusions and transcends the ordinary, deluded concepts of who you are. With time and practice, you will learn how to transform everyday reality through this highly polished consciousness. You will not be controlled by your own conditioned responses and therefore put out of control by vexations on the outside. You will be able to *use* every moment as an opportunity for greater awareness and greater power. When you reach this point, you will find that the most mundane moments have magic, the most limited people have jewels inside of them waiting to be brought to light, the apparently evil people have goodness darkened by fear and the people you would envy are people who are suffering—whether or not they consciously know it. To the very powerful mind that is able to *see* the universe in its day-to-day dance is not how it appears. The truth of it is always different than the appearance, and from moment to moment this truth keeps changing.

The practice of the Vipassana technique is a journey of discovery. When powerful and effective, it is a full-time undertaking, but it is an undertaking that actually takes you somewhere, as opposed to your own static beliefs.

The actual concept of Vipassana is very simple. It has to do with watching the contents of your mind as they arise and fall away through the participation of experience. It is best to begin by sitting alone in a quiet room. Your eyes are open and focused comfortably at a point in front of you. Clear your mind. And in *trying* to clear your mind, watch the thoughts that arise. Label them. Anger. Fear. Meaningless chatter. Confusion. Empty chatter. Worry. Pleasure. Chatter. And so on. Be mindful of how each arises and passes away. Let them arise. Do not hold on to them. If disturbing thoughts arise, watch them. Do not merge with them. Label them *disturbing thoughts* and watch them pass away.

What you are doing is watching your mind *move*. Each movement is a label called "Worry," "Anger," "Chatter," "Pleasure" and so on. When you are not deeply aware, each movement becomes an experience from which you attach emotional value and from which you form new beliefs. These beliefs contribute to your actions, which determine further experiences and further beliefs. And none of this has to do with truth. It has to do only with the movement of the mind.

In life, when you are bored, you tend to extend this experience by thinking "I am bored, oh this is boring." If you are angry, you extend the experience of anger by thinking "Oh, I am so angry, I am just furious." As these feelings arise on your mental screen, you identify your entire being with them, and like wild horses, they sweep you away. And when they sweep you away, who is left? When you can answer this question, you will have gained power and self-mastery that will enable you to deal with many difficult situations with ease. However, this answer must come out of your own perceptions. It must be a realization that you have from within about your own mind in order for you to have true insight into the situation that is empowering.

As a Gemini, you are enslaved by your mental attachments. They bloat your ego and they also pull your inner world apart. However, if you are practiced at contemplating your own mind, you will be able to watch this attachment, watch it as apart from you, and if you become patient and adept, you will be able to watch it pass away. From then on, as every negative attachment arises in day-to-day life, you will not respond to it through weakness, by being enslaved by it. You will watch it take form in your mind, you will watch your own emotions arise, and you will watch it all pass away.

I remember a time, about six years ago, when my Buddhist master put me into sitting meditation and left the room. He came back over six hours later and roused me. Smiling a big, enthusiastic smile, he said, "Well, how was it? Great?"

"Great? It was horrible," I exclaimed. "I thought you left me here forever. My entire body itched. Then my mind was so restless that I felt like I was suffocating and going crazy. And *then* everything passed away into this void and I felt like I was dying and finally, before you came in, I felt this emptiness and this peace."

"Good," he said. "You witnessed how everything passes away." I looked at him intensely, finally making the connection.

"It's just like the experiences of life!" I exclaimed.

"It *is* life," he replied quietly. "That's what life is."

As I developed this awareness, deeper and deeper, through constant vigilance during the course of daily life, a wisdom and understanding was born in me and began to glow like a light. Since then, I have had some devastating life experiences, and it was this wisdom deep within myself that gave me strength and got me through.

And so, in daily life, if you are trying to work but feeling tremendous anxiety and poor concentration, label each one of the thoughts as anxiety, mentally sweep it away and concentrate only on the moment. If you are walking, think walking, if you are writing, think subject and concentrate on the subject, if you are conversing, think conversing and become that experience in the moment. If you are dwelling in the past, let it go. Let your mind be a mirror, not a camera. If you are worried about the future, label your thought, some fear of the future and treat it as inconsequential, *not* a potential reality.

Always remember: *Everything is a product of your mind*. If your mind didn't move, there would be no distinctions, no dualities, no I versus you. If your mind is pure, then wherever you are in terms of time or experience, you will also be pure. If you have a heavenly mind, then you are in heaven. If you're feeling intensely miserable, you're in hell. With spiritual, Buddha wisdom, the nature of all experience can be directly perceived, and you have the power to be empty and to take into your heart the experience of the "other" and embrace it as you would the contents of your own heart.

When the pickpocket looked at the saint, all he saw were his pockets. When the saint looked at the pickpocket, all he saw was his soul.

IV

CANCER

June 22–July 23

Cancer Nature

Ruled by the tides of their fluctuating emotions, Cancers are Moon people, mysterious as the sea at night, delicate as a moon beam shimmering on the surface of a still and haunted lake. In their own unique ways, Cancers are haunted—by their fears and anguished fantasies, their attachment to the past, their driven compulsions and their quiet, self-obsessed dramas that sometimes move them to the brink of madness.

Self-enclosed and saturated with their own emotions, Cancers feel everything that they don't deliberately shut out. It is a highly strung inner world of intense emotional velocity that is ignited by any threat to their sense of control.

Sometimes sensitive and compassionate, sometimes cold and cut off from the impinging world, Cancers are influenced by both the inner and outer atmosphere. The result is a person easily pressured by onslaughts on their sense of self-preservation.

Because it is ruled by the Moon, Cancer is a complex sign: it is emotional, changeable, receptive, sensitive and subjective, and often so psychically attuned that it is engulfing to the conscious personality. Psychologically, Cancers tend to be sponges to their environment, emotionally absorbing so many divergent influences that it is often necessary for them to withdraw.

In whichever of the twelve signs the Moon is placed, it will have a predominant influence over the personality. Therefore, it is possible to know twelve different Cancers who are all very different. Yet one factor will tie them all together: a very strong, fluctuating emotional core.

When unconscious emotion is at the core of conscious reasoning, it does not make for an easy experience of life. Thus, Cancer is a remarkably difficult sign, claiming among its members a great many miserable people bounced back and forth between the demands of the inner and outer worlds. Add to this emotional turbulence a nature so sensitive that it feels assaulted by every sad moment and emotional nuance and you get a person painfully at war with themselves in what would be for someone else a perfectly cut-and-dried situation. Buffeted by mysterious emotional tides so strong that they can feel physical, Cancers bob up and down like buoys in a stormy sea, never knowing for certain from one day to the next what kind of person will meet their eyes in the mirror.

The composer Mahler was a Cancer, known for his music that stills the mind with melancholy. And, of course, Wagner, composer of the interminable *Der Ring des Nibelungen,* was a Cancer, clinging to and reveling in the tragic. On a more modern note, there is Carly Simon who sings, "I haven't got time for the pain."

Cancers compulsively preoccupy themselves with work and with creating and maintaining "secure" nests. But there is no security if the Cancer does not know herself or himself. Getting to know one's self is no easy business, since it requires calling up and facing all the inner demons.

In the Cancer mind, the unconscious is very close to the surface. As the first of the three water signs, much of

68

life is about learning to live with this emotional makeup in the middle of a cold and insecure material world.

In the Cancer experience, God often becomes the long-range future at the company, the children or the future marriage, the fully furnished condo, or the ego fully gratified by financial security. Often, it is as if these encumbrances come to have a life of their own which raises urgent claims and makes its list of dire demands.

Cancers are often criticized as being highly self-centered people. However, it is, in truth, as if there is no self, only a self-protective shell. With emotions so close to the surface, Cancers are hopelessly sentimental. They can be moved to tears by a love song, an old birthday card or a bunch of roses from a dear friend. In love, they are extremely jealous and quietly possessive—until something happens in which they make their voice heard. Generous to a fault, they can be fools for love.

When very immature, Cancers possess the conviction that they are what they cling to—until they lose their hold and, with horror, are brought back to themselves. But by looking deep into their souls, they have the potential of becoming whole individuals who no longer need a shell.

Cancer Strengths

The light of the Moon is subtle, inspirational and sometimes eerie. There is always a cold, quiet mystery, and magic that emanates from it. Sometimes, there is also a sense of madness. But it is its own power, nonetheless.

Ruled by the Moon, Cancers have their own subtle power. Often, they have to find it, just as they have to find themselves amid the onslaughts of moods that arise mysteriously. Nevertheless, the Moon is one of the two lights or planetary powers of the universe. To be ruled by the Moon can be a source of strength when you become conscious of it and do not live blindly.

The eighteenth-century Cancerian philosopher Jean-Jacques Rousseau once wrote, "Man is born free and everywhere he is in chains." Observing Cancerian behavior with great scrutiny, I have felt this many times. Cancers have to learn how to contact their own light. It is not like a solar light, which is obvious and often overwhelming. Cancerian light is subtle, poetic, emotional and contemplative. In contacting it and living through it, Cancers can find their own unique wisdom.

Cancerian sensitivity is a most powerful gift of this sign. However, one must know how to use it. Cancers often want to run from their own sensitivity because it can envelop and overwhelm them. But this is only when one is stuck in fear.

It is the nature of Cancer to give birth—in every sense of the word. The most enlightened Cancer makes life a continuous series of births. It gives birth to its visions. It gives birth to its creativity. It gives birth to its dreams and experiences them coming alive.

In every Cancer there is a beautiful, creative child struggling to come out. It is a child hot with life and mad with joy—the madness of children at dusk, still wild with play. It is the madness of being drunkenly in love or driven wild with the rush of the ocean in one's face.

However, so many Cancers don't allow that child life. No wonder Cancers often get depressed. They are denying the beauty in themselves and violating a fundamental rule. For the neglected inner Cancer child, every night is a school night and every day is a list of duties that must get done. However, when Cancers give birth to themselves as creations, they make every act a creative act.

The Cancer that is thriving on its unique vision lives vitally through the imagination. The inner child always has bright balloons with which to play. The adult makes an interesting moment out of many little ones.

Cancers are enormously intuitive, intelligent and aware of people. However, they must make their intelligence work for them. When their focus extends outward in natural sympathy and compassion, the heart can bring one out of the enclosure of the clouds into the limitless expanse of sky. When Cancer leaves behind its ego it throbs with life and extends the circle of itself outward. Looking deep into a Cancer's eyes one can see great depth and emotional power. It is just a matter of quieting the fear to allow the force to overflow.

Cancer Pitfalls

If I were writing a book exclusively about the Cancer experience, I would title it *Enclosures.* Psychologically, Cancers tend to be enclosed people. All of their problems stem from this.

From the enclosure of their mind's eye, the outside world is perceived and the inside world projected. Cancers project their fears, their demons, their fantasies, their past failures and their future hopes onto the people with whom they significantly interact. Quite often, these human beings are reduced to psychological archetypes in their personal psychodramas.

In such a manner, Cancer can be enormously self-centered. As the rational mind becomes swamped by the subjective inner world, Cancers can get caught up in little else. In the heat of such moments, Cancers can act impulsively and destructively, heedless of other peoples' feelings as well as of future consequences.

Unfortunately, emotionally retentive people who absorb inconsiderate behavior hold on to the bad moments and begin to look upon the person in a much colder light. However, Cancers tend to be oblivious to how badly their negative behavior can look from the outside. In fact, sometimes they use negative behavior as a psychological weapon.

This dynamic has to do with the disapproving "Mommy" within the Cancer punishing someone else they perceive as a "bad child." Or it can be the Cancer playing the bad child who conspicuously cuts off to punish "the Mommy" or the child's "bad playmate." Cancer can become exceedingly childish when hurt or disappointed. Quite spontaneously, Cancers can lapse into punishing as a self-justified means of communication.

Because of their inconsistent behavior Cancers are often looked upon as enigmas worthy of distrust. Likewise often perfectionistic, highly driven and compulsive in their work, Cancers don't trust themselves or anyone else who is capable of less. Too narrowly focused under pressure, they have a poor sense of the perspective from which they formulate the standards they impose on others.

The small, ego-bound state of the Cancer mind, buffeted about by extremes of like and dislike, desire and fear, deep anguish and the thirst for deliverance is a primitive enclosure.

How to get out of the prison? Cancers must let go, straighten out the emotional gnarls, and see beyond—beyond all the self-imposed postures straight to their own deaths. Cancers must see themselves dying in a difficult emotional moment. All the petty concerns of the small "I" will appear like what they are—small, transitory and not terribly significant moments. Death can be a powerful motivator for experiencing greater life. Playing with the idea of death may seem frightening, but what is even more frightening is someone who is dead *in* life. That is what the enclosure of the self does to the Cancerian sensibility.

It is the thick, wet blanket of negative emotional attitudes which doesn't allow the Cancer to expand. The small enclosure does not think in terms of thriving; it is concerned with surviving. This issue is played out on many different levels—actual and metaphorical. The Cancerian need for closeness, assurance and security in relationships can be extremely suffocating. When the pinchers of the crab finally click into place, they do not let go. Thus we have the classic Cancer problem of security. Cancerian neediness is highly narcissistic and not conducive to a healthy, generative exchange. In his book, *Honoring the Self,* psychologist Nathaniel Branden says,

"Emotionally mature, autonomous individuals understand that other people do not exist merely to satisfy their needs . . . [such an] individual does not experience his or her self-esteem as continually in question or in jeopardy. The source of approval resides within the self.

72

Emotionally immature Cancers seek completion and will control, manipulate, or cling until they get it. It is here, again, that the enclosure concept comes to bear. What such Cancers propose in the name of love, is, in truth, a containing and confining enclosure. This experience is also a highly controlling one because it is saying "Come into my little cage now. I'm going to lock you up and we will love."

But love is about freedom and possibility, not confinement and enclosure. It is about respect for one's beingness, which includes others' boundaries. It is not a grasping state. It is an open one. That is its power.

The essence of Cancerian pitfalls is that they proceed from and proceed to emotional powerlessness. And this brings us to the subject of anger.

Anger is a key problem for this sign, which often does not express itself effectively. There can be passive-aggressive behavior expressed in undercutting comments. There can be bitchiness, petulance, pouting, the cold shoulder or depression and complete emotional withdrawal. Anger is a terribly difficult issue for this sign, which literally is overwhelmed by its own feelings.

Cancer has to work consciously on creating responses to anger-producing situations that generate positive rather than negative communicative responses. Through communicating, Cancer must clearly explain its own emotional reaction rather than willfully and hotly accuse. Whatever the misunderstanding, it *can* be talked out and resolved without further injury if one tries to think about the perspectives of *both* sides. Once again, one has to get beyond the walls of the enclosure.

When the Cancer is able to reach out beyond the "enclosed self," when it is able to straighten out the cramps to spontaneously embrace, and when it is able to take the time and effort to show more compassion to those they are quick to judge or scold, it will be getting beyond old, crippling boundaries to live more powerfully within itself.

Power and Love: The Cancer Woman

The Cancer woman has such overdeveloped emotions that she could live without a body or a mind. Look into a Cancer woman's eyes and you see her emotions. They are her core. Indeed, they are a powerful source of intelligence and creativity.

"I believe in love," sings Cancer Carly Simon. The Cancer woman could have invented it. Love and often nurturance are her nature, and despite experience, she is never jaded.

Sensitive, kind and emotionally aware, the Cancer woman seeks deep emotional bonds that bring her back to her soul. She yearns to be awed by such connections, and lives for the feeling of closeness that comes with trusted, intimate sharing.

When a Cancer woman chooses to be receptive, she is all there. Yet at the same time, she is not indiscriminately moved either. However, consciously, she creates emotional boundaries which she maneuvers depending on the situation. Moody but not neurotically complicated, changeable but not capricious, when feeling emotionally fulfilled she is at her best. And she shows it.

Nostalgic, sentimental and sometimes weepy, a Cancer woman will dwell in memories and become profoundly moved by old, meaningful love songs. If unfulfilled by the present, the Cancer woman will inflate the past and gloss over the bad moments.

Blighted by bad mood swings, the Cancer woman can become obsessively internal, the thunder of her own thoughts silencing the sounds of the outside world. The feeling of love brings her back to a self that is fundamental. Love vitalizes her and fills her out in all the right inner places. She is restored through this nourishing state.

The Cancer woman's response to life is intensely personal and too often subjective. Princess Di, Jerry Hall and Brigitte Nielsen all fall into this domain. Such narcissism counters the feminine Cancerian power which nurtures and supports, generates and heals.

A Cancer woman who manifests the power of love

without using it to attract attention is pure and full of potential wisdom. The balance of giving and getting is her greatest challenge. When she achieves her emotion potential, she has a heart that is so loving it can heal the pain of all who pass through it.

Power and Love: The Cancer Man

The Cancer man is a kind of conundrum when it comes to the murky area of his emotions. Misunderstood by many and often puzzled by himself, he is an enigma who often gets in his own way.

Cancer is an unnatural sign for a man to be born in for a number of reasons. First of all, it is ruled by the Moon, the archetype of the feminine consciousness, which has to do with sensitivity, emotionality, nurturing, mothering and moods. Being a man with the emotional makeup of a woman isn't easy. But that's just the beginning. As the ruler of the tides, the Moon also involves change and fluctuation. And as the light of the night, its nature is one of mystery and lunacy, emotional instability and fertility cycles. Combine all of these peculiar factors and pour them into the brain of a masculine body, and there is bound to be a little turmoil. With the Cancer man this complexity has an uncanny way of forming the core of the character.

Emotionally and psychologically, the Cancer man is half woman. There are, of course, those Cancer men who strongly compensate for their makeup—Ernest Hemingway being one. A significant proportion of Cancer men are homosexual, a great many are emotionally masochistic, and all have an overbearing mother figure in the back of the brain that they are either bound to or want to run from.

The experience of love for many Cancer men is a very painful process in which they are challenged to know themselves in a more conscious light. Often compulsively attracted to the people who want to reject them and cold as stone to those they happen to attract, Cancer men writhe in a miasma of emotional frustration that does not necessarily get easier with time. Falling in love with several people is often like suffering a series of little deaths. Yet when the denouement of the emotional blight actually strikes, it is always with the severity of a *coup de foudre*.

It is so peculiar that so many Cancer men, right from the beginning, sense a rejecting situation and run for it. It must be stressed that this is a man who has extraordinary powers of intuitive perception. Yet when the red light goes on in the other person, the claws spring forth and lock into place. From this point onward, it is a progressive decline.

Suffering has a profound place in the Cancer man's life, and the men who don't want to deal with that often become completely promiscuous or avoid deep involvement altogether. The irony, of course, is that the Cancer man will talk of love like no other sign. They will chat on about their need for love and the "right" relationship. But in truth, all of those guys doing the talking are not doing any attracting. When, without conflict in one's heart, one really wants something, it manifests itself. In the case of the Cancer man, what often manifests itself is the feeling of profound emptiness. So it is here that he must begin to encounter the real person.

Cancer is a sign that does a great deal of psychological projection. What appears to be on the outside is really on the inside of one's mind. Many Cancer men get so caught up in their daily routines that they do not consciously deal with themselves, do not deal with the relationship between the masculine and the feminine within. Therefore, their unconscious contents are projected outward. The core of these projections have to do with one thing: power.

Cancer men tend to be power-oriented in emotionally immature ways. They seek to control others through negative behavior, and they in turn are attracted by cold, power-oriented people who have a very strong need for control and dominance. Often weak, fragile and passive on the surface, Cancer men, when masochistic, project their own unconscious desire for control and dominance onto the fatal attraction. They are enslaved in an emotional bondage that feels like closeness. But what a price! And indeed it is merely a matter of time until the bond is broken by it.

Like all water signs, Cancer deeply wants to merge, and throwing in a lot of security needs along with this can confuse emotional realities. What appeared to be intensity can turn into masochistic enslavement. Something deep within the Cancer nature feels it has to pay a price for love. This is because of the prevalence of fear which denies the right to have happiness. Therefore, the Cancer man's involvements are a way of finding himself—who he really is and who he isn't. What sorts out the illusions from the truth is a lot of emotional frustration.

The experience of love for the Cancer man is like the search for the Holy Grail. It is in essence spiritual because it involves the discovery of his own spirit through another. Therefore, the illusory projections that are experienced along the way are extremely painful because they are felt as loss of self, which, over time, can dwindle into an anguished emptiness, and in some cases, into suicidal despair. The despair is about emotional, psychological, spiritual completion, the absence of which is felt as a wound. Like Parsifal, there is often a naive, innocent quality about the Cancer man which can be seen in the most worldly and sophisticated of people. Deep inside, there is a vulnerable little boy with a wound that he does not know how to heal by himself. On bad days, that wound consumes him.

While the Pisces man increasingly perceives the oneness of the universe, the Cancer man perceives the separateness and is deeply threatened by these perceptions, expanding them into a ubiquitous fear of the loneliness of old age and death. The experience of love is the Cancer man's step out of the Garden of Eden and away from his mother's womb. Therefore, the subtle overtones of separateness carry an especially fearful unconscious undercurrent. Leaving his mother's womb is to discover his own wound. The course of his life depends on what he does with it.

Although he may not consciously realize it, because

the shell has become too hard, each intense love experience has brought him closer to his own soul. Until he experiences his own authentic soul and projects outward from that, all experiences along the way will be illusions destined to dissolve in time as truth unfolds. Only when he has finally found a home in his own soul will he find a soul mate with which to experience deeper, spiritual love, that issues from the spirit and that affirms it.

Along the way, many Cancer men get caught up in their own shells and make them into cozy nests that suffice for the purposes of daily survival. At a certain point, living in such a safe way, life becomes so deadening that pain begins to feel like positive feeling. Just the experience of being able to feel "emotionally caught up" is an overwhelming relief from the deadened, empty routine.

However, this reaching out, despite the eventual disastrous consequences is never really a disaster. It only appears so to the ego in the blinding moment of pain. The true disaster comes in cutting off all feeling and in being blandly narcotized by the deadened patterns of one's own existence.

As the first of the three water signs, Cancer is on earth to learn about the power of emotions. Like any power, its force can be used for or against. Thus, the challenge of the Cancer man is to learn the positive power of his own emotions as expressed in love, not need. And too, like Parsifal and the Holy Grail, he needs to allow the innocence of the little boy within to keep him on the quest until the wound is healed and he has become the light.

Cancer: Power and Work

When it comes to work, the classic Cancerian has the concentration of a brain surgeon and the drive to go along with it. Tenacious, task-oriented and intense, Cancers tend to be perfectionists who take their work personally—and sometimes a little too seriously. There *are* Cancers who leave the office at the office. However, it is likely that they work overtime, don't take time for lunch, and go home hours after the cleaning lady.

For the most part, Cancers care terribly about what they do, and should they find themselves in a situation that doesn't motivate them emotionally, the day-to-day drain could make them ill in a lot of different ways.

Basically, work can represent two things to the Cancer personality: self-esteem and security, the latter both financial and emotional. Quite often the self-esteem and security are tied together. The love of work is so intense that it manifests itself as prosperity on the financial plane (as with Sylvester Stallone). Then there are the Cancer types who are driven purely for the love of what all those dollars will do to the sense of security down the road (as with John D. Rockefeller).

Whatever the motivation, it is powerful and fueled by emotion. In that oceanic, swirling flow, an underlying insecurity adds to consummate psychological surrender. Cancers are highly impressionable people who want to be approved of by the powers that be—even if they personally can't stand them. Therefore, the work experience can mirror the love experience in that it has an emotional hold that challenges and also in terms of the challenges it poses to the individual sense of autonomy and power.

It is not uncommon for Cancers to lose themselves completely in their work or to see it as a sort of surrogate family that offers security and a sense of stability. Cancers are highly conscientious, industrious people who can easily put their work ahead of themselves at any given point. But not, however, without paying a price emotionally—and sometimes physically. There is a sense of grim determination about the Cancerian sense of survival and about the contracted sense of duty.

The Cancer sign boasts quite a number of creative people and writers in particular. However, you can also find your share of financiers and attorneys on the top along with drones on the bottom who simply try to get through the day. In the latter group, there is always a drained feeling that can be felt. They are drained of their own vital emotions, and somewhere along the line, they are not putting back what they have taken out. The signs are fatigue, emotional flatness, moodiness, irritability and low-grade depression. In the drive to create a dynasty as a life foundation or to put up with the grimness of the humdrum for a survival paycheck, Cancers can easily deplete their vitality, emotionally and psychically, stifling the creative, self-affirming visions that lurk somewhere in their soul.

When Cancers can summon the courage to operate from the heart and to show integrity to themselves, they can become very powerful in their chosen field of work. However, when they discipline themselves to endure their fear, they are weakened, powerless and contracted. And whether or not they are aware of it, it shows.

To be powerful in their work Cancers must look at themselves, not lose themselves unconsciously. Secondly, they must decide what they are willing to give up for what they want to get. Finally, incorporating the lesson of the next sign, Leo, they should try to do what they love, and the rest will follow. This often means taking risks that threaten one's sense of security. However, there is something much more important than security. It is *yourself.* The powerful Cancer knows that and treats work as a meaningful part of life, not as a means to an end of a deadened existence.

Powerful Cancer Psychology

> A human being . . . is an ever-widening
> circle of meaning, forever making new
> connections to new aspects of exis-
> tence. . . . Every second of life is to be
> welcomed as the proper time for ad-
> vancing in the quest, every aspect of
> human behavior must be seen as holy
> and meaningful and rife with opportu-
> nity. . .
>
> —Walt Anderson, *Open Secrets*

Cancer

Cancer is a sign with very powerful emotions. Therefore, it is necessary to work with that power and to make it work for you rather than against you.

This involves many considerations. On the most basic level, you must pay conscious attention to your environment. As a very receptive water sign, your mind is strongly influenced by your surroundings. Emotionally and psychologically, you ingest your surroundings without even consciously realizing it. Therefore, you should, whenever possible, create an atmosphere that is congenial to your sensibilities by paying special attention to such specifics as light, beauty, and music.

All forms of light, from sunlight to candlelight, will have a positive effect on your psyche. Light is a part of your inner being, even if it is the mysterious, changeable light of the night.

Beauty in the form of colorful fresh flowers and meaningful *objects* can also serve to harmonize your environment in a very positive way.

Finally, music is very important in its effect on the mind and emotions. This has been scientifically documented. The psychiatrist Roberto Assagiolo, founder of Psychosynthesis, was one of the more renowned people to place emphasis on this point. Classical music, the Baroque period in particular, with such composers as Bach, Handel, Vivaldi and Telemann, has a particularly uplifting effect on the mind. On the other hand, in a state of mental agitation, the more modern, Impressionistic composers such as Ravel, Debussy, Gabriel Fauré and Erik Satie have a soothing, meditative effect.

Essentially, to transcend negative emotional states, Cancers have to alchemize themselves. They have to move on the awareness of the next sign, Leo, and learn how to change lead into gold. In daily experience this lead can be a disappointment, a frustration, a hurt, a heartache, a devastating piece of news. Or it can be a big depression that is part of a process, a death-and-rebirth process in which part of the self is dying off and being reborn. Whatever the negative experience, you have to learn not to sink further into the negativity, but to see the opening, the door, the meaning that will allow you to rise up.

A fundamental psychological guidepost word for the Cancer mind is *renunciation*. In this case, renunciation means quite simply renouncing all negative thoughts in order to be free. We all create our own prisons by holding on to the wrong things for the wrong amount of time. However, Cancers do this more so than most other signs because they are both so emotional and so subjective.

When negative, Cancers are given to "wrong" thinking. This thinking is contracted. It does not take in the whole picture. *And* it is tainted. It is tainted with negative emotional overtones that perpetuate the life of the negative emotional state which I prefer to call an emotional cluster. In the negative Cancerian mind, it is as if beads of emotion compounded by attitudes cluster together to form a ball of sizable weight and proportion. In turn, this ball becomes an experience or sometimes a depression that grows heavy. However, the entire substance of the experience—all the little beads—are merely individual examples of negative thinking.

Begin by challenging yourself. Whenever you have a strong emotional feeling that is negative, say to yourself the opposite. For example:

NEGATIVE: I feel so sad and lonely. I know I'll never find emotional happiness. Other people are happy in love and don't suffer. But I'm not like them. I'm not lucky. I'm not meant to have anyone. Deep inside, I feel like nothing. I feel like my life is nowhere.

OPPOSITE: I look at so many people in such rotten, miserable relationships and I'm so relieved that I'm not one of them. Other people are so eager to entrap themselves because they're frightened and lonely. But I'm free, free to choose the right person for me. I know, deep inside, that I'm meant to find harmony and happiness. I'm going to do that, no matter what.

Even if it doesn't happen on my ideal, fantasy time schedule, I'll eventually meet the person who is like a part of my soul, who reflects all of the things within myself that I value.

This is a very powerful psychology which can be practiced all day long, every day on any area of emotional difficulty. By yourself, you might want to keep a notebook and actually write everything out. And what will happen eventually is that

1. You will become more conscious of your own thought patterns.

2. You will have canceled out each negative "bead," planted a positive one, and prevented the formation of a negative cluster.

3. The positive beads will eventually form a cluster that takes powerful hold in your subconscious mind.

When unhappy, water signs (Cancer, Scorpio and Pisces) tend to seek escapes that dull the feeling. The obvious escapes, such as drugs, alcohol, and food, are there, but there are others, too. With Cancer, it is frequently obsessive work patterns and compulsive involvements that serve as a negative means of coping with the painful contents of the inner self. Such Cancers are often control freaks, compulsively tidy, compulsively work-oriented—to the point of emotional deadness, depression or exhaustion, or compulsively attached to the idea of a relationship with the "wrong" person. Unconsciously, the compulsion serves to block out painful emotions regarding one's deep relationship with one's own inner world. It allows the Cancer to continue in a chosen manner on a chosen path and to avoid confronting the self.

Many such Cancers lead essentially joyless existences, in full pursuit of what is outside of them. However, to be fully alive, it is necessary to experience yourself fully and consciously. Once you've done that, you can extend your boundaries outward to incorporate a deeper, more compassionate experience of others.

The more you are fully conscious and the more that the heart of consciousness is developed, this heart experience begins to replace compulsive experience and the need to clutch. The more you take in, the more the entire experience of self grows and flowers. When you are less concerned with self-protection and more able to feel for many different kinds of people in many different kinds of ways, you will become radiant from within. The more people that you take into your heart, the less you need the protection of your shell. Your shell only serves to preserve you in your own limited attitudes.

Free yourself of limitations and shells and negative attitudes. Act with your soul, not your defenses. Let go of all compulsions and find God in your own heart. Then feel each person, each tree, each flower, your enemies and the almighty sun as yourself.

The word *enthusiasm* comes from the ancient Greeks. It meant, around sixth century B.C., in the Orphic cult, to be at one with the gods. To be in that exalted state. Beyond shells, and fortresses and fears and entrapments and compulsive work mania. To be boundless through the heart. To *be* joy.

Regardless of the problems, fears and frustrations of your life, you *can* enthuse. But first you must *will* to get beyond your small, petty self to see and feel as if from the sky. But you don't have to go anywhere.

It is all within your own heart. Every day there are miracles there. There is joy. But you are missing it because you are living in limitation defined by your own tiny boundaries.

Dissolve these boundaries! They are nothing more than your own ego. You make them exist. When romantic love gives you joy it is because your ego has dissolved into the other and you have become something else. But you can become something else *at any moment*, without falling in love.

The great psychological limitation of Cancer is that it

seeks expansion only through the totally personal realm: the conventional romantic love experience. However, there are also so many other ways in which to feel, expand and transcend one's small self. There are many, many joyful ways to dissolve when one lives through the heart.

Dissolve your boundaries and become infinite possibility—the Possibility that permeates all life and that lives within your own soul as an eternal light.

Maximizing Your Cancer Power Potential

Essentially, what holds you back from experiencing greater power in various aspects of your life is fear. Cancers have many fears regarding money, security, performance, loneliness, love, old age, death, and so on. With age, the fears change and grow new fears. However, they all are born from one fear factor deep within the personality. It is this factor that must be dealt with consciously. Cancers are Fear Full. In order to become Power Full, they must become full of their own inner light. This must become their Source, their intelligence, their sustenance and their inspiration.

Cancers are deeply afraid of the depths of their inner world. To escape, they project their fears outward. When a person or situation becomes menacing, it victimizes them. However, in truth, what is on the outside is not really important. It will change. The real threat exists deep within.

There are many Cancers who live sterile, humdrum lives, enslaved by tedium and defined by triviality, compulsive about each task.

Deadlines must be met, projects must be completed at any cost.

Cancers tend to cling to their patterns of powerlessness and sometimes change the focus of their direction. To become more powerful, it is necessary to change the workings of your own mind. But change takes a great deal of courage. If you can get into your soul and face fear consciously, you will then be able to get beyond it to something else. That something else is the light within you. The Source within your own mind. This place, which in most people remains unconscious, is truth. When you live through truth, you are totally aware. You are deeply connected to everything around you. And you are in tune with its intelligence. Where there once was loneliness or emptiness, now there is joy. Where there once was fear, there is possibility.

One Master put it this way: "It is just as if the current of a river is flowing towards the sea and you are trying to swim up current. So you feel the river is against you. The river is not against you. It has not even heard about you."

Your life is a series of moments. It is your mind and your emotional attitudes that connect them. And that becomes the substance and quality of the connection. However, try leaving your mind out of it. Be free of anticipating the next moment. Be fully aware *now*. Don't get detoured by your inner voices.

You suffer, not from insecurity, but from your own needs which are contaminated by fear. Let go of all the tight grasping and look to see what is there. What would happen if *all* the things you cling to were lost? Who would you be then? That answer, like the response of a Zen koan, can bring great power.

To silence your mind, to get beyond the fear, to arrive at truth, there is a powerful mantra that you should use every morning. It is *Sô Hâm*. It literally means "I am that." *That* refers to the powerful Source of light within, the place beyond fear.

Say this mantra along with conscious awareness of your breath. Inhalation and exhalation has to do with expansion and contraction of your own parameters. Concentrate on the *so* for the inhalation and the *ham* for the exhalation. Perform this exercise for at least twenty minutes every morning. It will bring great inner stillness, in which your higher, superconscious self, the self which has all the answers and wisdom that you will ever need, has great power.

The more you use this mantra, the more this high, pure awareness will take over your mind, and the more you will cleanse your inner world of all of its negativities.

Cancer

During the day, in fearful, stressful moments, say this mantra to yourself, and a different, powerful, consciousness will come into being. The more you incorporate this mantra into your life and your unconscious mind, the more you will access this internal power.

Only meditation can stop your suffering and empower you because only meditation can make you see. Your suffering is because you do not see far enough. When you are able to see everything with your highest, superconscious faculties, there is no more suffering. There is only experience through the prism of power.

V

LEO
(July 24–August 23)

Leo Nature

Leo is the sign of the sun, and like the sun itself, Leos shine with stellar incandescence. Leos' magnetism makes them highly memorable people who exude power and personableness.

Personality is the Leo strong point. When so desiring, the Leo charm can tame serpents and turn the world at large into an adoring enclave. At their best they give off a scintillating sort of radiance. They are positive and enthusiastic, spirited, dynamic and larger than life.

Leos expect the best from themselves and everyone around them. It is this attitude that helps them to realize their dreams. Should disappointment dawn, Leos are dauntless and have a way of transforming disasters into golden opportunities. However, should they be betrayed, they can become another person. Their need for loyalty is very deep and leaves them feeling deeply wounded at the thought that their trusts have been misplaced. It is much easier for them to admonish than to admit that they're hurt. At this point they withdraw their warmth and retreat into icy silence. They are capable of turning their feelings on and off like a light and can appear to be many different things at different times to different people.

Suddenly, the person who seemed so totally focused, interested and engaged, can become a stranger. The reason for the paradox? Leos' internal life is strong and demanding—sometimes so demanding that it shuts out the voices on the outside.

Leos are *highly* self-centered. However, like no other sign, they manage to pull it off with an élan that usually doesn't offend anyone because they are so generous and enthusiastic. Along with this comes a sense of humor that is dazzling and childlike. This includes a great ability to laugh at themselves and to fill others with mirth as well. They make other people feel privileged to participate in their larger-than-life drama, even if the action happens to be going on at the supermarket. Like no other sign except Pisces, they have an innate ability to transform the boring and banal into something bright and shining.

Leos love to mythologize experience and have the ability of living out their own myths. They see themselves as unique, and quite frankly they are. They bear the wisdom and the magic of selfhood along with the breath of human potential. It is only when all movement seems to stop that Leos lose their light.

The experience of nothing to look forward to is the dreariest one for Leo. It can make their eyes lose their spark and their sense of humor turn to cynicism. Despite their courage, Leos do not ride out depression well and when the sun goes down can easily turn self-destructive.

This is a far more complicated sign than appears on the surface. As fixed fire, Leos seek life-sustaining meaning in goals and dreams. If the means of attaining them is seriously blocked, they are not quick to change course. Leos can hold on too long and get stuck in old patterns and plans that have come to define their lives. However, when they do leave someone or something behind, they never look back. Once Leos are finished with an affair of the heart they can be just as cold and indifferent as they were originally passionate. These hot and cold aspects of Leos' personalities can appear to be slightly paradoxical. One might indeed say, how could a person who is so warm be so cold? The fire goes out and the light fades. For the fire to remain blazing Leos have to be captivated and fueled by the idea of who or what they're involved with. Leos hate, loathe and despise feeling confined or bored. Conditions must answer their expectations of how they think things should be. This brings us to another curious subtlety: the split between the head and the heart.

Although Leos have a reputation as pleasure-loving partygoers, this is also a strongly intellectual sign associated with an extremely high intelligence and a tendency to think rather than feel. There is a wonderful story of two friends, Aldous Huxley (a Leo) and D. H. Lawrence (a Virgo), who out for a walk in a meadow, come upon a beautiful flower. Aldous Huxley verbally rhapsodized about its beauty. D. H. Lawrence, being an earth sign, simply touched and sniffed it.

In a similar vein, Leos are fond of talking and thinking about love. However, mysteriously in the midst of all the thinking, all the feeling fades which then leads Leo to analyze the nature of their own feelings. As one Leo woman I know put it, "I am totally sick and exhausted from analyzing. I just want to have a good time." Two weeks later she was back at home alone analyzing.

The one thing that usually gets Leos away from thinking is large doses of love. Yet again, this is not at all as easy as it might appear. Leos also love their freedom and loathe confinement. Hand in hand with this goes the fact that *they* want to be the one to make the choices. After all, its *their* drama and everyone around them just gets to play along.

Therefore, it is not surprising that despite their larger-than-life dose of charm, intelligence, and vivacity, this is still a sign that is not especially lucky in love. Once Leo finally makes its choice, the chosen then becomes the most and the best in the greatest of all grand schemes. (Leos nourish themselves on superlatives.) However, their choices often tend to be terrible and reflect their idea of a romantic experience rather than the virtues of a particular person. As a matter of fact, Leo can so easily become blinded by their idea of love that the other person feels left out of the relationship. This brings to mind two Leos I knew who were quite happy for quite some time in a relationship where they hardly ever saw each other. One day on the telephone the male Leo said to the female Leo, "I think we have a wonderful relationship." The female Leo replied, "That's because we never see each other. When we see each other we fight." Nevertheless, the two Leos, who were both *terribly* busy and compromised for time, continued to have a perfectly satisfying situation over the phone. The haphazard dinners that infrequently punctuated the distance usually ended early and in disaster.

This is a sign that is determined to do things its own way, at all costs, with no patience for the opinions of others. When this works, the Leo energy and willfulness can create miracles. When it backfires, it's probably more comfortable hanging out in a towering inferno.

Leo is the sign of the child, and when provoked, it can be enormously childish. If pushed too far, Leo can be like a vociferous member of the "terrible twos." During such moments no one else exists. However, the storm usually doesn't last long. The clouds are impatiently blown away, and once again the sun comes out. At this point, everyone hiding under their chairs should bear in mind that all should be forgotten.

It takes a serious betrayal for Leo to bear a grudge. Minor transgressions are usually reflected on and forgiven with great magnanimity. Leos are impatient with negativity and therefore hold their heads high above their wounds. Moreover, they love to love, whether it be a person, a place, an idea or their dog. This is the source of the utter magic of this sign and the spellbinding effect it can have on those around them.

This ability to be so positively responsive to so many people and things is a personal power that simply comes along with this sign. It's the kind of power that turns frogs into princes and makes dreams into miracles. It's the power of the self to recognize consciously the glory of selfhood and to see in all experience and in all people infinite potential. At the heart of the pure Leo experience lies God unmasked, unmythologized, a consciousness that is the Source and from which light transforms into life.

Leo Strengths

Leo is the sign of strength, being ruled by the Sun, the planet which gives light to the Earth. Like the Sun, the Leo nature shines with an incomparable radiance. However, a most wonderful quality of this solar nature is its ability to shed light upon the lives of others.

Perhaps it begins with the Leo smile. There is a childlike sparkle in the eyes and a sense of knowing something terribly amusing. Possessing a stunning sense of humor, Leo loves to laugh and to make others laugh as well. There is a Leo I know who tells the worst jokes, but he so amuses himself in the telling that its worth suffering the ridiculous punch line just to witness his childlike glee.

Leo, being the sign of the child, has a way of bringing a fresh innocence and joy to its experiences. Leos know how to enjoy themselves, and because of that, they are a pleasure to be around, creating "moments" out of the most mundane experiences. I am reminded of one client's comment about her Leo boss. "Out of the blue he's roaring at me to get into a cab. I suddenly find myself sitting in this beautiful restaurant and surrounded by people taking his orders. I think to myself, 'What am I doing here? How did I get here?' and then I realize that it doesn't matter because I'm having a great time."

This is true Leo style. Leo is a great host or hostess. It loves parties and it loves showing others a good time. To be around this sign at its best is to feel that you have a key part in a Metro-Goldwyn-Mayer production, minus the camera cuts. Even if down to their last dime, Leos will find a way to pull things off in grand style.

This is a sign that is so generous that there are times when it should seriously be locked up. One Leo friend tells a story of being terribly irked by her mother's anger when she gave away her winter coat to a needy college friend. "How could I not give her my coat?" exclaims my friend. "She didn't have one." Of course it didn't occur to my Leo friend that through this act of spontaneous generosity she would not have one either. However, when this realization did dawn, she didn't make it a problem. Instead, she enthusiastically found money to buy another.

Such is the maganimous Leo spirit. Not only are Leos generous to a fault, but they also loathe pettiness, selfishness, greed and people who try to rain on their parade. Another unusual virtue is that after they've done their good deed, they forget all about it and fly on to another. It's their way of having a good time. In turn, good things magically come to them because they generate so much joy from goodness.

To the higher Leo mind, doing good things is intrinsic to having a happy life, and happiness is something Leos consciously strive for. Even if they go about their quest in the wrong ways, their sheer zest and enthusiasm is contagious and intoxicating. It is no wonder that people born under this sign are usually ridiculously popular. Even if they don't always live it, Leos have invented the good life and all the glamour that goes along with it. Dreary circumstances depress them; they unconsciously ignore people with negative attitudes. No matter how bad a moment may be, Leo feels obliged to make the most of it. Leos deluged with problems will still smile and tell the world they're terrific. Then they try to become terrific, and usually succeed. Leos are born with the power of positive thinking, and that is partially the key to their success. Not only do they make the best of a bad moment, they also have a knack for bringing out the best in people. Leos are quick to seize upon the good qualities of the most problematic person and to compliment them with great effusiveness. They can turn a weed into a flower simply through their sheer enthusiasm.

Although everything about the Leo nature is larger than life, Leos also possess a sense of wonder about the "little things." They have difficulty perceiving limitation, and they experience limitation far less than other signs. The Leo mind is so expansive and future-oriented that a bad experience is viewed only as something to be followed by great opportunity. Leos also have a way of creating their own opportunities and then forgetting about all the hard work that went into the results.

Leos have so much mental and physical energy that they don't consider working hard as working hard. Part of this is because they tend to love what they are doing. Even if they don't love staying up all night studying, they do love excellence. The great psychiatrist Carl Jung was a Leo, and with his great genius created a revolutionary form of psychology that was totally beyond the consciousness of his time.

Creation is the source of the Leonian center. Leos define and exalt themselves through their creations and transcend the boring, routine and mundane in the process. Their visions are idealistic, as are their expectations. Because they are so idealistic, Leos make the best friends. The Leo nature is noble, generous and loyal, and it expects the same in turn. The Leonian attitude toward the people around them tends to be so positive and loving that it can actually act as a vehicle for the transformation of others. This is the sign of the miraculous, and the secret to each miracle is the heartfelt love that is brought to all experience.

Leo Pitfalls

A big secret regarding this sign is that Leos are not quite as fearless as they appear. There is a great deal of anxiety associated with Leo, and likewise, a tendency toward drug and alcohol abuse.

Leo is the sign of the tense, extroverted overachiever. Leos have classic Type A personalities and tend to race through life driven by an inner gyroscope that will never allow them to stop achieving. They tend to take on too much and are at high risk for heart attacks. One Leo of my acquaintance, upon receiving his Ph.D. in English, promptly moved on to another school to work on a Ph.D. in psychology. Friends speculate what new career he'll take on from there.

This sort of overachieving attitude seems perfectly natural for Leo, which has a deep need to create itself and also to define itself by what it happens to be doing. A Leo that isn't doing anything is indeed a dark person. Therefore, the nagging fear of failure experienced in this sign is not due simply to pride and egotistical projection but is due to an insistent urge for self-creation.

In the horoscope Leo is associated with the fifth house of creation, and as such, Leos tend to look upon themselves as their own creation, quite apart from maternal or paternal influences. This is the sign of *the* individual, the self-made person. The extraordinary attractiveness of these people comes partly from the positive way in which they project themselves and partly from the ease with which they'll enthusiastically share their light. The basis of this luminous quality is a consciously defined and self-created self. It is this pressure of always having to be something just to be which is the source of the deep-seated anxiety associated with this sign.

Taken to its extreme, the rapacious drive to be one's own person can lessen the simpler enjoyments of life and lead to people problems. Loved ones often have to compete with Leos' acting out of their endless ambitions. Although they possess an extraordinary amount of energy, they can also be exhausting to keep up with when possessed by their private world. These personalities are prone to extremes, and when out of control, Leos can make themselves tense and tempermental by refusing to calm down, cool out and put things in perspective. Because internal pressure is a constant, external stress can trigger explosive situations as well as physical illness. Troublesome skin conditions, gastrointestinal disorders, headaches, frequent flu symptoms, minor accidents and depression are all examples of how the unbalanced Leo energy can bring about its own undoing.

The first step to ameliorating these situations is to

recognize consciously what is happening. Sadly, this is part of Leo's problem. Leos will not listen unless they have asked for advice. They are also not open to being told to relax. Either they feel totally in charge of a situation or they feel that the situation is out of control. If it is out of control, they pull stressfully upon themselves to get it back under control.

This need for control, augmented by the desire for perfection, can make this sign an enemy unto itself. It is true that we attract what we dwell upon, and if we dwell upon fear, we will eventually see it realized in our lives.

One way fear and anxiety crystallizes in the Leo experience is in the form of blocks. This manifests either as stagnancy or in an approach-avoidance pattern seen more often in female Leos. In male Leos, the blocks are more often experienced in their love relationships. As a matter of fact it is not uncommon for a male Leo to focus and direct all of his energy into his work, giving nothing more to his marriage than material support. I have a number of divorced women who shudder at the memory of years spent in such lonely, soulless connections. Yet to the minds of these Leo men, who were not villains, there was no alternative. Their vision demanded that they keep creating themselves, and being future-minded, to keep becoming.

Creative self-expression is the key word to Leo. A purposeful existence is the breath of life for this sign. At the same time, to suffer from confusion and to feel no sense of purpose is as painful as the idea of death itself. Deep down in the psyche of this sign there is a morbid dread of mortality. This fear often remains unconscious but expresses itself in a tendency toward hedonism, thrill-seeking, and living on the edge. The ability to flout death is the quest of the hero. And Leo, with its powerful ruler, the Sun, is the sign of heroism. However, unlike the innocent and unwitting Parsifal, the loneliness of this quest is consciously felt, as is the fear. Like the cowardly lion in the Wizard of Oz, Leo struggles sometimes pitifully to hear its own voice.

This is the sign of the actor/actress, and like the

thespian who disrobes on a silent stage, the question Who am I? always remains. This issue may not be consciously confronted, but nevertheless it is a vital issue that can lead one closer to his or her own potential.

Leo is a sign that can become jaded, dissipated and even suicidal in the exhausting, compulsive quest to feel more alive. In such extreme cases, self-obsession can give way to cynicism, sadism and a viciously destructive self-enclosing life cycle, as seen in the highly idiosyncratic Leo, Andy Warhol. The sun becomes blackened, yet it is not the dead of night awaiting dawn. Rather it is the hollowness of a self-centered mind that is unspeakably lonely in the light of other people. The dark side of heroism is tragedy, and it is that fine line that the Leo must tread every time the self is tested. The sign of life must rescue self from its own mortality, and there is no help that it will allow itself along the way.

Because Leo is the sign of selfhood, it epitomizes the mystery of a human existence. We are born alone. We die alone. And given a life, what do we do with this preciousness along the way? The fierce independence of this sign carries this weight as if it were self-invented. Ironically, Leo can carry this independence to such an extreme that there is no freedom. Every compulsive step creates a new shackle that the mind, turned too far inward, can no longer control. Underlying this is a haunted sort of anguish that whispers, If I have not become something, if I cannot see myself reflected back to me, than I am nothing.

Self-consciousness can be the source of Leo power. But when it becomes obsessive, it is an insidious source of unhappiness. At the end of this spectrum there is self-victimization. These blocked Leos hold themselves back from the things they want most. For all Leos there is a struggle that goes on behind the scenes. Achievements are not easily gained as they appear. There is always the anxiety of "Am I good enough?" which leads sometimes to the false arrogance associated with the lower aspect of this sign.

The most fundamental lesson Leos must learn is how

to trust their power all of the time. Along with this goes the ability to take joy from their gifts and their natural, spontaneous luminosity. At the moment of entry into this world a door was opened. There is no need to search fervently for a doorknob. The name of that door is possibility, and possibility exists in every circumstance.

In the end Leos have to look upon themselves as the doorway and smile at the light shining through that as the most intrinsic part of their nature. Then the creative aspect of life will flow naturally and quietly like the poem that must be written.

Power & Love: The Leo Woman

Leo is the sign of love and romance, and because of that the idea of love has always been important. However, Leos are also so idealistic that they are easily disillusioned. When Leo women think they've found the man of their dreams, they tend to mythologize him and see both him and the romance as larger than life. However, should their lover look smaller than their dreams, Leo women can quickly fall out of love, forgetting even his first name.

Because Leos possess such an intensely individualistic and independent nature, relationships are not easy unless they also have a lot of freedom. They have a restless, searching nature and cannot bear feeling caged or closed in. For that reason Leos can be quite content playing the field as long as their suitors meet their lofty standards.

Leo women are queens and cannot bear being bored for the sake of having a boyfriend. Consequently security is less important than a feeling of exhilaration and excitement. For that reason, Leo women are initially captivated by generosity and grandeur and turn a cold shoulder on crudeness, rudeness and poor presentations. Leo women would rather be alone than with someone they felt diminished their self-image. Their dignity precedes them and determines their expectations. Left to her own devices, the Leo woman can find love in a lot of different people and pastimes. However, should she encounter that "per-

101

fect" person, she will take great delight in lending herself fully to the drama.

There must always be a touch of drama to kindle the queen of the zodiac's incandescent passion. Through her active imagination she will generate such color that it might appear that she will never be so in love again.

This, of course, is not the case. This woman is an intricate blend of fire and ice and can quickly turn off her feelings if her pride is offended. Leo women will let their pride get in the way of having things they want most. Although they are loyal in love and generous to a fault, they also have the strongest sense of self and will not allow anyone to compromise that for any length of time.

This fiercely individualistic nature can often be intimidating to more insecure men. That is why Leo women need strong men they respect, and who, in turn, show respect for their persona. The Leo woman has an intense need to shine in all of her endeavors and shine, she usually does. However, when her light is too bright a lesser man will feel overwhelmed.

Herein is a paradox. While strong, powerful men may excite her, they may also try to control and dominate. This is not the sort of role that the Leo woman sets out for in life. This is a woman who values her own expectations. Being told what to do and how to do it is for other people. This sort of romantic setup is guaranteed to get in her way, and it will not be long before her attention drifts in another direction.

Therefore, it is not unusual to see this larger-than-life queen with a wimpy but devoted man whom she allows to adore her. Should the adoration and self-conjured drama be great enough, she'll convince herself that he is deserving and will make do.

Leo women are capable of generating vividly romantic scenes and settings and love to give love. This comes from a nature that is both magnanimous and abundant. When a Leo woman is in love, her creative powers are enhanced and her inner world transformed. All Leos secretly believe in fairy tales and in their being destined for sublime love. The dark side of this mindset is cynicism, which comes from romantic overexposure and which results in emotional satiation.

Every Leo woman has to learn that she already has all the power within her for attacting the "right" love. She must trust this power with the full force of her heart. Past disappointments do not matter. All that matters is the mental attitude of the moment. There is no need to cut herself off or to compromise. However, the Leo woman must be totally clear about what is most important in a person. Conning herself will only lead to confusion. This sort of confusion will only delay the whole process.

Leos' childlike responsiveness to people is magical. However, sometimes they mentally "make up" the person they're responding to. Leo women have an overwhelming need for men to mirror their ideals. Deep down, they desire a hero. However, heros are self-created. It's not enough to give them the idea and help them along.

Such is the tendency with the Leo woman, who can exhaust herself through self-convincing. The most wonderful quality in her nature is her ability to turn black into gold. However, even though they do bring out the best in people, they can't completely re-create them.

Finally, the Leo woman must allow herself to receive and must see receiving as a value. When she is ready to receive, she *will* receive. It is that simple. Only her mindset can make obtaining happiness in love more complicated. And the Leo woman can negate her own power to attract. The Leo woman must affirm this power every day and tell the universe that she is now ready to receive. She *will* receive and will experience the power of her own heart reflected back to her.

Power & Love: The Leo Man

It might be said, and rightfully so, that the Leo man invented romance. When in love, or when ardently impassioned, the Leo man can set the stage for the grandest love. With great pride he bestows his creative energies on his chosen. However, the chosen one must in turn make him look good and must reflect the self-image that he wants to see.

The Leo man has his own view of himself as larger than life and likewise seeks this experience from love. This man can mythologize love so much that the object of his desires may feel second in importance to the drama. He is an idealist who wants the best and expects the most. In the long run he usually gets it.

Although he exudes a mesmerizing magnetism through the sheer force of his confidence, energy, and charisma, it also takes the Leo man a long time to grow up. Leo is the sign of the child, and childish it can well be. When the infamous Leo Mick Jagger was asked by the press what his political affiliations were in Great Britain in the seventies, this graduate of the London School of Economics replied that he never spent time on it because he was too busy chasing girls. He added that his greatest life challenge was becoming mature.

The Leo man can be quite a lothario who will tell you he loves women. However, what is more often the case is that he loves the sport and the entertainment of it all. Because this is the sign associated with amusement, Leo men, especially in the early years, tend to be playboys who make the most of their playing.

The more serious, success-driven Leos ultimately seek a mate to fill in the picture and feed the ego. In turn, they will generously support the situation and reward the mate by supplying the props. Their willingness to support the situation financially is due in part to their generosity and in part to their need for control. When unevolved, the Leo man can be a highly controlling, tyrannical person who dictates rules that must be obeyed unquestioningly. This is a sign that has more than a coincidental number of political dictators under it, from Fidel Castro to Napoleon to Mussolini. Likewise, it is not unusual to see the Leo man reigning at the top of his profession like a king, covetous of power and unable to delegate authority.

Being married to this type of person suits a cold-blooded fortune hunter who wants to be taken care of. However, a more emotional woman may have serious problems if she wants to feel she is really married. This brings to mind one highly emotional client who complained of her fiercely ambitious live-in Leo lover. To her it seemed that every time she wanted to see him, she had to make an appointment.

Although the Leo man may be romantic when it comes to dispensing material tokens, it can be quite another thing to take up too much of his time. Eternally busy, he is always pressured in the moment and jam-packed with plans for the future. One woman said of her son, "He doesn't have a life. He has a resume."

And so it goes that this man fares best with a self-sufficient, independent type woman who doesn't threaten him with her self-sufficiency and independence. Therefore, a delicate balance must be struck—one that usually requires a lot of feminine compromising. Although he may be too busy to be around, the Leo man still needs to feel loved. If he doesn't, quite magically droves of women materialize who make him feel life and love. Once committed, this man tends to be loyal in his own fashion; however, if forced into another's arms out of loneliness, he can manage to have an awfully good time.

Self-image and performance are inordinately important to this man—so much so that he will take love where he can get it because it serves an ego as well as an emotional need. It is not uncommon for this sign to suffer from intimacy problems and impotency, since sexually he is self-conscious and more concerned with his performance than the actual experience of love.

When the Leo man is able to get beyond himself successfully and allow himself to go deeper, he is then able to receive a spiritual, soul-felt satisfaction from the love experience. However, as too often is the case, his controls will not allow him the freedom, especially in the earlier part of his life.

Another negative character type of this sign is the Don Juan who verifies his existence in the act of conquest and who carries no abiding interest in the quality of the contact or in continuing the connection beyond the moment.

This type of man carries a great deal of anxiety beneath the surface and can become so successful at his game that he completely kills off his ability to love. In the extreme, sexual perversions, from pornography as a substitute for intimate sexual love to psychological sadism as a means of contact, become the avenues through which his sexual drives find their outlets.

To be powerful in love the Leo man must first see love as a value which exceeds his own personal need for power. However, the power urge is so primal that it usually leads the way and the result is a well-meaning person who is emotionally detached and highly compartmentalized. The psychologist Erich Fromm says in *The Art of Loving* that "love is a power which produces love; impotence is the inability to produce love." However, the determining factor in this ability to love "depends on the character development of the person."

To be truly powerful in the act of loving the Leo man must outgrow his narcissistic impulses and recognize the value of *two* people. If he cannot grow up and get beyond the infant in his nature, what he will give to the relationship will be glossy but empty and will deteriorate with time. I have had many wealthy women clients who have emerged with a deep sense of relief from these dead marriages. It is as if they have finally gotten their life back after so many years of being put on a shelf and treated as a token. Through these marriages they gained a great deal of financial security, security that other women might find enviable. However, the price paid was their own life force and the feeling of death that comes from living with a person who cannot express love.

Leo men have clever ways of making themselves look compromised to give themselves **emotional distance**. Quite easily they can be self-sustaining, and it is this factor that prevents them from coming to terms with the concept of two.

Only if two, rather than one, becomes a value and only if the need for relationship is based on the desire to relate, will the Leo man find a way to communicate on a deeper level. When the Leo man lives through his heart, he is indeed a powerful creature, able to transform himself and others through the power of his love. His magnanimous heart is the source of his splendor as a person. If he relies upon it also as the source of his emotional intelligence, then with a remarkably small amount of effort he will have it all. When mature, he can be the most endearing, emotionally supportive person a woman could ever have. He generates love and life like a brilliant flame emits light. His love shines right from his soul. And that, in a simple word, is power.

Power & Work: Leo

Although Leos are overachievers with highly successful track records, they tend to underestimate their accomplishments. The anxiety deep within them concerning performance never allows them to rest and gives them problems delegating authority. They embrace perfectionistic standards and feel contempt for mediocrity.

Leos were born to lead and have a difficult time following. In addition, they don't enjoy working for someone else—unless it's someone they hold in high esteem. For these reasons Leos function best working for themselves and living out their dreams.

Work is extremely important to Leos, perhaps too much so. Leos tend to be workaholics and tensely employ the highest standards to their performance. Work tends to occupy a great deal of their waking thoughts, and if it is not satisfactory, it can make them physically ill. Leos can literally die of unhappiness. Therefore, it is important that they do something they love. Some Sun signs can force themselves to do work they hate just for money. But with the Leo nature this takes a terrible toll. Because their attitude toward work is all or nothing, they seek a lot of happiness in what they do.

Leos are highly ambitious, goal-oriented people who love the idea of having an objective to work toward. Should they suffer confusion about their direction, it can be an extremely painful experience that can actually reduce vitality and resistance to infection. Because Leos are so idealistic, they have a difficult time viewing career problems objectively and panic at the possibility of failure.

Fear of failure can be so profoundly rooted in Leos' personality that it can cause blocks, stagnancies and career limitations. Leos have a high intelligence along with a creative mind and limitless potential. A greater conscious appreciation of their gifts will free them to express more. Fear is the source of confusion, and this must be dealt with reasonably. Instead of looking at themselves as either destined for success or doomed to failure, they should concentrate on the pleasure along the way. Love will be its own reward. Moreover, it will also bear the shining Leonian quality of excellence. However, when Leos try too hard, rather than relaxing and letting go, their gifts do not flow from them and they have a tendency to get in their own way.

All Leos have to learn how to relax and trust the shining sun that is their source. From this source comes the creative genius that is the natural inheritance of this sign. This trust is easiest when they are doing something they love. Action arises spontaneously and freely from a higher intuitive faculty.

If they concentrate on the fact that their mind is beyond limitation, they will start to live on this level and things will come easily to them. However, if they become driven by fear, their minds will turn against them and they will bring about the failure they most fear. It is extremely helpful to detach the ego and proceed from a pleasure principle. They *can* make magic and make dreams manifest if they let go and give up to the God within them.

Before Leos attempt to achieve something, they should sit quietly in meditation. They should blank the mind and then think about the qualities within themselves that they most enjoy. They must concentrate on the feelings of that enjoyment. Rather than feeling the pressure of having to perform, they should think about the achieving of the goal as having a good time. They should think upon it as something that will bring them pleasure and think about the qualities within themselves that bring them

108

pleasure. Forget about perfection. The enactment can be looked upon as a game. There is no need to suffer for success. That is powerless thinking. Cultivating a positive attitude about one's self and taking pleasure from one's endeavors is the only way to become more powerful in what one does. When one experiences the pleasure of one's own power as a person, rather than worrying about the possibility of failure, one will shine with the success for which one was made.

Leos are blessed with extraordinary energies and abilities. On a daily basis they must give thanks for them. They must never forget to give thanks to themselves for all the good deeds in past lives that made them the powerful people they now are. This acceptance and self-affirmation is the most powerful perspective one can cultivate. You are your own source. Love it.

Powerful Leo Psychology

Into every abyss I still bear the blessing of my affirmation. . . . I live in my own light, I drink back into myself the flames that break from me.

—Nietzsche

There are two selves in each of us. One is a small, ego-bound self that has to *be* something in order to have a face to show to the world. The other, higher self is a lofty experience of consciousness that comes from an elevated heart. This self does not have to be anything. In fact, it has no self-consciousness, because it merges with the fabric of experience, and in the process, transforms the most mundane moment into the transcendental.

Leo is the sign of the heart, and of the potential higher self. Its pathway is to live fully through the heart to become its own divinity. This heart, when it is developed, and the person has risen beyond a petty, selfish ego consciousness, is not only the source of Leo power, it is the source of all power. In this state of divine love and trust it is possible to create miracles. The entire being becomes a magnetic force that generates opportunity. This personality shines more brightly than neon, is noticed in a crowded room and is always rewarded for its luminous essence. The scaffolding of material power will always fluctuate and shift, but this soul power that is born of a higher, purer form of love and union with the Source never dies. Its joy can only be dimmed by the noise of an undisciplined mind.

This transcendental experience is the legacy for each Leo to claim. It is for them to rise above the deadening structures and entanglements of the outer world to achieve a greatness of being. It is for them to realize their unique destiny and to rise to it, unencumbered by fear or doubt. It is for them to create from their own hearts their unique myth that will help guide them to greatness and give others inspiration. Leo represents the mirror and miracle of the human heart, what a human being *can* become, what life *can* be, and how humans are capable of living.

This light of consciousness is an eternal light erasing bad karma and the mortal fear of death. It is the radiance born by the sense of oneness with the Source that is the great mysterious potential of human existence. There is no power greater than this luminosity translated into experience. It is the challenge of every Leo to become miraculous and help others attain through the magnitude of their inner light.

Maximizing Your Leo Power Potential

Every day, preferably early in the morning, create a space of solitude where your mind becomes still. In the quiet of an empty room, concentrate on the rising and the falling of each breath. Momentarily forget the obligations of the day, the problems, the anxieties. Let your mind quietly follow the movement of your breath as it flows softly like the ocean tide eternally lapping at the shore. Relax gently into this rhythm and feel gradually a sense of peace overtake you.

If your mind wanders, bring it back.

Leo

When you have relaxed sufficiently to have left the world behind, see in your mind's eye the summer sun at high noon. Feel its heat flow through your heart and watch its blinding radiance expand until the light fills up the entire expanse of your mental screen. Then say to yourself:

I am created by divine light.
I am sustained by divine light.
I am protected by divine light.
I am ever growing into divine light.
My heart is a miracle.

Say these words from your heart and feel your heart rise with a passion that uplifts you totally. Surrender your entire being to this light and feel it expand your heart. You are now a vehicle of this light. Say to yourself:

I surrender my consciousness to the light and I accept the joy of being one with it as it manifests itself in all aspects of my life.

Then, with your whole being send love out into the universe to all sentient beings, ask that they may be healed of their ignorance and suffering through the power of this light. Then ask that divine love surround and illuminate you.

As you go through your day, bring your mind back to this experience and embrace the feeling of upliftedness. Give thanks for having entered this life as Leo, the sign of divine light, and at all times, when frightened, when tired, when anxious, when feeling stress, remember that you come from the Source of divine power from which all things are possible.

VI

VIRGO

August 24–September 23

Virgo Nature

Commonly known to be the sign of the nitpicking perfectionist, Virgos often consider themselves to be discriminators graced with divine sanction. Seeing flaws like Librans see beautiful faces, Virgos are often controlled by their own visions. In time, their visions go into what makes up a life.

The single most important challenge in the Virgo experience is to see things in larger terms. Virgos' visions determine their career success, quality of experience in relationships, health, and overall quality of life.

Shy and cautious, Virgos tend to underestimate themselves and other people. Their attitudes become self-fulfilling prophecies that prevent a joyful experience of life that is spontaneous and open-ended.

The perfectionism so often associated with this sign, has in fact far less to do with perfection than with a diminished view of the whole. It is the sort of perception that focuses in on the loose thread rather than the color of the fabric. Consequently, Virgos are victimized by a deadly dreariness that is born of duty and discipline, self-control and routinized regimes.

People born under this sign often have to wake up to the possibilities of their own life and the power within themselves. Shortsighted, Virgos settle easily for the minor roles that are so often assigned to them rather than stretching beyond and utilizing the gifts of what could be a superior mind.

However, a mind alone is nothing without a sensibility to go along with it, and it is here that Virgos stop, sit down for a rest and then fall asleep. Upon waking, there are the omnivorous demands of the day's duties and errands, and their minds are once again assaulted. What this sign never seems to understand is that the trivial has its place in *everyone's* pattern. However, it will eat you alive if you let it become the pattern itself.

Not infrequently Virgos are indecisive, so they are reduced to following rules. This way, right and wrong and black and white become infinitely simple. This kind of mind feeds on its own rigidly formed principles. When deeply entrenched, these contracted attitudes often bring on disease.

Love is a curious experience for the average Virgo. Their deepest, darkest secret is that it is something they crave. Yet when in love, it usually makes them uncomfortable.

Virgos can be loners, never feeling equal to the risk of possible rejection. When venturing forth, they will do it from a position of control which ensures their security. However, the preformulated mindset often prevents deep emotional surrender. Consequently, there is often emotional distance between the head and the heart.

Virgo needs to be enlarged by love in order to feel the magnitude of life first hand. However, Virgos do not often choose people who make the best partners. Easily disillusioned, they can easily turn off, and in the process cut off their capacity to feel.

Body and heart awareness are absolutely essential for Virgos to unify themselves. Beauty is also important as a tonic for a more expanded life. Those Virgos who allow their sense of order and discipline to infuse their time for pursuits which invigorate them are rich, rewarding people. Their positivity promotes growth and like a lens on a camera, captures a life perspective that is colorful and generative. These Virgos are healthy and alive because they have made a simple choice: to be alive, *fully*. Likewise, they affirm themselves through involvements which promote a sense of possibility.

Commonly known as the sign of work, Virgos can work to get beyond their own attitudinal limitations. If they can sort out what is really important, it becomes a fine base for filtering out the dross of life that, on a daily basis, imperceptibly brings them down.

Our attitudes have tremendous power over the course of our existence. Attitudes can be consciously formed to shape a rewarding life with greater meaning. What is meaningful heightens life and makes it truly worthwhile. However, appealing to the uniqueness of each individual, there can be many experiences and endeavors that can be meaningful in many different kinds of ways. Through time, these can and will change, leaving room for new experiences that bring one to a new stage of life. There must always be the sense of change and movement for the life to be healthy and wholesome. To be conversant with its own unique power, Virgo must become master of this positive sense of change and must actively translate it into a panorama of possibility which works for the life. Consequently, the life itself should become a vital and colorful expression over time, like a richly textured painting that is an experience in itself to behold.

Virgo Strengths

The most capable person in the office, Virgo is quiet and indispensable. Conscientious and highly responsible, Virgo needs to feel needed. Few things in life make Virgo feel happier than saving a dire situation. Virgo's competence is never questioned. It is assumed. Caught in a life-

or-death quandary concerning the maniacal office computer, all one ever has to do is find the nearest Virgo. Virgos are more helpful than the Yellow Pages and a lot faster. In a blink, it's all right there in front of you like a freshly made bed.

In ways that they find meaningful, Virgos love to serve, and it so happens they serve exceedingly well. Virgos make excellent doctors and nurses, psychologists, astrologers, healers and high-level aides in many different areas. Possessing a keen mind, sharp perceptiveness and a patient penchant for detail, they are highly gifted at organizing others and doing the behind-the-scenes work.

There is a painstaking quality to the Virgoan performance that might put a Renaissance iconographer to shame. It is part of the perfectionism that this sign is so commonly known for. Virgo is the sign of the master artisan who *cares* about what she or he is creating. Virgos make the most marvelous artists and architects, possessing an innate eye for detail, perspective, structure and form.

At their best, Virgos have impeccable taste and a refined sense of style that they communicate with considerable élan. This is often part of a mind that can be enormously fertile, inflamed by the desire to learn and improve. Virgos are the eternal students of the zodiac, turned on by new, unexplored systems of thought that they can put to practical use to improve their lives. Their highly developed sense of discipline enables them to excel and endure in areas in which enthusiastic dilettantes fall by the wayside. There is a great deal of self-direction in this sign as well as self-motivation that makes for substantial and enduring rewards.

When mature, Virgos are kind people, caring about the animal kingdom, the underdog, their trusted cohorts. Virgoan sympathy is subtle rather than sentimental; it is practically oriented and prepared for action. In a crisis, Virgos can be called upon to function through a mental framework that few can successfully master. A substantial force in the face of sickness, death and severe depression, they can heal as well as help immeasurably. Reliable, responsible and dutiful, Virgo is the breath and light of a better person, who thinks, discriminates and displays compassion quietly.

Highly intelligent, Virgos also possess a clever, sarcastic sense of humor that shows an awareness of the absurd as well as a droll sense of what appears to be serious. When they are able to transcend their *own* seriousness and have fun for fun's sake, they can rise above the banal and become people of infinite possibility—the people they were always meant to be.

Virgo Pitfalls

Virgos have a unique way of shooting themselves in the foot and then looking upon the rest of the world as the enemy. When negative, a Virgo is a dreadful person to be around. On the sunniest day, the sky spits acid rain in the Virgoan mind's eye. Other people are rude and overpoweringly stupid, and the entire atmosphere of life is like stale beer—flat and depressingly smelly.

When really down, this type of Virgo pulls others into dreariness. The negative Virgo's vision is pocked with imperfection and misgiving, with guilt and the kind of resentment that leads to rancid rage. There is an obsessive quality to this kind of mind, and in its emotional patterns it comes to define itself. The perspective is narrow and subjective, tinged with an unexpressed anguish and fraught with a jealous, competitive sort of anger. This sort of Virgo sees itself as "the other," which means the first to get slighted, snubbed, stepped upon, passed over, ignored or willfully taken advantage of. When the defenses have a chance to develop their muscle, an "I don't care" attitude takes over. Then we have a Virgo who takes great pride, not in actually being something, but in dwelling in what other people are not.

In all kinds of ways the Virgo mind can diminish its own quality of life, and it can easily become an insidious pattern that brings disease in time. When one breaks the word *disease* down, one finds the meaning of this experience: not at ease with one's self. And here we have the essence of the negative Virgo pattern.

Early on in life, feelings of inferiority and the fear of being rejected form a psychological base, which becomes a prism through which the world is viewed. Combined with a low physical vitality, Virgos feel powerless to change things. Especially in youth, this experience is very painful. There is the idiosyncratic sense of being shut out or viewing the world through a filthy window. Unfortunately this lessened sensibility drags on into adulthood.

Negative adult Virgos have ironclad defenses which further prohibit them from becoming more involved with life. The nagging sense that something will go wrong or will be taken away persists. This becomes an onerous weight that is never openly expressed, only accepted with silent resignation and an emotional stiffness.

Negative Virgos begin to take pride in their capacity for cutting off anyone who poses a threat to their crystallized ego center. In their mind's eye, they still see the lonely child, possessing an amorphous need for recognition which made the subsequent terror of rejection more traumatic.

The most unfortunate fact about negative Virgos is that they bring about their own fears. A turned-off person is inevitably turned away. This often becomes the subtle self-fulfilling prophecy of the sad, embittered Virgo myth. This can happen in all kinds of ways, from the obvious, sullen projected rejection, to a compensatory grasping of attention and power, to a savage criticalness which magnifies the flaws of others and uses them to fuel a sense of superiority.

As with Gemini, Virgo is ruled by Mercury, the planet of thought, investigation and opinion. All Mercurial people egotistically align themselves with their ideas. And so, the negative Virgo mind can be like a fortress, shutting out all other possibilities of perception, strongly fortified against truth, holding on to a hollow mental perception that grows more dismal with time.

Such a quality of life is a droning, duty-bound nexus of meaningless, minuscule actions. Or, it can be a bleak battle with chaos and the deadening demands of one's inner demons, inexorably rising up to shut out the light.

From this perspective it is understandable why so many negative Virgos would prefer to sleep their life away, while those with more energy power-trip on their extraordinary stamina and superhuman control.

Negative Virgos abuse their child within because it bears a truth that is intolerable. That truth is a need for love, for acceptance, for trust and for a freedom from the fear. Only when the adult Virgo breaks down and embraces these feelings can he or she have a hope of mature love, meaningfulness, possibility and authentic power. In the end there has to be conscious acknowledgement and a will that wants more. This will can be a tremendous source of power, or like a self-inflicted sword wound, can be a lifelong source of unutterable pain.

Power and Love: The Virgo Woman

Serious and intelligent, the Virgo woman can bring new meaning to the word *goodness*. Kind, caring and usually generous, she has patience and sympathy for other people's needs. Wrapped into one, she is a dutiful daughter, a best friend, an indispensable employee, and an all-around fine person. In a world of self-centered people, the Virgo woman is someone you can count on.

The Virgo woman is her own person, and this is often projected in a cool, contained aloofness that may be misconstrued as cold. On the contrary, she is reserved but very much aware of what's around her. Cerebral and discriminating, she is someone to befriend.

As with everything else that comes under the guise of her life, Virgo takes her relationships seriously. Unless she has a great deal of Leo in her horoscope, she does not know how to play at love and tends to have an all-or-nothing attitude whereby involvement implies commitment. Saying "yes" with her heart means saving a special part of her life for down the road.

Such caution, then, is understandable. However, this attitude can sometimes cut her off from experiences that could be enriching.

Deep in the Virgo woman's psyche is a stern, primordial father who demands to know each suitor's intentions. Immediately he is sized up as to his deficiencies and assets, his seriousness of purpose and his acceptability concerning his choice of life path. What tends to be omitted along the way is fun. The Virgo woman needs to be able to have more of it. Likewise, she needs to relax around her rules. Criteria are not necessarily truth. With time, even the best criteria can change, and the situation can fall apart. There is no security in life apart from the comfort of our own illusions. Therefore, flexibility is essential for maintaining both sanity and truth.

Upon finding what appears to fit her criteria, the Virgo woman will serve quite selflessly. And here we have a problem and a paradox: a self-contained person that can also be so selfless.

To the Virgo woman this is not a conflict of which she is conscious. Yet it is a highly significant undercurrent in her life. Her reason and her emotions are often bitter bedfellows, and because of this, many Virgo women serve the wrong people. When their reason returns, the connection becomes shriveled, and so does their heart.

Needing to feel needed, Virgo women can easily fall in love with someone they feel sorry for. Or their power of reason can be reduced by the mere presence of a person they hold in the highest esteem. However, neither necessarily has the ingredients for a good marriage, or possesses essential characteristics that they would consider important in a friend.

Idealistic as well as realistic, the Virgo woman can be taken in and bamboozled by her own ideals. In addition, her emotional reticence does not enable her to establish parameters that could become guidelines to situations that are out of control. The shadow side of all that salient sensibleness is chaos, excitement and electrifying passion. Often when these rear their ancient heads, Virgo reason disappears into an oceanic void.

And so what we see is perfect self-containment versus perfect lack of self. In each, the Virgo woman is like a vessel to be contained. Virgo is a highly obsessive sign, and when losing reason to love the Virgo woman becomes obsessed to the point of irrational thinking. Many such Virgo women serve frantically in order to feel secure, setting up a love situation as if it were a system of barter. Of course, they don't consciously conceive of it this way. Nevertheless, this sort of compulsive giving does set up a situation of inequality and often brings on problems and resentment down the road.

It is not uncommon to hear a Virgo woman talk of her past relationship in the light of pure saintlike martyrdom. As a person who is so responsible in so many other respects, it is amazing to perceive the lack of responsibility she displays toward her self. In the moment, when she is busily setting herself up, she is blinded and there is no stopping her. However, down the road, when disillusionment dawns, she is totally divorced from her daydream and quite cut off from her part in provoking the scene.

The balance between reason and emotion is not an easy one for the Virgo woman. However, it is only here that she will find the truth of her self. When she acts from this balance, she will be acting from her own authenticity and will therefore express the power that is her potential. In everything she does, this power will generate a greater quality of life.

To attain that balance, she must listen with her heart to the truth that is there before her. Instead of merely reason, she will have a wisdom that will guide her and expand her as from a tiny sunbeam to a dawn of radiant light.

Power and Love: The Virgo Man

Astrologically speaking, Virgo men so often get short shrift. They're treated as someone who has as much flair as an overworked accountant at tax time. Not exactly alive in the areas of imagination, spontaneity and electrifying excitement, these poor fellows are condemned to drone on to the top of the next list in a future of interminable lists, routines and responsibilities. And, of course, this is both true and not true.

Virgo men who grow beyond the conditioned boundaries of themselves to live through their individuality can be very exciting people. Mentally, they are explorers who perceive everything around them and from this make connections that are penetrating, enlightening and often pervasively witty. At their best, Virgo men can see through the masquerade that others exhaust themselves to present. Intuitively, they understand the absurdity of pretense and the power of authenticity and truth.

Because not many people or women embody this ideal on a daily basis, Virgo men often become sarcastic and cynical, inwardly revolted at the lies that people create and call life. Deep inside, they long for someone to *really* talk to, and sometimes give up and out of loneliness settle for someone who seems pure but simple.

The challenge of the Virgo man's soul is to see beyond. In a society based on such superficial values, this is not an easy challenge. There is often so little stimulus and often such little reward. As a result, the most natural path is to become cynical or withdrawn. Reduced to automatic routines, the Virgo man succumbs to a norm. There is no power here. There is only the perpetuation of habit and the hanging on to the most bland sense of emotional security.

To experience power in love, the Virgo man must expand through it. Whether through manipulation or tyranny, Virgo men, often quiet or helpful in public, can be domineering monsters at home. This is partly because deeper, vulnerable and compassionate emotions are cut off and partly because his mind has created a tyrannical script that he believes.

Such a Virgo has created a version of reality which forms the basis of his security. This contributes to a rigid, steellike modus operandi designed to eliminate any potential of emotional pain. When this delusive powerbase begins to dictate the options of his daily life, it leaves little room for love. Virgo men may be kind and helpful but only as long as their partner falls into place on schedule.

Aristotle Onassis was a Virgo, and the stories are legendary concerning his coldhearted control and domination of the women in his life. Emotionally impaired, he

Virgo

brought his women, psychologically, to the brink of death. Interestingly enough, by the time of his own death, he had lost complete muscular control of his eyelids, a metaphor of his inability to see with his heart.

This idea of "seeing" is a particularly relevant one as it applies to the Virgo man. Virgo men often see the outer picture of others with sharp clarity. However, they do not see the depths of *themselves*. They do not look *into* themselves. Instead, they look outward.

The experience of love is a vast, mysterious one that brings into play many psychological factors. Some of them have to do with need, some with fear, some with desire. However, for mature, rich love, there has to be courage. This kind of courage allows one to be honest with one's self, a remarkably difficult task for the Virgo man. However, courage brings its own kind of miracles. The world looks larger and brighter, and there can be joy that comes from the heart and the power of feeling the grace of one's own aliveness. When it comes to the awesomeness of love, the Virgo man must learn that there is no power in the head. There is only power in emotional courage, and for such a controlled person, this courage will be tested day after day.

In the end there is the authentic, expansive give and take of love, or there is the experience of selfishness, which can be called by any name the ego chooses. But always, the choice is there, and it will dictate the life and the quality of the experience.

Long before it was considered fashionable, Virgo was considered the original workaholic. Meticulous and precise, conscientious and super-responsible, Virgo is a worker bee that functions best when praised and appreciated.

While some signs perform for money or power, Virgo works for love or duty. Virgo takes every detail personally. Seeking professional satisfaction rather than personal glory, Virgo thrives behind the scenes, providing that it can see that it contributes to overall performance. In such a setting, Virgo will be the first to arrive and the last to leave. With no extra pay, Virgo will eagerly take on a

125

terrifying load of responsibility as long as it feels that it is
improving an otherwise besieged situation.

Virgo is born from an old-world artisan attitude that
historically took great pride in excellence. The problem is
that a trend of impersonal power psychology pushes this
selfless work ethos far into the background. Therefore,
Virgos are the first to overwork themselves into a state of
exhaustion, and being quiet and humble, the last to asser-
tively ask for a raise.

Their natural tendency, therefore, is to give more
than they get, and in the long run, to feel foolishly compromised by the situation. Sad to say, the best of Virgo's
work intentions are seldom rewarded. Therefore, a lot of
emotional conflicts arise concerning their professional
choices.

A repeated theme in the Virgo experience is to give
out what it can't afford—and then afterwards to resent it,
turning the recipient into an avaricious demon. Work,
therefore, becomes both a rite of passage and a test of
power that is increasingly difficult to avoid. More than any
other sign, Virgo, being the astrological sign of work, must
encounter its self or lack of self in this realm of life. In the
process, many life challenges evolve.

For Virgo, worth is deeply experienced in the work
place. Yet seldom do Virgos voice expectations and establish successful parameters. It is here that they must begin
to deal with themselves.

Virgo can find great soulful meaning in work, and it
can also find significant lessons concerning its own personal expression and power. Summoning the courage to
deal with one's self in a manner that determines rather
than undermines one's own professional desires is a Virgo
challenge. In the process, it is necessary to be more
conscious of the cause and effect of their own behavior
and how it works for or against them. In the superficial
work situation, we are very often rewarded, not for our
worth, but for how we project ourselves as *worthy*. And it
is here that so often, Virgos mentally let their shoulders
slump while their back gives out with deep resentment.

Resentment is a very real issue in the Virgo realm of

work achievement. Another is the temptation to envy the underserved privileges or unpunished liberties of their coworkers. The only successful attitude is to look straight ahead in the mirror at the person who is *really* boss. When all is said and done, Virgos must learn how to manage themselves and must consciously develop that sense of responsibility. Power comes from self-worth, and self-worth is not dependent on compliments and hearty pats on the back. It comes from knowing the truth of your own strengths and from using that as a starting point for proceeding upwards, *regardless* of the bumps along the way. Sticking to this course is the light in the forest. In time, this light will come from within and it will be its own reward.

Powerful Virgo Psychology

What is great in man is that he is a bridge and not an end: what can be loved in man is that he is an overture *and a going under.*

—Nietzsche

To work toward and to achieve their potential, Virgos must expand their boundaries and consciously live with that vision of expansion in mind.

When Virgo is its own worst enemy, it suffers from not seeing far enough. Quick to condemn others as stupid and to feel snubbed, the Virgo mind judges subjectively from superficials and stops there. Always be able to go further, to penetrate deeper and you will arrive at pure truth. With truth comes the understanding and wisdom that is enlightening and uplifting.

Virgo must rise out of its narrow, self-invented world, dictated by routine, control, "efficiency," fear and jealousy, and tap its own creative source. When creating, Virgos transcend their own mental thought patterns and are affirmed by the creative act. Flowing with their intuition and sensibilities, experience can become magical and open-ended. Creation can enlarge the scope of life and bring one to the brink of infinite possibility. And it can be extended to one's daily acts. All it takes is imagination to change your world, to open it up and make it pulse with life. This active, disciplined use of imagination can become like an internal light that colors your world.

When too narrow, the Virgo world is colorless. Interpersonal experience is shallow and confined to lifeless communication centered around trivial, mundane experiences. There is no expression of vitality or possibility. This sort of Virgo's mind is painted with the earth, and it is a canvas that is depressing and lackluster, with the sense of a dwindling away with time.

Virgo has much to learn from its opposite, Pisces, the sign of infinite possibility and primordial chaos, expansive emotion and the magic of the muse. When we are able to embrace the wisdom of our polar opposite, we transcend ourselves and extend our boundaries. Consequently, life becomes a source of joy even in the "little" moments when, in passing or for a more prolonged time, we are able to take someone into our hearts and feel the rise that comes from the beauty of the connection. Like Pisces, Virgo needs to be more susceptible to beauty in all of its subtleties: the beauty of another person from whose heart there is something to learn, the aesthetic beauty of nature or the environment, the beauty of one's own inner world being brought to light.

Virgos who have transcended their own narrowness, yet have maintained their own impeccable eye for the perfection of form already think in terms of possibility. However, this must also extend to the emotional plane. You can multiply your life's potential if you can see with your heart. True power is the ability to do this through conscious depth awareness.

In any given moment, the more you are able to perceive, take in and incorporate into your private world, the greater the content within the form of your life. It is the content of your inner world that will allow you a powerful or powerless expression in the outer world. Every moment, whether appearing negative or positive, can carry its own power if you can rise to it and see beyond. Seeing beyond boundaries is the challenge of the Virgo mind. It is a power that can transform the entire life with time.

On a daily basis, get up in the morning, look at the sun and feel thankful that you're alive. Regardless of your problems, life is a miracle. Your life is a miracle if you are able to *see*. Learn to treat the small, "insignificant" moments of your life like the Japanese treat their tea ceremonies. Each detail is treated with the still freshness of beauty. Each gesture is one of concentrated, centered awareness. In everything that you do, cultivate this awareness as if it were a beautiful garden.

Maximizing Your Virgo Power Potential

A fundamental problem that many Virgos suffer from is fear—fear of failure, of rejection, of the future, of being betrayed, of growing old alone, of anything that could go wrong. Deep inside, the Virgo mind tends to fear the worst, and when this becomes a mental resting place, fears begin to manifest themselves as reality.

It is crucial that you develop a distance from your fears. Watch yourself generating them, and as each fearful thought pops up, mentally say to yourself "fear" and dismiss it. Don't identify with it.

Go into your inner world and select a couple of your deepest fears, the ones that give you the most trouble and that threaten your inner peace. Call them up in full color in your mind and then say to yourself "garbage out." See that image as contained in a clear plastic beach ball. Then visualize a huge blazing funeral pyre such as one sees in India with powerful, furnacelike flames that reach ten feet high. Throw your ball of fear into these flames. Hear its contents explode. See the contents of your fear disintegrate into nothingness in the sea of flame. Then say to yourself "garbage gone."

Your fears are mental garbage, and they do not have to have any power if you use your own power to destroy them. As you go through your day, monitor your mind. Be conscious of its contents. Whenever the contents are destroying your inner well-being, mentally destroy them.

The second Virgo power blockage is a diminished mental perspective. The following Buddhist mental exercise, called Ajikan, should be done daily, preferably in the morning. It will strengthen the mind while it also makes it flexible and elastic and capable of perceiving more with greater depth.

The exercise itself is extremely simple, yet powerful. See before you a small circle of your favorite color. In your mind, expand the circumference of the circle outward, further and further, until the circle disappears and you have nothing but space. Now, pull the circle in. Slowly, make it smaller and smaller until you have the tiniest dot. Finally, expand this dot into a circle and slowly bring it out once more into infinity.

The more you do this exercise, the more you will be stretching your own mind. Use this exercise in daily life. In a situation that is troublesome and confining, stretch it outward with your mind. When a situation is problematic and overwhelming, contract it in your mind to a tiny dot.

In truth, the experiences that we often see as so overwhelmingly significant, in the eyes of another person would be merely a dot, and vice versa. Our subjectivity tends to rule us. However, reality is never a fixed thing. Nor is it ever *one* thing. It all depends on your inner perspective.

Great, powerful masters are never bound by their own subjectivity. Through mental training, they can dominate their own moods, characters and qualities as well as the surrounding environment. They are not moved like pawns by their own impulses, by other people or by the "stars." They are so strongly centered that they radiate outward like a beam of the most powerful force. It all begins and ends with the mind, a mind so highly developed that it encompasses all, but is contained by nothing.

Much greater power can also be yours. Your fears are merely phantoms which you can destroy for good. But first you must be willing to move beyond your own imagined boundaries.

VII

LIBRA
(September 24–October 23)

The Libran Nature

In many respects, Libra is a sign of paradox. Librans
sprout from a series of contradictions: self versus nonself,
mental versus emotional, pleasure versus pathos, help-
fulness versus helplessness, generosity versus greed,
kindness versus coldness, control versus chaos. Underneath the smiling face and stellar charm lies a character
with many convolutions, confusions, frustrations and am-
bivalences concerning its identity. Combine this with very
high intelligence and you have people who think a great
deal about how they ought to be, how they should have
been, how they might have been and how they will be if
only . . . and so on. While this complicated process
sounds highly self-centered, it is in fact the workings of a
self that doesn't feel complete *by itself.* It always seems
that something is missing, and whether that appears to be
another person, a significant promotion, or a successful
project that will prove one's worth, the day-to-day drama
is often a torturous spiral.

The need to affirm one's self is so strong in Libras that it makes many of them burn with ambition. In the intensity of striving and accomplishing, one leaves the sense of lacking behind. Alas, the fuel for such ambition is the kind of anxiety that never lets one calm down. The satisfaction that comes from having achieved one's goal is soon supplanted by the necessity for a new creation. And so continues the rise and fall of doing and being. In between each gap is like a gasp in which a threatening, self-diminishing voice sneaks through.

That voice always whispers, Who am I? Am I this spectacularly smart, efficient, high-profile person that important people respect and value? Or am I a fearful fraud who will eventually be found out? The truth, of course, most always tends to be the former. However, should something fall short in the scheme of things, Librans fear, with a sickening sensation, that their demise is imminent. From this perspective, with a single-minded greed, Librans often envy the privileged who don't have to pay any price and get to keep the goods.

Success never seems terribly real to Librans unless they work very hard at it and pay a lot of dues along the way. Deep inside there is a bubbling fear that everything will disappear or be taken away. To live on this roller coaster of fear and vacillation is like facing a future with a plastic heart. The choices afford remarkably little freedom and only the most fleeting sense of control. Deeply anxious in the present, they let their dreams drive them toward a future in which they might one day feel like the person they most want to become.

Less ambitious Librans lose themselves in relationships or immerse themselves in a state of misery because of this lacking. Here, the need for authenticity is projected onto other people or onto a partner to whom they assign total power. It is through this realm that they seek satisfaction. Now instead of the agonies of "Who am I?" and "Whom might I become?," the record flips over to "Do they love me?" and "Will they leave me?"

In their overworked minds, Librans are always making comparisons. This has a great deal to do wih the extraordinary unhappiness and confusion seen so often in this sign. In any number of ways, Libra gives away its power and then feels pitiful and uniquely put upon. The question posed then is "Why are those people out there doing all this to *nice* me?"

The laments of this kind of Libra are like the cries of persecution during the time of the Spanish Inquisition. Quite often, the pain is just as inexorable. The story usually goes something like this: certain, significant people have simply ignored them or beaten them up or stolen their lottery ticket. In addition, their secretary treats them like a worn carpet, their upstairs neighbor has taken up the trumpet and the cleaning person mistook their new ten-thousand-dollar sculpture for an ashtray in which she burned her boyfriend's picture.

Such an unfolding of information usually involves many digressions and repetitions, during which one finds out a lot of other incidental information bearing no connection to the story line. Librans can be good listeners. However, they rarely hear themselves, and that is because they are so worn out by the internal dialogue playing itself out inside their head.

Likewise, Librans do not perceive the power their own behavior wields when life appears to go against them. Consequently, they tend to see themselves only as terribly nice people whom terrible bullies take advantage of or use like wilted lettuce between two slices of rye.

The truth is that Librans can be conciliatory. However, they can also be argumentative. They can be generous and gracious. They can also be selfish and determined to receive at any cost. They can be diplomatic, but they can also be insulting and provoking. They can be enormously kind, but they can also give just to get. They can also be as cold, remote and uncaring as a terrorist aiming a machine gun. They can be great peacemakers who love beauty and harmony. They can also be extremely ugly and vicious when turned inside out with rage.

The scales tip two ways—such is the true nature of Libra. However, it might be said that Librans tend to make up for their negative side through the spontaneous outpouring of their positive side. Their greatest limitation is that they never appreciate their gifts quite as much as other people do.

However, mature Librans stop worrying about this and their ego needs. Rather than being immersed in competitive thinking, they have reached a quiet place of self-acceptance. From this perspective, their involvements are generative outpourings of love, rather than piteous, consuming cries for attention.

Libran Strengths

Libra could have invented the good life. This charmed person exuding social grace is *persona grata* at formal functions and is everybody's favorite dinner guest. Dazzling hosts themselves, Libras adore their own parties and know instinctively how to create a highly memorable occasion.

Libras have an unsurpassed talent for bringing out the beauty in life. They relish and revel in beauty in all forms and find it everywhere they look. And as is usually the case, they are always looking for it everywhere.

The fact that their ruler is Venus implies that Librans are highly pleasure-oriented. Librans' communication of this can be like a religious experience. The classic Libra personality is highly perceptive and alert to all the seductive subtleties of life. Their own beauty comes in their ability to create from their sensibilities.

With a flourish they can create "a moment" out of the most banal circumstance. What was merely a floor becomes a picnic ground in February. The iridescence of champagne shimmering in crystal, a perfectly staged flower here, a brightly colored "floor setting" there, and of course candlelight everywhere, and what better way to forget the February blahs? Life is as large as the Libran imagination, which can be pure magic. Librans love luxury. However, they can also make a humble circumstance look luxurious. The pleasure they convey through their creations would be inspiring to Aphrodite herself. Beauty

136

is not simply beauty for beauty's sake. It conveys a transcendent spirit of life which is a gift for being alive. It whispers, Leave the pettiness and the sorrow behind. Feel the rise in beauty, feel the glorious ascension and celebrate it. It is everywhere and in everything. Just learn how to look.

It is this ability to see that sets Librans apart from most other people. It is their gift. Librans notice everything and how everything fits in with everything else. Instinctively, they understand relativity and interrelationship, harmony and proportion, the importance of perspective. They bring this sense of symmetry to all experience, not merely the aesthetic. It is in the field of human relationships that they live out the search and struggle for the sort of balance that brings peace and harmony.

Librans have highly conciliatory ways of communicating, the essence of which is that they make you understand that they understand your side. While so many people suffer from subjective thinking, this sign is able to see clearly the different perspectives that make up a conflict and the best way to satisfy both sides to achieve the most workable outcome. Libra is an air sign which has to do with thought and mental processes. Therefore, they are able to sort out a sea of feelings without adding in their own emotion. In doing so, they remain detached yet sympathetic and understanding. It is this ability that enables them to get to the truth of a situation without being pulled in. Even their way of communicating emotions makes them clear, understandable, manageable and in control. The talent for perceiving truth and communicating with precision often puts them several steps ahead of people who get locked into distortions and delusions.

Given this, it should not be surprising that Librans make excellent lawyers, diplomats and couple counselors. This sign also has razor-sharp intelligence supported by excellent communication skills. This highly developed verbal ability combined with a refined aesthetic sense also lends them much talent in the arts, especially in the areas of music and writing. John Lennon and F. Scott Fitzgerald were two Libran notables whose respective trademarks had to do with their striking visions of life.

Libra is also a sign known for its lively wit. Again, this pervasive sense of humor comes from an ability to *see* the ludicrous in all circumstances, to find keen enjoyment in it and to take pleasure in communicating it to others.

The Libran desire to share is a higher octave function of Venus. Librans love to share their bliss as well as the lackluster moments of their bad days. Knowing how to share is one of the boons of their nature. They can be the best of friends and the most inventive lovers. At the very least, Libras tend to be a lot of fun. Their laughter and love of a good time lights up the space around them and leaves one feeling as if on holiday—a holiday much awaited that has only just begun.

Libra Pitfalls

Despite the arresting talent, intelligence, charm, grace, beauty and sheer capability seen so often among natives of this sign, Librans have a strong tendency to make themselves miserable. They lack the capacity to appreciate, enjoy and be thankful for their own gifts, though these same gifts in someone else would be cause for envy.

There are several reasons for this. Fundamentally, the sun in Libra bears the quality of the sun in its fall. This means that the ego and the sense of self is very weak, leaving Librans with the nagging fear of being somehow deficient. It is as if a cold, critical father quietly pursues them, not allowing them to incorporate meaningfully the positive feedback that they receive from the outside world. The behavior of the classic Libran personality is alternately self-critical and compensatory. One moment they obsess over a sense of inadequacy and possible rejection; the next, they obnoxiously show off some quality that they see to be a source of power. Three days later, they are down again.

What is the middle ground? Where is the truth? This question is the focus of the classic Libran's entire life.

Libra

Libra is the seventh house sign in the zodiacal circle. The seventh house has to do with the experience of others. It is also called the house of open enemies. Therefore, the psychological experience of Libra is intrinsically tied into the experience and perception of others. Thus, when you have an ego or sense of self that is weak and uncertain to begin with and you add to this a strong orientation towards others who can easily be perceived as highly threatening (open enemies), you have a person who suffers a great deal of confusion in terms of self-perception. Many Librans suffer from a perpetual identity crisis that can continue well past middle age. Small emotional crises arise in their life on a frequent basis, crises initiated by their own nagging sense of uncertainty and the tenuous place this leaves them with regard to significant others. Being an air sign, which has to do with communication, they feel they need to talk about their fears and uncertainties with friends. It often appears to those patient people who lend their ears that while the circumstance may change, the story remains the same. This poor Libran is being battered about by his or her parent, boss, business partner, lover, spouse, erstwhile friend. In point of fact, Librans' feelings are being battered about by their own brains, and the bottom line issue is *not* what someone else is doing to them, it is what they do to themselves, or don't do *for* themselves.

Poor pitiful Librans assign all of their power to other people. They do this for several reasons, none of which are they ever conscious of, unless, of course, they have had successful psychotherapy. Librans can be highly responsible people to other people. However, they don't like to be responsible for themselves. It is something they neither enjoy nor know how to do terribly well.

Therefore, what they tend to do is put all of their supersonic intelligence into manipulating other people into taking care of them. And they do this quite artfully: they set up situations in which they appear to be the one who is giving. At the time, the person receiving is much too flattered, charmed, teary-eyed and breathlessly taken aback to realize that there is a sizable agenda down the

139

road. Giving, for this type of Libra, is no impulsive act, but rather a clever, long-range investment. Harold Pinter wrote a brilliant play around this very phenomenon. Interestingly enough, the play is entitled *The Servant*. In it, the butler, who begins the play as the obsequious servant, ends up controlling his boss.

The not-quite-conscious intention of the terribly generous and often obsequious Libra is not so much control as it is a deep desire to have needs taken care of. Sadly, what happens, as can happen to *all* investments, is that the bottom often falls out. Once again, a lonely, sniffling Libran is the victim of someone else.

Librans tend to talk a lot, and never hear themselves. If they could possibly hear their own words and how they are repeated, they might gain an insight into *their* behavior, which is the source of *their* problem. Librans have extraordinary expectations of other people, while the expectation they maintain of themselves is "nice person despite all circumstances."

What this nice person tends to do is lose himself or herself in other people. Being ruled by Venus, a highly self-indulgent planet, Librans are fond of indulging themselves and those who serve their needs.

It is this element of self-indulgence that makes immature members of this sign difficult to deal with. Because the influence of Venus is a strong one, many Librans remain immature for most of their lives. Those who are mature understand that the issue of relationship is the issue of relating to another, not of losing one's self in that other. Consequently, they take responsiblity for themselves, their decisions, desires, mistakes and achievements. Their achievements come about because they focus their strengths on their positive, self-affirming goals.

Immature Librans create emotion traps in which they remain stuck. In the end, the only way to emerge, is to claim one's own personhood and take responsibility for it. This conscious choice of who one is to become is the first step toward owning one's own power and sense of possibility.

Power and Love: The Libra Woman

The Libra woman is in love with love, in all its gauzy and phantasmagoric manifestations. However, this is not the emotional sentimentalism of the Cancer woman, who experiences the feeling of love through her emotions and sensual memory. This is the longing of a woman who lives and loves through her mind.

The Libra woman would have you believe that she is highly emotional. And certainly she seems to sound it. However, what she is expressing is her emotions concerning her thoughts. This is a woman who is in love with the *idea* of grand love, the cinema of a Technicolor takeoff of a great classic: the *idea* of waltzing on a moonlit beach in white silk with a man so handsome his eyes separate the waters of the incoming tides, the *idea* of a modern-day dragon slayer, strong, muscle-bound and motivated only by the desire to protect her. In her mind's eye, the Libra woman lusts for a hero, the kind of old-fashioned fellow who is fated to become godlike. However, the sad truth is that the initial reviews are too frequently misleading. For instance, the powerful and courageous prince is really paranoid. The screen of the Metro-Goldwyn-Mayer goes up in flames and starts to look like a smoldering Bronx fire. The towers of the castle crumble and the ominously silent phone starts to make nasty faces. What is a serious, committed romantic to do? It truly seems that there is only one solution. Start over.

At the end of act three, we have a woman who is about as emotional as John Wayne. What happened to the man who inspired such beatitudes, such bliss, such revelations? Oh, he was just a jerk, she mutters absentmindedly and cleans his remaining belongings from her closet. Off she goes into the great beyond and before long, a new stud emerges in her life whom she briefly elevates into a mystic vision of romantic bliss.

One Libra woman I know openly admits that she married her *ex*-husband because he was a *great* dancer, another because he was voted best looking in his high school class. Others I know went for rich and handsome, exciting and handsome, almost famous and very well dressed. But should he break a leg or the boredom set in, there unfortunately goes all the fun.

When it comes to love, the Libra woman tends to lose her power not so much to the *man*, but to her own psychological projections, which actually prevent her from allowing him to be real. Her experience of her lover tends to be the shallow one which suits her fantasies at the time.

Besides looks, what a Libra woman sees in her man of the moment are the qualities in herself which she feels or fears to be lacking. If she came from a poor family, he might be from a wealthy or socially prominent one. If she is fearful and has many problems making decisions, he will be confident and adventurous. If she is insecure about her intelligence, he will display a strong intellectual prowess and perhaps have an impressive education. If she sees herself as very short, he will probably be very tall. And so on. In embracing these qualities in another person it is as if she is taking them into herself. However, one of the difficult lessons of life is our own aloneness and the acknowledgement and acceptance of our own individuality. If we are frightened and insecure, we are going to remain frightened and insecure until we confront the demons within that are keeping us this way. Other people can help, but they can't take away who we are.

The Libra woman must look for truth in her relationships rather than illusions if she is going to grow with them. This truth implies psychological freedom because it demands that she give up roles and stereotypical visions to communicate with real people—both herself and her partner. In order to do this, she has to want to dig beneath the surface and feel something for the humanity of the man she claims to love. And if she can't, then she should choose for a time to be alone to discover for herself who she is and isn't, whom she desires to be, and whom she might become.

When a Libra woman is repeatedly disappointed and disillusioned in love, it has to do with *her*, her illusions, her lack of an affirmative selfhood, her lack of power as a person. The Libra woman who loves through the grace of her own power shares her complete self with another self. She connects *to* rather than trying to escape *from*. Instead of stultified thinking, she feels compassion—compassion for human limitation, because she is aware of her own limitations. And because she knows her own worth, she is able to care for herself and communicate the same caring to another.

Power and Love: The Libra Man

When involved, the Libra man mentally begins all of his sentences with "we" and ends them with "us." This is a man who understands the principle of partnership as well as the sort of give and take that baffles men of many other signs.

Unless immature (which we will get to), this is a man who actually *wants* a relationship. The Libra man does not like being alone and always surrounds himself with people, even if the situations are superficial and the personalities quickly come and go.

The Libra man is an extraordinary romantic with refined sensibilities. He is highly susceptible to beauty in all shapes, colors and forms. A beautiful face makes his day—but also makes him dreadfully insecure because a fearful voice deep inside of him says he can't have it.

Because his nature is so other-oriented, the Libran man sees his associations as self-reflections. Therefore, one of his favorite fantasies is to walk into a party with a stellar beauty who is blind to all but him. The Libran man is a strange combination of deeply insecure and strongly idealistic. Therefore, he seeks to fashion his future on his dreams.

When his mental freeze frame is satisfied and in full operation, Mr. Libra will then begin to feel. If he feels secure and in love, he will most likely want to get married. To this man, marriage is the apogee of partnerships. He completes himself and, in the process, finds a new facet of experience which makes him feel less afraid. Those Libra men who choose to live alone always have a history studded with less-than-inspiring relationships that have fizzled and left them feeling distrustful, disillusioned and drained. However, living on the loose is not the nature of these fellows either. Too much time alone can make them unbalanced, moody, depressed and dangerously susceptible to drugs or alcohol.

Happily married, Mr. Libra is a model husband, one who will remember birthdays, anniversaries, Valentine's Days and the exact day of the first date. If he doesn't cook, he'll do the dishes. He'll probably also take out the garbage, frequently suggest going out to dinner, and when dining in, supply the perfect flowers for pizza by candlelight. He also has a superior sense of humor, which can smooth a bad day into the beginning of a great evening. Not only is the Libran man considerate and romantic, but when caught in a conflict he will communicate constructively—with insight, intelligence and reason. Above all, he sincerely desires to please.

This is when he is in love. When out of love or when immature, he can be cold, conniving and motivated by a selfish ego. This is a man who must hear "bells ring" for the most superficial reasons. Should he hear gongs or feel that the romance is fading, then he will find his own way to disappear. Suddenly, a situation with so much promise quickly becomes a thing of the past. Libra is an air sign, after all. Air has to do with mental pictures, not emotions. Because he is smart, quick-witted and insightful, the Libra man can *understand* emotions. Yet what he *feels* has more to do with what he thinks and what is externally influencing his thought processes at the time.

He has an uncanny way of turning complex emotions into statements of cool reason. All at once, adumbrated feelings seem so tidy and so *terribly* in place. The Libra man likes to figure it all out. And when he doesn't, a few times falling on his face and getting messed up from his own tears is great for helping him to grow up and get beyond the demands of his "baby" self.

When successfully past the thumb-sucking and capable of hearing his own heart, the Libra man has the capacity to experience great love. There is great power in this because it requires a delicate balance of the mind and the heart, the self and other, love and self-love. Higher emotions come into play that are personal and compassionate rather than merely romantic and based on illusion, projection and ego. A caring evolves which enhances the ability to perceive each moment. In all its majesty, love illuminates two minds and hearts and brings them together as one. From the depth of this experience, each individual can be reborn into the best of what they already are. The light goes forth as energy into a darkened world.

Power and Work: Libra

Workwise, Librans are both masterful and efficient. Their thinking is keen, logical and objective. They have an intuitive sense of timing and a highly creative mind that abounds with ideas. Librans are also perceptive, aware and know how to make ideas work for them. Combine all this with excellent communication skills and a strong ability to work with people and you have the raw material of a multimillionaire entrepreneur.

The Libran problem is insecurity. Librans have a terrible time trusting their position. Consequently, they tend, sometimes unconsciously, to put obstacles in their own path. These obstacles might have to do with timing— procrastinating or a hindering situation they have unconsciously set up out of fear. Or it might have to do with becoming professionally involved with the wrong person because they were proceeding out of emotional needs rather than confidence and objective awareness. Librans find countless ways to sabotage themselves because of the fear factor. Unfortunately, at such times, a tendency to be self-indulgent overtakes their personality and leaves them writhing and contorting with the feeling of being victimized.

Many Librans are chronic complainers who dump responsibility onto other people. They want aid, support, soothing and someone who takes charge of all the areas that they are loathe to look upon. When this heralded ideal turns into a fire-breathing dragon, the anguish and the anger can foment for a very long time.

On the other hand, I have known a number of Librans who are *totally* successful people. Their talent, intelligence and capability aside, one very important factor defines them: they succeed *in spite of*—In spite of time problems, in spite of people problems, in spite of momentary failure, in spite of their own fear. They have a flexibility and a positiveness that completely paves the way. These are the people who turn visions into vistas that steadily unfold their fruits with time. These people don't whine about what they don't have. They concentrate on what they do have, and using all their strengths in a conscious and constructive manner, they multiply their holdings and the sense of who they are.

Librans often have a way of communicating their problems that makes them sound very complicated. However, the problems are always very simple. It is their lack of mental discipline that creates the sense of confusion. Librans need discipline in order to know power first hand. Discipline is fuel in the down moments. It is the drive that keeps things going over humps. It is not enough to be smart, clever, brilliant, original, have a head full of ideas. An undisciplined, self-indulgent mind is like a car with no wheels. Librans tend to steer toward dreams, ideals and self-indulgence and veer away from discipline. Consequently, many of them are like bright, shiny sports cars with nothing to drive on. The power is there but the car is going nowhere. The ego craves the end result but the undisciplined brain cannot command the effort. At a certain point, it wants to be elsewhere—usually with a lover in which it can lose itself and its fears—if for just another day.

There are Librans who are so insecure that they stop striving altogether. Afraid to compete, afraid of a failure that does not even exist, they withdraw into the lull of a safe, inconsequential existence. Inordinate safety is the *sine qua non* of such a person who sabotages her or his special gifts through allowing them to lie dormant. Thus, this creative, supertalented personality can be the classic underachiever terrified of risk, unable to move beyond the sanctuary of self that has become, with time, a prison.

When a Libran is able to take pleasure in work, the fear recedes and a deep, inner power is born that is confident and in control. In order for this to happen, the person has to so merge with the work that he or she loses all self-consciousness. This experience is much like the one-point-at-a-time attitude of the successful player on a tennis court. There is no sense of "I." There is only the concentrated sense of the experience.

Again, without discipline and self-control, this magical concentration cannot come into play. Achievement and accomplishment must begin somewhere. For Librans, there must be a conscious choice to use their powers—not to lose them to their fears or to any other people along the way.

Powerful Libran Psychology

> What happens to a man is characteristic of him.
>
> —Carl Jung

Characteristically, Librans assign power to other people and events to the detriment of their own power. Each time this happens, they forfeit the joy of experiencing their own talents and of projecting their uniqueness to the world.

Powerful people are directed from within. They trust their own intuition and they rely on their own judgment. It is here that Librans tend to lose their footing. There is a great deal of internal dialogue in the Libran mind that often interferes with confident, concise, linear thinking. In troubled times, the thoughts issue from fear and insecurity and become obsessive-compulsive. Fueled by anxiety, the Libran mind doesn't focus on the resolution to the matter; rather it dwells on the emotions caused by the problem. When negative emotions feed Librans' thought processes, they cause greater anxiety and more fear, all the while undermining the sense of confidence.

Words and thoughts have great power. Negative, fearful thoughts diminish power. Positive thoughts create strength. In a weakened state, Librans tend to talk endlessly about their problems, repeating the story again and again as the negative emotional power grows. While it is beneficial to share problems thoughtfully to obtain perspective, the Libran mind tends to become immersed in its own words and consequently brings itself down through the telling.

In this manner, the emotional weight of a problem tends to mushroom in the Libran mind, rather than decrease with time. When undisciplined, the Libran mind dwells in the reactive stage. Stuck there, it relives the situation obsessively and thereby dampens its own powers of reason and intuition.

In order to become more powerful, you must build your own powerbase. Consequently, you must control your negative thoughts and coldly concentrate on the dynamics of the issue. You must also stop feeding yourself the negative dialogue that goes nowhere.

Become aware of how your thoughts control you. Cancel out those thoughts that undermine you and concentrate on a detached perspective of the problem. Talk to your negative thoughts as you would to a very negative person. *Out*talk your own negative thoughts and listen to the kinds of words you are using to combat the negativity.

In order to experience yourself more powerfully, you must will to do so. If you want to radiate from your own source and stop depending on other people, you must work very hard at trusting your own mind. When you succeed, you will have preferences rather than needs and dependencies. You will operate from your heightened intuition and honed awareness, and your behavior will be calm, appropriate and exacting. You will never complain that someone else slighted you, because you will look at experience from a perspective of power and beneficence. You will use your will with consciousness and take responsibility for all of your decisions. When problems create minor upsets, you will live through them with fluidity, dignity and exactitude, and then you will move on.

Self-acceptance, self-love, courage and compassion will be the rewards of consciously canceling out your mental negativity. Peace and inner harmony will be the by-products.

What all this adds up to is a different kind of life—a life in which you are at the top of the mountain instead of staggering back and forth through the hills and valleys. You have everything inside of you to have the emotional fulfillment you want, *right now*. But first you must stop giving the power away. Take responsibility for yourself. Develop yourself. Then enjoy the self that you are sharing. When you come from a place of wholeness, what you bring out in other people will be the most positive reflection of yourself. Cultivate your self-love and live through that discriminating intelligence, and your experiences will become a statement of it. That statement will be the stamp of your life.

Maximizing Your Libra Power Potential

We attract what we dwell on. And what we dwell on, we become. Librans tend to dwell on their insecurities and misgivings. In their minds, they tend to relive the past and to become deeply embroiled in the emotions that arise from what is essentially mental labor.

As already stated, Librans have a high intelligence. Yet they so often use their minds to make life more difficult. Decisions are difficult. Emotional confrontations are difficult. Keeping to their center when negatively swayed by another person seems so often impossible. The quagmire of emotions surrounding unresolved issues can be consuming.

Essentially, Librans make the basic bumps of life far more complicated than they are. To become more powerful in the day-to-day dilemmas, they must first learn how to simplify.

The self-esteem of the Libran is based on the number of snags in their own thinking. Their subjective experience of life is based upon their self-esteem. Librans are so often miserable because they don't trust and respect themselves in certain situations. They don't trust themselves, because their thinking becomes jangled and muddled.

To change this pattern, you must begin by watching your thoughts. Perceive them and separate yourself from them. Are they negative? Are they repetitive? Do they go in circles? Do they create anxiety? If so, these are garbage thoughts and you must get rid of them. Mentally picture yourself throwing them out as if they were garbage. In doing this, you will clear your mind and you will access more mental energy.

Replace these thoughts with positive thoughts and ideas. Focus your mental energy on these thoughts and feed yourself with them. Make this little exercise a routine part of your daily life. Observe yourself thinking in the shower, on the way to work, in conversation with another person. The more you train your mind and direct your thinking, the easier it will become. Eventually, it will be the way you think, and this will show in your life.

It is also extremely helpful to work with affirmations. Affirmations are written statements of positive goals that you want to achieve. Write your positive goals down on index cards. Carry the cards around with you and read them every day, several times a day. When writing them out, use such positive, affirmative language as "I am in control of my own mind and will powerfully eradicate all negative thinking today"; "I am eliminating my fear of lack of money and now see large sums of money as a symbol of my positive self worth"; and so on.

It is also helpful to carry around inspiring quotations that motivate you and make you feel as if you're listening to a helpful, understanding friend.

Eventually, what you will see is a new person. You will find yourself dealing positively and powerfully with yourself as well as with others. You will have a sense of confidence that is real and that projects outward. This confidence will help you deal more effectively with your day-to-day problems and will enable you to create what you want from life.

Libra

This undertaking takes discipline, patience and persistence. However, watching yourself grow steadily more powerful should be greatly satisfying. Every day can become a new adventure in which from a very private perspective, you watch yourself unfold. You will feel excited and inspired by what you see!

VIII

SCORPIO
(October 24–November 22)

Scorpio Nature

Scorpio might be the most misunderstood sign of the zodiac. It is a convoluted sign, commonly associated with mystery, sex, power and intrigue. At cocktail parties, the simple confession "I am a Scorpio" can send crowds scurrying in different directions. In social gatherings where the communication has descended to the most superficial astrological chitchat, Scorpio gets more than its share of abuse.

Much of this has to do with the fact that at any given point a great deal of the Scorpionic agenda remains hidden. Intensely private, strongly secretive and rather suspicious, Scorpio does not reveal itself to anyone, nor does it form close friendships overnight. For the most part, members of this sign stand aloof from more obvious social interactions. Scorpios prefer one-to-one situations to large parties at which people present their social facades. This is a sign of depth and depth perception. Scorpios see and feel far more than most people, and not infrequently these feelings are complicated and problematic. Because of this, at a very early age, they develop a deep need for control, along with a list of goals and game plans that will take them where they want to go.

The need for control and power are key factors in the Scorpio personality. To many signs, power has to do with the cause and effect of external events. To Scorpio, it has to do with the experience of self and self-mastery. "I will, therefore I am" is the core of the Scorpionic scheme of things. To be out of control or to be under someone else's control are deathlike experiences for the classic Scorpionic mind. Scorpio is the sign of death, sex and transformation. Herein lies the divinity and the mystery of this sign, for each of these experiences has deep psychological value, the potential of which is great power.

Sex has profound power in the Scorpio mind. This influence is vast and psychologically pervasive. Sex is a psychology for Scorpio which enters into all things. Sexually tuned in to all circumstances, this awareness can lead to an emotionally intense experience of life. Or when the feelings are cut off and compartmentalized, the quality of sex can remain shallow, compulsive and lascivious.

The power of sex is the power of connectedness. Sex can connect all aspects of ourselves—our minds, hearts, souls and sexual organs. It can connect this complex whole with the complex whole of another. However, this sort of transcendental, passionate sex which makes the gods sigh and which is transformative by its very nature is not what the majority of people, cut off by their deadening routines, are capable of. Likewise, many Scorpios, bearing the legacy of the sexual sign of the zodiac, have in fact cut off their feelings into neat compartments which fuel their desire for material power.

However, still erotic by nature, Scorpionic sexual urges will seek satisfaction in all kinds of ways—from pornography to promiscuity, inflamed by intense flights of fantasy. When cut off, Scorpio makes its connections pornographic, that is, there is only a genital connection but no deep, inner mind-soul connection. Thus there is no emotional content. Many Scorpios remain so disconnected that they never know the mind-shattering power of sex. However, they do sense a deep, inner loneliness and a confused desire for something more. This they usually bury under their hardened, life-denying routines, which in turn bury *them* under years of their own life.

The more alive and connected we are, the more we are able to become fully alive in ourselves through sex. This is the power of sex: the power of life and possibility. However, like all power, the only way one can enjoy it is if one has really earned it. Otherwise, the strain of pretense will begin to wear on the mind with time.

Possessing an extraordinary lust for power, the Scorpio mind is often worn away, turned in on itself and turned off to others. In the extreme, this results in emotions that are swollen with turbulence and turmoil.

Unsublimated Scorpionic emotions are the substance of hell. The mood swings, depressions, obsessions, compulsions, fears, anxieties, anger, rage and bouts of deep inner loneliness bordering on alienation are enough to send an average person around the bend. In its rawest moment, Scorpio sees the inexorable ugliness, horror, brutality and cruel underlying truth in life. It is the excruciating discomfort of this vision which makes them fear helplessness with a gut-wrenching aversion. Control and power then become the means to security and transcendence in an otherwise savagely chaotic world.

The pathway of the Scorpionic archetype takes an individual, at some point or another, through the depths of intense emotional experiences. Each step of the way they are challenged by inner voices as well as the capacity for maintaining control. Often there will be a painful descent into their own underworld, yet they will ultimately emerge changed and reborn. The new personality sees, hears, desires and is fulfilled in a different way. However, before this renewal can take place there must be the serpentine shedding of the skin—the release of the old condition—and this will inevitably involve pain.

Something within the psyche, deep within the fabric of existence, must die to make way for the miracle of rebirth. When this death occurs, when this psychological surrender to the unknown, to fate, or to the "finger of God" takes place, it is a moment that defies both courage and control. Old conditions on which securities, expectations, trust and need were based are annihilated. Here is the hope of new life, a life very different from what was previously known and accepted.

Scorpio has the most extraordinary power of self-renewal and self-mastery. Hardened criminals can turn into firebrand ministers, "hopeless" alcoholics into evangelical teetotalers, terminal patients into "miraculously" healed healers. But first there must be the descent, the surrender, and the pain of sacrificing the past. The miraculous, which is inherent in this sign, bears witness to the fact that new life does come from death. However, it is not the life that the ego envisions. It is life that comes from a higher truth and a transformed way of being.

Power is the central focus of the Scorpionic experience. In its baser forms it is power in business and sexual power. Behind this kind of power is the manipulative psychology "In order to get something I will look like I have something to offer." However, this kind of thinking generates shallow, empty human connections, the opposite of what the Scorpionic soul needs for emotional and psychological nourishment.

The word *power* comes from the Latin word *potere,* which means "to be able." Power is important because it implies an enabling situation instilled with possibility. Part of this possibility can be a richness of content, a depth, a boundless ability to comprehend with the heart and not with the ego. This is a critical Scorpio test and one not easily mastered. What the average Scorpio knows as power is ego power, and that is why it needs so much control. When the ego is on the line, it must be both fed and protected. Ultimately, this can require a great deal of energy focused solely on self. On a very deep level, under all of the games, maneuvers, manipulations and power plays, Scorpio may be the most vulnerable of signs. This is because Scorpio desire is far deeper and more intense than any other sign. The tentacles of this desire are so far-reaching that they often come to define the sense of self and self-esteem.

When the do-or-die-1'll-do-it-my-way-or-not-at-all syndrome of Scorpio controls the person, there is often an individual who in one way or another cuts herself or himself off from other people. The paradox of this sign is that it can cut off with the same degree of urgency with which it deeply desires to connect. Appearances to the contrary, Scorpios cannot shut off their feelings like a water faucet. However, with remarkable control, they can cut off their outward responses. There are Scorpios who have learned how to live on this low threshold of life in a monotonous, deadened existence where there are no rises, but no falls either, no gains but no pain. This kind of Scorpio entertains a certain ego-dominated satisfaction from self-control and the sense of superiority experienced by watching others suffer who are not equally in control. In fact, this kind of willful, egotistical response often becomes their only source of energy in an empty existence lived through head games and a deadened heart.

Scorpio is symbolized by three members of the animal kingdom: the scorpion, the serpent and the phoenix. The first of these stings others, and when trapped, will sting itself to death. The second, the serpent, has to do with Scorpio wisdom, change, death and transformation. This stage of development marks the beginning of being able to see beyond the self, and beyond the needs of the small, egocentric existence. It is the first stage of yearning for something higher, brighter and vaster that adds meaning to the life. This is a level of profound emotional and psychological change. At the phoenix level, emotional desire largely becomes transpersonal. Low-level power urges are transformed into compassionate responses. A wisdom has been born as a result of many deep emotional changes. As a result, a strong, affirmative center has come to define the consciousness. This center which is like an internal light, is true power as opposed to the compulsive, egotistical need to grasp and manipulate for purely selfish ends. Along with this comes an ability to perceive and proceed toward a higher good that in itself has come to be emotionally nourishing and meaningful.

At this stage of evolution, there is a quiet, joyous inner freedom. The tensions and consuming life struggles have given way to an elevated level of consciousness that has become a level of being and a way of life. This is the payoff of psychological power. The bumps, of course, still happen on the outside. However, there is no turmoil within. When wisdom and understanding come to play, crises come to have meaning and imply a greater sense of possibility. When one has accumulated enough personal power, the mind can create miracles in the most mundane circumstances of life.

In the end, the only real power that one can possess is in one's inner space. One can be chairman of the board, or ruler of a vast domain. However, one must still die alone. One must experience physical suffering alone in one's body. One is alone with one's own inner demons and fears. In view of these essential experiences, the Scorpionic question is, Who are you *in total truth?* Who could you be given your own limitless potential? The answer is, *Everything.*

The Scorpio who no longer *has to be* anything because of ego needs, is free to be themselves. In the depths of that freedom lies limitless potential, which is the apotheosis of true power. This sort of individual is authentic, wise, at peace within, and is able to connect deeply with others. All emotional trials lead to this ultimate self-mastery. When this essence spurs one on towards greater power within, all emotional and psychological struggles begin to have meaning. Each is a metaphor and each unfolds a parable of one's uniqueness. All that is required is to trust the courage, the intelligence and the truth of one's own soul.

Scorpio Strengths

When intensely focusing their will, Scorpios can accomplish anything. An invincible force, the Scorpio will enables Scorpios to rise above against all odds. Notable

Scorpio

Scorpios are Actress Katharine Hepburn; the artist Georgia O'Keeffe, who lived and worked in the desert by herself into her nineties; and Teddy Roosevelt, known for his motto, "Speak softly and carry a big stick." Inherent within the highly evolved Scorpio is the warrior spirit who defies insurmountable obstacles and attains heroism as if it were a divine right.

Scorpios can invent themselves, give birth to new selves and transform old dying selves. Scorpio is a sign of extremes: of great suffering and the most deeply felt joy, of insidious death and superhuman resurrection. In a lifetime, Scorpios often die a series of little deaths and experience ascents born from turbulent psychological labor.

Death is often a critical factor in the Scorpionic life. A beloved person dies, a highly significant relationship dissolves, a business, goal, achievement or cherished hope turns to dust, and the result is a deep inner sense of devastation, usually self-contained and sometimes leading to a depression that is deadening.

However, it is from such profound experiences that a new strength is born, usually through a combination of willful assertion and enhanced insight. In the wake of these onslaughts, a powerful psychological energy is released and a new level of performance comes into being.

There is an archetypal and godlike quality about Scorpio strength. A superhuman will issues out of the depth of pain and comes to bear with powerful emotional and psychological intensity. On the surface, the Scorpio personality may appear cool and removed. However, their emotional energies are volcanic.

Such engulfing emotional transformations serve the purpose of tremendous psychological breakthroughs, shattering the protective veneer and bringing about freer and more elevated ways of coping. Through such an experience a power is often unleashed that enables one to see circumstances, one's life purpose and emotional depths take one beyond the dimensions of the old self, into a life of greater possibility.

However, because of the deep, often unconscious

161

emotional convolutions that can influence or distort the logical thinking pattern, this still remains a most challenging sign where one is often at war with one's self or where various aspects of one's life conflict or even contradict each other. Scorpio is a sign associated with highly successful business executives, financiers, and world rulers, Jordan's King Hussein being an example of the latter. Such people are able to use their superior concentration to channel emotional energies to fuel their goals. They create highly systematic worlds where control is achieved through orderly thinking and foresight. The flow continues as anticipated as long as life does not seriously challenge them or they do not challenge themselves by yearning for greater meaning. It often seems that crises are necessary in order for this sign of fixed water (emotion) to change.

Due to its propensity for becoming deeply attached and security-seeking, Scorpio suffers intensely when its props are pulled out from under it. Yet this is a sign that usually understands suffering and its inevitability. This can be a great strength from which profound wisdom can be born. Scorpio has the capacity to perceive truth in all circumstances. It can see beyond comforting illusions and attachments into the most painful aspects of human existence. It is as if there is a vast coming together which enables the mind to be beyond the veil of *maya*, the monotonous and mundane world—and from there to find meaning which does not exist for the complacent pursuers of pleasure and security.

This kind of Scorpio is aware of death in life and the kind of life that can proceed from death. There is a richness to the character that comes from a superconscious source. And there is a compassionate heart that extends itself far beyond itself to love, to share, to attest to the miraculous power of human connection devoid of falsities and pretense. Through a heart that is pure, Scorpio can heal psychologically, and in the process can extend its own boundaries. Through this capacity, it is a sign of infinite possibility embodied in its capability to perceive, to feel and to understand with depth.

162

As the sign of the unfathomable eighth house, Scorpio is associated with the Divine Mysteries. These Mysteries involve the power that can be born from surrender to a higher power. This surrender can be pure, simple and quiet, or it can be the resulting emergence from an experience of emotional, psychological or physical disintegration. However, it is the portal to a beatific joy that is boundless and infinite. The ultimate archetypal strength of Scorpio is the experience of the infinite contained from within, the miraculous housed within the self that is each human being's potentiality and power.

Scorpio Pitfalls

Probably like no other sign, Scorpion pitfalls have great potential for a positive conversion of power. The Scorpio soul is a battleground of the forces of light and darkness playing themselves out on many levels with the overworked mind ticking away in the middle. The great intensity of this sign will find no relief until it finds its soul, its true center in its involvements and attachments. All detours to and from this source will bring on a gnawing, deep-seated anxiety, a need for withdrawal and escape, and a simultaneous desire for connection and control.

Classic Scorpios have calm, sibilant voices and a cool demeanor. However, deep under the surface, this nature is so intense that in ordinary circumstances disturbing emotions are driven under cover. In many cases, when there has been early psychological trauma, the emotional response is cut off altogether. Scorpios who have suffered often use their natural facility for control to deaden their feelings completely. Denial of feeling can issue from the deepest levels of consciousness, while on the surface, calculated power plays and mental manipulations motivate the individual at every turn.

An extreme example of this malaise is the diabolical murderer Charles Manson. Although Manson's mind has moved into the realm of the psychotic, it is still highly emblematic of Scorpionic extremes. When Scorpio power and control become a complete substitute for love and compassion, the complete personhood is diminished to a cold, ruthless will. This type of person is difficult to contact. Such people cannot love, because at some time they would have to become vulnerable. Distrustful to the bone, they fear ostensible bastions of security because on some level they have known abandonment and look at life as a series of small deaths. To compensate for the possibility of pain, they have developed a steel will. This will is the mortar of their emotional survival. However, merely to survive is not enough. This sort of severely alienated Scorpio often seeks to thrive at others' expense, inwardly nourished by its own ego power. The more challenging the conditions of the immediate world, the more the power drive becomes a battleground of the brain.

Such a negative Scorpio is a pleasureless, lifeless individual, flushed with an internal darkness that swells and sometimes rises from the depths in the form of powerful mood swings. These savage moods swings are like dim prophets of an invisible yet encroaching doom. And day after day the exhausting, paralyzing obsessions drain and torment this devoured mind, which cannot connect with its own heart.

The Scorpio who has completely lost control has mentally disintegrated into chaos. Thoughts collapse, and the psyche becomes engulfed with dread, rage, violence, despair. Yet a dramatic break in the conscious controls that usually comes from a deathlike experience in life can bring renewal.

As every psychologist knows, emotional growth has a symbiotic relationship with suffering. Old, wise Scorpios know this too, and are no longer afraid of it. From living through their deepest fears, they become freed from them, and in the process have come to experience a true, lofty power within themselves. This is like a prophetic and compassionate voice that can be trusted. With emotional growth there is less need for the kinds of experiences or defense mechanisms that had previously served as psychic supports. With growth, there is also greater psychological freedom, inner lightness, and an ability to experience and appreciate meaning from many sources.

Scorpio

One of the great paradoxes of the Scorpionic experience is that while devastating emotional pain originally forced the consciousness to become frozen, it is only devastation that can open it up. At such times there is a sense of going under, of drowning, of even dying and watching the self in some significant aspect disappear. This is followed by a curious loss of feeling and along with it a loss of the fear, while a subtle energy emerges that is strangely uplifting. At this point, if the individual has enough character to view his life with even a modicum of honesty, he or she will inevitably be moved to wonderment.

It is not possible to attain this level of wonder simply through enforced will. It is the result of a rite of passage in life that must be experienced through the fruit of emotional and psychological pitfalls. Subtle or flagrant, self-undoings are doing the person in and she or he must emerge from them rather than merely relinquish them if deep and authentic freedom is to be obtained.

The theme of insidious self-destruction is one that is classically Scorpio in nature. It is interesting that when the scorpion is trapped, it will sting itself to death. There is a similar urge in the Scorpionic human being. Indirect forms of suicide, whether it be drug abuse, alcoholism, sadomasochistic relationships, or self neglect, is not uncommon.

The motivation for suicide in the Scorpio experience usually has to do with deep feelings of failure or unbearable loneliness. Scorpio is the most deeply passionate sign and needs to dissolve into whatever it happens to be most deeply involved in. This instinctive desire is at the core of every conflict, unconscious fear and carefully thought-out act. Concomitant with this need is a deep-seated fear of abandonment that forms the basis of both serious decisions and severe depressions. While Scorpio may be loosely considered a loner because of a tendency to brood in private, it is far more distinctively a sign that thirsts for deep connections and is loathe to grow old alone. Scorpio has a great deal of intense emotional needs, and the more that aren't met, the more unbearable the emptiness becomes. A Scorpio that feels deeply alone also feels desperate and disconnected. It is in this state that self-destructive tendencies will most likely emerge.

The fear of abandonment and the anxiety of loneliness are primordial Scorpionic problems. They are deeply rooted within the character and spring from an inability to emotionally handle perceptions. Fundamentally, we are all alone, regardless of the daily illusions we embrace to enable us to forget. But because Scorpio naturally feels more deeply than the other signs, the fears are also inflated in the imagination, which can at times be morbid, especially if it gets encouragement from "circumstance."

Scorpio is a highly complex sign, and thankfully, one in which there are great powers of self-regeneration as well as the self destructive tendencies. However, in order to transform, one must first get beyond the stage of bondage.

The anger factor alone is an emotional issue so convoluted that many Scorpios simply get depressed rather than deal with it. Scorpios tend to hold anger in, to brood, obsess, dwell and relive the past. They bear grudges, bitterly cling to injustices and without a word, are capable of cutting a person out of their life forever. When they do express anger, it is often indirectly. A viciously sarcastic comment here, a meticulously timed story there. Scorpio will watch and wait for the perfect moment. Behind the scenes of this cool delivery lurks a seething mess of feeling that has long been festering and feeding on itself.

There are Scorpios who are so out of touch with their feelings that their reactions are delayed for days and finally surface in depression. There are also Scorpios who will put their fists in someone's face. However, these are most likely to be under the influence of alcohol. Stone sober, Scorpio usually has more than enough control to dampen any propensities toward physical violence. However, when the inhibitions are markedly reduced through chemically induced substances, what we have is a person who actually enjoys his own anger.

This is a sign of extremes. Scorpios are volatile. Add to this a heavy dose of compulsion and you have people who do not know when to stop until something stops them. This is a sign that can take pleasure to the point of abuse. Unfortunately, because the compulsions are so strong, Scorpio does not learn quickly from experience. When under the influence of alcohol, the emotions and impulses of this sign are so overwhelming that they rule the person.

The dark energies of Scorpio have a Shiva-like essence. In Hinduism, Shiva is the god of both destruction and regeneration. It is a most powerful deity because at the core of its essence lies the truth of existence. Likewise, within the destructive behavior of Scorpio lies the power to transform, the power to renew one's personhood, like new skin. Just as the serpent sheds its skin in order to grow, Scorpio possesses an inherent power to renew itself through surrendering to experiences that challenge the ego, the sanity, and a subjective point of view that had heretofore been passing as objective.

To attain this new skin, there must first be a tearing down and gradual elimination of old structures and boundaries that are no longer meaningful in the individual's life. This is often very painful. There is a feeling of the ground crumbling beneath one's feet, a feeling of the sense of self melting, diminishing. This is the destructive aspect of Shiva, the dying off of conditions, making way for new life. The unknown looms ahead, and it is questionable whether anything will again be born that will bear the same critical meaning.

Despite the horrifying pain of this experience, it is also one that is miraculous. Regardless of the dialogue of the ego, a new condition will be born slowly, in its own way. This new condition will breathe new life and greater meaning. If there has been a profound surrender, there will also be a ressurection of the spirit. Like a gradual new aliveness, there will be a new phase of existence that will bring new involvement.

Scorpionic evolution is like a funnel in which the energy will either expand or contract, often quite dramatically. Learning how to trust the power within, it is possible to benefit greatly from one's suffering, to look at one's self and one's life in a way that had previously been unimaginable. It is like skipping from one level of schooling to another, and consequently seeing more, understanding more and becoming more.

In the Scorpionic experience, every pitfall has its own potential. It is not an easy climb, through the subconscious caverns of one's self, yet, regardless of the momentary limitations, power lies ahead for those still open enough to seek meaning from themselves. We are ultimately all alone. Only when we attain, through the depths of ourselves, the answers to our deepest and most difficult questions, will we have earned freedom and authenticity. This is the divine mystery of Scorpio. To live through it, to become it, is the only true power.

Power and Love: The Scorpio Female

Whether striking or self-effacing, plain or ravishingly beautiful, the one adjective which best suits a Scorpio woman is seductive.

To the Scorpio woman sex is as natural as breathing. It's a psychology deeply rooted in her being. Her sexuality permeates the atmosphere around her and accounts for a great deal of her attachments.

Scorpio women love men or they need men or they hate men because they love them and they need them. It's all part of the same story. With many Scorpio women the story can become very complicated.

When a Scorpio woman is emotionally involved, nothing is simple and a great deal can become convoluted overnight. By nature, the Scorpio woman is shrewd and intuitive. However, once she has been in the bedroom too long, her brain does not serve her well.

Essentially, Scorpio women are all or nothing in their emotional response and have a tendency to become galvanized by powerful attractions that are highly problematic. The man may be married, emotionally immature, insensitive to significant subtleties or downright egotistical and selfish. Yet in this Scorpionic mind an invisible string connects and its fibers are sex.

168

Scorpio women have an emotional memory in their bodies which can haunt them for days and even months. The power of a powerful sensual attraction stays in the cells and speaks through ripples of desire and longing. The desire nature is immensely strong in this woman, but its origin is deeply psychosexual and not the sort of shallow fascination with a handsome face.

There is usually mystery, power and great sensual appeal underlying the Scorpio woman's magnetic attraction. Often to friends the real mystery lies in what she sees in him. Nonetheless, to the Scorpio woman's mind, the *je ne sais quoi* is all-consuming.

It is not terribly uncommon to see an awesomely attractive woman in this sign attached to a man who should not be let out in public. However, usually the couple does *not* go out in public. Quite often he doesn't even bother to call. The fact that they get together most likely has to do with her patience, positive thinking and exclusive obsessive-compulsive preoccupation. When a Scorpio woman is obsessed, she is inclined to give all—reason, emotion, energy, inventiveness—to receive less in return. In her mind, she is being fulfilled to the depths of her body's intelligence.

To the Scorpio woman this sort of connection breathes of myth and eternity. Through the mystery of her own body she is able to become another person—a person perhaps no one else knows, but nevertheless, a person she most wants to be. Perhaps it is a wanton woman or an adored damsel or a female who is fed by the power of an imagined protector. The Scorpio woman can play it out within the confines of her bedroom—with or without the knowledge or consent of her lover. Through her response, a subterranean reality evolves that becomes increasingly involving. The power of sex, the power of her lover in the moment, the power of her own consuming sensuality is psychosexual. Whatever or whomever the lover may be in reality, when there is great sexual passion he takes on the identity of it in her mind. Therefore, it is the power of her own response which arouses and transports her. Her passionate lover is a psychological projection, not a person, but he is a powerful projection nonetheless.

A Scorpio woman caught up in a passionate projection is a person who can't be reasoned with under any circumstances. This sort of passion is a druglike and addictive experience, simultaneously enhancing surrounding sensual stimuli and reducing a reasonable, practical, logical mode of thinking. The power and problems of the real world recede while the internal pull of the projection takes over and can take on a life of its own.

There is a man I know, an archetype of Taurus, solid, steadfast, practical, and plodding. For many years he has been completely committed to a Scorpio woman who has turned him inside out with her passionate infidelities. The interesting point is that each man she left him for was less successful, less attractive and less financially solvent. Nevertheless, these experiences represented passion that she needed and did not find in her stable marriage. Even more for the Scorpio woman than for the man, passion, when evoked, is an enormous pull. It can become a total immersion into a netherworld that is primordial in nature, issuing from the depths of her unconscious, leaving her feeling powerless in the face of rational choice. The core of her identity becomes an obsessive-compulsive thrust which can have a wearing effect with time.

There are many obsessive Scorpio women who fail to learn and therefore, benefit from the lessons of their passions. In the vein of fixed water, they repeat the essence of their experiences and cling to emotional behavior patterns that are self-defeating.

The ego drive—which can include the desire to seduce and conquer—can be very strong in the Scorpio female. This is a sign that is particularly vulnerable to the presentation and trappings of power. There is often a sense of exaltation that comes from tasting power first-hand and through signficant others. At times power can become a priority over more compassionate considerations. The drive toward it can become a compulsion that diminishes personal happiness in time.

Scorpio

In the Scorpio woman there is either a need for power and dominance or a need to attach to a man of power—and sometimes both. The late Princess Grace of Monaco was a Scorpio, and in her lifetime, achieved great worldly power—but at a cost of considerable personal unhappiness. The struggle for power can be such a passion in the Scorpio woman's personality that it dominates and dictates the tone and guidelines of every relationship. When so driven, Scorpio women can be consuming—to both themselves and others. Yet at the same time, they cannot simply pull the plug on their emotions. They must live through them. They must allow their emotions, drives, compulsions and complexes to take them somewhere—to a place within of insight, clarity, wisdom and compassion. In short, the Scorpio woman must learn how to live with herself successfully before she is able to live with anyone else. This is a test of true power.

The inner world of the Scorpio woman is a vast, deep, often adumbrated terrain. Emotions lurk behind every turn. Some ignite under the full force of the will, and some never really surface and are felt as dark downswings of moods. It is not easy living as a Scorpio woman. Likewise, it is not that easy loving. This intense nature is strongly expressed in its attachments. Such intense attachments often seem doomed from the start by their very intensity.

Scorpio can be a cold, ruthless sign when seeking control. When a Scorpio woman is betrayed, or sometimes ignored, a slow, burning ferocity is born that can be merciless. This need for control can be so deep within the personality that she may avoid relationships altogether. Although Scorpio is commonly considered the sign of sex, it is not uncommon to see Scorpio women who completely withdraw from sexual relationships until they feel a deeper sense of control. To reiterate, sex to a Scorpio is deeply psychological. It is always the attitude about themselves in relation to the partner which constitutes the strength of the passion. Unlike the beauty-conscious Libra, a Scorpio woman can become fatally attracted to someone who, by society's standards, might

171

be considered unattractive. However, something in the psyche must feel the "switch go on" or else the moment will not amount to much. When not emotionally involved, a Scorpio woman can treat a man as if he died but doesn't yet know it. That mysterious, elusive pull away from reason *must* put them in a place of silent wonder. When properly in love, Scorpio dies, goes to heaven and is reborn.

Especially for Scorpio women with their enormous emotional intensity, love can be a vast learning experience which can be transformative and lead to great personal and spiritual power. It is the power of being able to hear with the heart and see through the eyes of wisdom. The Scorpio woman who has gone through many evolutionary stages, who has encountered herself along the way in many guises—some pretty, some unpleasant, some hopeful and inspiring—will eventually be able to claim her richness and become a vast source of power for herself and others.

Power evolves through the Scorpio woman who becomes aware of the true value of love. In her psyche, power and love will both evoke their own myth and mystery. The path it will take will be through her own uniqueness. For the Scorpio woman, this is a path of infinite possibility fueled by her compassion and capacity to learn from day to day. The reward for the journey is a constantly renewing inner self, steadily emerging from the darkness to cast its own light through love, a light that quietly leads the way.

Power and Love: The Scorpio Male

It is commonly considered that the Scorpio man is a sexual mastermind. This is probably not far from the truth. Sex is an integral part of the Scorpio man's psychology. It is a way of looking at the world and himself that determines many of his choices and creates a lot of his problems as well.

Scorpio men have a magnetism that frequently has an arresting effect on the opposite sex. It centers in the eyes.

172

Scorpio

They are riveting and intense, and linger for a provocative extra beat. In that one second a Scorpio man can see a great deal. He has a perceptual ability that is both penetrating and intuitive. He knows instinctively how to go about getting what he thinks he wants.

The Scorpio man is smooth and calculating, seemingly nonchalant and usually more than a trife manipulative. With great deliberation, he thinks things out to their successful consummation and never leaves anything to chance. It is an interesting fact that many monarchs have been born under this sign. Likewise, we see, even in the average person, the desire to rule, the tendency to covet power and the need to impose control. Many Scorpios are politicians. They tend to make excellent world leaders. However, when it comes to love, their need to control and their inability to compromise create a great deal of problems.

The Scorpio man is a very complex individual with a great deal of intense feeling and passion—so much that he doesn't know what to do with it. Add to that his extraordinarily consuming drives—egotistical, emotional and sexual—and you have a person who needs control to function effectively.

The Scorpio man is so intense that he cannot live spontaneously. He is so complicated that he can't believe that things can actually be simple. Therefore, he feels compelled to organize every aspect of his life in terms of a master plan. An important part of these calculations is the Scorpio's wife or lover. Because he has a deep-seated fear of abandonment, death, and ultimate aloneness, he always marries. While there are Scorpio men who remain faithful, most treat their marriage like an office out of which they manage their affairs. All it takes is one long look back over the crowded room from a beautiful body to put the motor in motion. Once the power is on, there is usually no turning back.

Each time the Scorpio man is possessed by passion he feels reborn. Passion is the fuel of his nature. When any person or involvement rekindles it, his response is profound. An illustrious Scorpio lover was Richard Burton,

173

who flamboyantly expressed his passion both on and off the stage.

In general, Scorpio men tend to be much more subtle, indirect and enigmatic in their emotional expression. When merely sexually attracted and not emotionally consumed, they can be aloof and downright cold. This man is motivated by *intense* attractions. While the superficially erotic will most definitely appeal to him, he can be bound by deeply psychological ties.

Sex must have a powerful psychological effect for the Scorpio man to become deeply involved emotionally. What determines this is usually a psychological projection in which he experiences a quality in the woman which is, in fact, his own hitherto unexpressed female rising to the surface. Such was the "soul" contact between Richard Burton and the wife he referred to as his mistress, Elizabeth Taylor. Interestingly enough, Elizabeth's moon (psyche, soul, deep emotional nature) is in Scorpio, which evoked Burton's soul.

This was, by no means, harmonious contact. Fraught with the extremes of passion and brutality, it was a steamy, obsessive and often savage attraction. Caught in the depths of it, Burton found himself vacillating between extremes of utter possession and psychological repulsion.

There is within the Scorpio man a deep ambivalence regarding the issue of surrender. While one aspect of the psyche relishes the ability to experience his emotional and sexual nature, to relinquish control demands that one pay a price. In this case, with such a consuming emotional nature, the price can be quite high. Loss of concentration, the ability to focus, the ability to function—all can come to pass when a full-blown Scorpionic obsession takes hold. The mind is possessed and it may be a divine madness, but it is still a madness nonetheless.

That is why a great many Scorpionic men never venture this far, into the dark, swirling waters of Aphrodite. Instead, they satisfy their security needs by marrying someone steady and reliable. From there, they satisfy their erotic fantasies by engaging in shallow yet highly secretive liaisons.

Power is a profound drive in the Scorpio personality. Power satisfies the primal desire for control, security and self-importance. Underlying this power drive is the desire to feel autonomous, a desire which contradicts the demands of any relationship. Therefore, Scorpio men are deeply torn, but are nevertheless determined to have it all. Perhaps that is why they can appear so enigmatic and ambivalent when engaged in a relationship. They need a relationship. They also need to not need a relationship. But with time they usually find a relationship in which they can experience autonomy and control.

Scorpio men are highly self-centered in a unique way. Somewhere in their psyche is a warrior, a lone wolf who doesn't believe that anyone could understand the often troublesome complications of his intense, introverted nature. The typical Scorpio man doesn't even look for someone he can talk to. Should he encounter that profound connection in a woman, it is likely that he would be truly startled and on his way to becoming obsessed, especially if he finds himself strongly sexually attracted.

It is unlikely that such a situation would occur. However, in the event that it did, it would consume him and cause him to rise up and then sink down into the depths of himself, perceiving and then losing his soul.

When deeply attached, the Scorpio man will hold on to a situation until the smouldering ashes slowly recede. Despite their strong controls, Scorpio men can be ruled by their emotions to the extreme of great misery. The Scorpionic poet John Keats dramatically expressed this in his well-known poem, "La Belle Dame sans Merci," which means "The Lovely Lady without Pity." In the poem he refers to himself as "Alone and palely loitering," yearning painfully for the woman who makes kings, princes and warriors "pale."

These images link deep, passionate Scorpionic love with death. To reach the extreme of surrendering such reason to the love projection is a deathlike experience which can be simultaneously pleasureful and painful, psychologically disintegrating and spiritually transformative. Along the way, to be caught, controlled and propelled through the entanglement is to be like Dante crossing the rivers of hell. It is in fact a voyage through the shadows and the light spaces of self into the deep, dark, murky waters of the primordial unconscious. By being submerged and resurrected, it is possible to become reborn into a new state of consciousness where a higher, purer, more conscious love is possible.

Suffering is a significant theme in the Scorpio experience. The Scorpio man who has suffered through life and love has a greater capacity to be enlarged by love. It is a combination of this dearly won compassion and largesse which allows him to extend himself spiritually and psychologically. He no longer has to be *bound* by love or by the fear of it. At this level in his evolution he can be affirmed by the loving experience and can share his own affirmation like a blazing light that profoundly radiates through and enriches another person. This is the potential of a Scorpio man—to become a very powerful heart that is heard in many, many ways.

Power and Work: Scorpio

Scorpio is the power behind the throne, and has the substance of which CEOs are made. Success is a *sine qua non* in the Scorpionic scheme of things and with thoughtful precision, Scorpios know how to set the scene in motion.

Scorpio may have been the secret inventor of the seven-year plan. And secretive they are! Quite ruthlessly, they calculate all the subtleties and possibilities in a significant situation. Then shrewdly assess how to take over, using their coworkers' weaknesses to their best advantage.

Work has a way of consuming a great part of the Scorpionic mind power. Members of this sign are highly goal-oriented, possess a strong memory, and have supernormal powers of concentration. Likewise, they can become intensely caught up in work to the exclusion of everything else. The passionate Scorpio personality often sublimates personal dissatisfactions into intense career drives. However, unlike the equally ambitious fire signs, Scorpio has a patience and forbearance. Therefore, Scorpios are able to deal with the sorts of situations that make others scream and lose control. Likewise, they are able to handle the mentally cumbersome details that can panic impatient personalities. What it all adds up to is, simply, superior executive skills. Scorpions have them in abundance and are able to carry out all that they undertake.

Once a Scorpio has attained a chosen pinnacle, he will continue to gain through strong interpersonal skills and an ability to communicate effectively. With the exception of those who are emotionally undeveloped, Scorpios have compassion for the problems of their coworkers as well as paternal concern for upcoming underlings. In dealings with both, they have the strength to use their power prudently and to delegate authority with a thoughtful understanding and calm.

However, when the Scorpionic need for power and success is severely thwarted, the psychological pain can be profound. When the steam heat of the Scorpio nature is seriously blocked, it can result in a deadened person who can neither feel nor find an adequate outlet for compensation. Scorpios who give in and wallow in their negativity can waste years of their lives. Down the road, the layers of fear and resentment can result in physical illness.

A deeply frightened Scorpio becomes paralyzed, marking time, making excuses and often arrogantly overcompensating for his or her fears. As the internal life grows tense, the quality of life loses its potency.

Such deep feelings of dread are difficult to fathom in the minds of significant others. However, to the deeply troubled Scorpio, the anxiety of loss is excruciatingly painful and imposing. For good or ill, Scorpio is a powerful sign, and when the energy of this mind works against itself, the effects can lead eventually to despair or an insidious sickness. However, when one is able to release emotionally, often from hitting a low point, the experience can bring one to a more powerful level of existence.

Along the way, what is transformed is the old ego power. It is the ego which attempts to hold on, to gain control and to perpetuate the struggle. However, there is also another kind of power, a higher power. When the fuel of this ego power is put through some intense frustration that is stronger than the will, the higher power flows through subtly yet miraculously. Life starts to become simple. Once the obsessional garbage of the mind has been silenced, a higher voice can come through. This powerful voice is the voice of truth, and its guidance and direction is infallible.

It is possible to contact this source and use it powerfully in a work situation. However, when the mind is undisciplined, the tendency is to focus on fears, frustrations and fantasies that divorce the consciousness from the power within. The more one can proceed from this inner source, the more one is able to benefit from negative work situations that might otherwise leave one at a disadvantage.

The tendency of the Scorpio mind is to view power merely in terms of material success. This view is both superficial and deluded. Great power can be unleashed by facing one's failures. It is possible to transform these weaknesses into strengths by developing a deeper understanding. However, this requires a conscious will directed toward self-mastery and an ability to look to experience for the lessons that can be learned about one's own psychological limitations.

Work is a vital expression of life that is becoming increasingly meaningful to many people and to the Scorpio in particular. Therefore, it can also be an excellent area where one tests and maximizes one's personal power through consciously working on one's total awareness and insight. How we get along with others, how we experience success and failure, how we deal with our fears around both all have great import. The challenge of Scorpio, workwise, is to multiply and elevate one's self by encountering the truth through painful conflicts and problems. These lessons, especially when the cause of inner turmoil and turbulence, can provide a doorway to a more successful way of being that the small, ego-bound self cannot foresee.

Powerful Scorpio Psychology

The mind of the perfect man is like a mirror. It does not move with things, nor does it anticipate them. It responds to things, but does not retain them. The Sage is able to deal successfully with things but is not affected by them.

—Chuang-tsu

You tend to be controlled by our own need for control. This can create significant blocks to your experience of your own power.

In your lifetime, you must learn to trust your own boundlessness. Likewise, you must not allow yourself to be bound by your own caution and fear. While it may appear that your caution is a gateway to greater control, it is through your developed intuition that you are able to transcend limitation and move on to new levels of power within yourself.

It is important for you to come to terms consciously with the fact that your control does not always serve you well. Often it is limiting in that it diminishes rather than clarifies your experience and the way you force others to relate to you. Likewise, your way of looking at things can be subjective and off center when you are dealing with an issue that is emotionally charged.

In order to be free and operate from your highest intelligence, you must never remain rigidly locked into an attitude or perspective. Always be able to go deeper. In depth perception there is truth. In summoning the courage to live through truth, you will find both meaning and power.

In order to be psychologically free and luminously intelligent, you must never remain rigidly locked into an attitude or perspective. Always be able to change your course and to go deeper. In depth perception there is a powerful awareness. And in living through this awareness, you will stretch your emotions and your mind.

Your fears, your controls, your compulsions and obsessions are merely stopping places. But there is a great Source within you that is boundless. Once you learn to let go of the small, constricted vision that cuts you off emotionally, you will perceive the illusions underlying all problematic areas of your life. Eventually, as your awareness grows, you will gain power over them. Once your personal power grows, you will no longer be controlled by the old fears and anxieties. You will have a penetrating mental perspective that allows you to monitor and eliminate old negativities.

Scorpios have a strong tendency to take themselves too seriously. You benefit by standing back and seeing your own seriousness with a sense of humor. Being able to laugh at yourself in all circumstances is a great power over your self-imposed tragedies. Scorpios create a great deal of their own suffering through their intense and emotionally constricted way of perceiving and responding.

In truth, heaven and hell have the same dwelling place: the mind. The difference between these two states is what fills that empty space. Many Scorpios carry around a great deal of darkness which they become resigned to. And this resignation, which is its own negativity, cuts them off from a full, vital experience of their own life. Scorpio is the sign of death and regeneration. Those Scorpions who live blindly from control and who do not confront and regenerate their own negative emotions are often dead in life.

On the outside, you may have many attainments and material rewards. However, until you become master of yourself and your inner world, you will remain haunted and trapped in your own intensity.

Force yourself to lighten up. Expand your way of looking at things. Stretch your mind. Develop compassion for others. Nothing is as serious as your obsessive mind can make it. Instead of getting stuck in your own moods and self-centered absorptions, allow your depth to take you to a better understanding of your own personal experience. In every experience there is a lesson that can expand your life. However, you must get beyond your old rigid mental patterns to be *able* to perceive. Your mind is a miraculous vehicle when you know how to cultivate it properly. Part of this lies in formulating a fundamental goal: of moving out of your own darkness.

As one Master so beautifully put it,

> **In darkness you were groping, in darkness you came in conflict with others, in darkness you stumbled upon things. Not millions of acts have to be answered; only one thing has to be done and that is, don't remain ignorant, become aware. Once you become aware, all that belongs to the world of darkness disappears. It will look like a dream, a nightmare.**

This awareness, which implies precision and impeccability, is the only real power. It is the power to be beyond chaos. This autonomy, *despite circumstance*, is the only real control.

The challenge of Scorpio is to become a conscious warrior, who, through time, moves into a larger luminosity of self. Through joy, pain, hopelessness, fear, and sudden insight always keep in mind:

> Everything we do, everything we are rests on our personal power. If we have enough of it, one word uttered to us might be sufficient to change the course of our lives. But if we don't have enough personal power, the most magnificent place of wisdom can be revealed to us and that revelation won't make a damn bit of difference.

Maximizing Your Scorpio Power Potential

You have an obsessive, compulsive mentality, and at all times you must direct it in order to not be controlled by it. A very effective way of doing this is to cultivate a "witness" which stands watch in your inner world. This witness is your own mind, which watches itself and labels its own emotional twists and turns. As you do this increasingly, when a disturbing situation arises, you will not be dragged down by it, even if you have a spontaneous emotional response. Therefore, instead of being turned inside out by frustration or anger, *witness it*. This means that instead of feeling terribly frustrated or deeply angry and letting it ruin your day, watch your mind having these experiences, label them "anger," "frustration," and so on, and then move on to witness new emotional experiences. Note how many different experiences you will have during the course of one day.

Eventually, what you will become aware of is how your mind changes and how your reality changes along with it. However, your mental-emotional responses do not have to be your reality. When they are, they consume you and can put you out of control. When you feel out of control, it appears that a condition is controlling you from the outside. However, at all times, you are the thinker and therefore you can change your own thoughts.

Your mind is like a movie screen, across which thoughts arise like phantoms. They play around for a time and then drift away. If you identify with them when they're on the screen; you become them. You become fear, rage, depression, anxiety. However, if you watch them scampering about in their various costumes, you can witness them doing their thing and then disappearing. As the day goes on, new thoughts dance out, and the show goes on and on.

When given a strong emotional charge, thoughts have great power. On the inner, subconscious plane, they form images and when these images are called up repeatedly, they can actualize as external events. In this respect, we create our own reality.

An obsessive mind can either get stuck in its own obsessions, or it can repeatedly direct and control its own thoughts to control its own reality. Put your mind to conscious use. Let it work for you at all times, even in moments when it does not appear to be working.

If, at first, this practice seems awkward or uncomfortable, in a rather short period of time it will nevertheless become quite natural, and like a game that requires no effort. The more you do it, the more power you will derive from it and the less you will be controlled by either your negative thoughts or negative circumstances. On deeper and deeper levels, you will be able to perceive the essence of your own reality. And more and more, you will be able to perceive how *all reality* has the potential of working for you. This, in one word, is power.

IX

SAGITTARIUS

November 23–December 21

Sagittarius Nature

The essence of the Sagittarian nature is possibility personified. Diminishment of any kind depresses the classic Sagittarian, as does anyone or anything interfering with the Sagittarian's sense of freedom. Sagittarians always want to feel free to make choices and to move in any direction that suits them. Sagitarrius is the sign of the adventurer, bound only by his own beliefs. Sagittarians have expansive minds and are eager to learn, and experience, always restless and impatient to move ahead.

The classic Sagittarian is a democratic individual with ideals that often define the lifestyle. The Sagittarian soul desires expansion at all costs and is sensitive to social issues that affect the functioning of self and fellow man. Sagittarians want the best of all possible worlds. They will never stop searching until they find it. For a great many members of this sign, the entire experience of life is one endless exploration. Sagittarians see possibility where other signs perceive limitation. They also have a

187

genius for seeing splendid things that the common mind might consider silly.

Deep inside, Sagittarians believe they can do anything that they want. "No" is a foreign word in their vocabulary. Sagittarians don't believe that words of limitation apply to them. Therefore, they are left free for the consuming quest of their personal utopia.

In the natural horoscope, Sagittarius is associated with the ninth house of adventure, higher philosophy, religion, travel and foreign lands. The ninth house is also the house of knowledge, values, beliefs and ideals. Thus, the archetypal Sagittarian mind seeks to live through or move toward something greater. Sagittarians tend not to see life as it is but how they would like it to be. Therefore, living on this materialistic and often mercenary earth can pose a few problems.

The Sagittarian nature wants to soar, and after landing, to remain unimpeded. This can cause some unsettling problems when encountering the situation called "daily life." Sagittarians want life to be perfect, and they don't want to waste their perfect time dinking around with petty, boring details or being bothered by a moronic boss with no vision. A Sagittarian will give away their last thin dime to the needy. However, they have no compassion for a mediocre mentality that manages to get in their way. The Sagittarian sense of justice extends only as far as its ideals.

Born under the sign of travel, Sagittarians easily take flight when faced with confinement of any kind. This is a sign not terribly comfortable with the notion of commitment. "What works, works as long as it works, but not after that," could be the Sagittarian motto. Sagittarians tend to live life as if on a layover in an airport. They suffer from terminal anticipation, hyperventilating for what is next and comes after that and after that.

The Sagittarian mind is deeply at home with change because it is so restless. At the drop of a hat, it can pick up and move, without any preparations. The Sagittarian nature is not the most practical, yet it is also oddly pragmatic.

Sagittarians can perceive truth in the absurd and can do some pretty absurd things in the name of truth. So many times their self-confidence can create success out of sheer pandemonium.

Typical Sagittarians also tend to be very lucky. Opportunities come to them, and they often tend to be in the right place at the right time. The typical Sagittarian has a sanguine attitude and optimistic expectations that circumstance will create an uplifting turn. More often than not, it does. Therefore, unless hit by midlife crisis, which can make them feel they should be an "adult," the typical Sagittarian is never down for long. Upon arising, a Sagittarian usually tries to find meaning in the down moment that will expand the future.

The Sagittarian mind is like a restless child's. It is fresh and alive, idealistic and expectant. There is an inherent buoyancy in the Sagittarian nature which makes even boring moments in life seem like highly amusing anecdotes. And this brings us to Sagittarian charm. The typical Sagittarian has a lot of it and it serves them well. Sagittarians can be memorable rascals or deeply thinking philosophers, adventurers, entertainers, or all of the above. Whatever the momentary pursuit, when the charm shines, it is invincible. This is a person who can make an adventure out of a rainy day or a comedy out of what appears to be the most miserable circumstance.

Sagittarians are the comedians of the zodiac. That is not to say that every Sagittarian is a stellar wit. But it is to imply that an overriding sense of humor seems to be a birthright of the sign. Quite naturally, Sagittarians see the funny side of every situation—even if they can't appreciate their vision at the time. The popular humorist Spalding Gray is a Sagittarian, and in typical Sagittarian style, he fashioned his humorous monologues out of his life experiences. It is Sagittarian genius to be struck by the sheer absurdity of a serious situation and to be able to communicate that with hysterical intensity. Sagittarians can also be pranksters and clever, witty caricaturists, stand-up comedians and the most rapid tongue-in-cheek deliverers of an acerbicly witty line.

Humor is part of the great Sagittarian life adventure. It gives breath to the banal. It startles. It expands. It wakes things up and in the most boring moments, makes things bearable.

When not terribly grown up, Sagittarians are not terribly serious—about anything. Getting them to show up on time—or at all—can be a bit of a problem. Commitment, to this kind of Sagittarian, means that they may not even make it through the evening. And certainly after that, nothing should be assumed. With great ease and remarkable cleverness, immature Sagittarians can play musical chairs, beds, houses, and "long-term partners." The variety of people and settings in their past attest to the sense of adventure which spurs them on.

The mature Sagittarian tends to be seriously intellectual. Knowledge, philosophy and higher learning are significant pursuits. It is here that the idealist comes to life with aspirations that define the person, the presentation and the goals.

To a serious Sagittarian, their beliefs have life and carry meaning that can affect the world. A Sagittarian devoted to a philosophy or belief system is a person who soars above the earthbound banality into a plane of possibility. Sagittarius can be overcome with the need to express their expansive ideas and in the process, change the world. Jane Fonda is a classic example of the sense of a burning mission that always seems to be beginning anew.

Sagittarians search for the sublime and shudder at the sorts of earthbound encroachments that deny possibility. Their dark moments come when they feel they have to compromise to conditions antithetical to their ideals. Some Sagittarians will choose to escape and evade commitment. Others will drop out or rebel. Still others will seek an avenue to express their frustration and vision of truth.

Sagittarius is a sign of expansion. And expand, they will, in any way they can. They might eat too much, drink too much, fall in love too many times, think too much or have too many undertakings that go unfinished. Whatever the experience of expansion that they are tied in with, the feeling is one of being boundless in a moment in time. It is this sense of being blessedly pregnant with a moment, a vision, a flash of truth that will take them somewhere that keeps Sagittarius going. And the more substantial the journey, the more they come home to their own soul.

Sagittarius Strengths

It could be said of typical Sagittarians that they are so generous that they would write a bad check to help out a friend in need. The spirit of Sagittarius is so expansive that they are like air-born elfs, soaring between dew drops in the middle of a huge forest.

Sagittarians are forever in search of the beatific, and because of that, they look toward lofty places. The Sagittarius nature is a highly idealistic one that sees life, both as it is and how it ought to be. The discrepancy between the two is sometimes difficult for the Sagittarian personality. Sagittarians can never understand how anyone could be less honest and magnanimous than they are. After all, large-mindedness only promotes joy and more good times. And they are right.

Sagittarian positivity shines like a beacon, and to stand in its glow is to feel embraced. Sagittarian positivity is the harbinger of possibility. It opens doors, dissolves barricades and creates opportunity where none previously had a hope of appearing. This is what is loosely known as Sagittarian luck. It is an attitude—all prevailing, that things will ultimately work out for the best. If they don't, it's for a very *good* reason.

The Sagittarian urge to soar, to be free of limitations and trivial perplexities is instinctive and very powerful. We become what we think. Sagittarians demonstrate this. It is the legacy of their spirit. It is also a gift they have to share with others who are weighed down by their own vision of limitation.

The Sagittarian personality has the natural ability to be happy and to make others happy. When misfortune arises, there is an ability to rise above circumstance, to see beyond momentary negativities and to search for some meaning that will be liberating. Sagittarius is associated with the ninth house of higher philosophy and wisdom. It is also the house of joy, of travel and of higher understanding, formally termed religion. It is, in essence, the ability to reach up and call upon a higher power within one's self.

The experience of Sagittarius has to do with elevation and transcendence. The Sagittarian vision is one of idealism and infinite potential. Given all that, there is tremendous strength in this sign, but it is a pure strength, a strength of spirit, rather than an intestinal fortitude. When expressing their best selves, Sagittarians bubble with life and bring the absurd to bear in the drollest fashion. The Sagittarian sensibility evokes humor through its expansive ability to connect with the comic undertones of a situation and to communicate this vividly. Sagittarian mirth is incandescent. It can light up a gloomy room and bring the dullest party to life. Amid all the sparkle a conversation will take hold that in some way will be captivating. Noël Coward, Woody Allen, Winston Churchill are good examples of Sagittarians.

Even the quieter Sagittarians have an expansive nature and a respect for life that includes all the furry (and even the scaly) creatures. Sagittarians are notorious animal lovers, people collectors and cause supporters, staunchly believing in betterment and in being able to make positive change in someone or something's life. Even if they never follow through on all of their initial enthusiasm, they sincerely mean to in the moment when impulse overtakes them.

The mail of one Sagittarian friend includes solicitation from an organization called "Adopt A Whale." Her front door is papered with slogans on nature conservation. One day, having noticed that her cleaning lady had just left and nothing looked any different, I asked my friend what she did. "Nothing," replied my friend nonchalantly, flipping through her "Adopt A Whale" mail. "But she has all kinds of problems and she needs the money." I pointed out to my friend that she also needed money, and she admitted that that was a good point, one she had never thought of. Typical Sagittarian story.

Sagittarians can also be outspoken and in such times are quite capable of saying "no," but not to anyone in need. I also suspect that they say "yes" more than they should. Sagittarians try to make everyone happy, or at least, less unhappy.

Sagittarians are also highly idealistic and respectful of everyone's and everything's freedom. They have a habit of being shocked when the rest of the world doesn't conform to their humanitarian standards. However, it is no use trying to explain that there are many situations and people who do not accord to the divine. A Sagittarian's values and ideals are as precious as their best friends.

There is a nobility in this sign that all signs could benefit from embracing. The sheer, unself-conscious positivity, the generosity, spontaneous warmth and expansiveness speaks of a sort of utopian possibility. Old, evolved Sagittarians are rich in wisdom, deep in understanding and filled with joy at life's simple things. They reflect what man can become—for himself and for others. All the time, they are never stopping, their spirit moving, changing, growing into a greater manifestation of eternal becoming.

Sagittarius Pitfalls

In an exuberant moment, a Sagittarian can promise to deliver the Atlantic Ocean on land. And who could not believe those twinkling eyes, that beguiling manner, that generosity that could captivate the IRS? However, unfortunately, on-time delivery is not a strong point. At the moment, Sagittarius means every bit of its grand plan. However, X number of days later, the impulse seems like an idea of a decade ago. It doesn't have anything to do with the present moment, and to get it in motion again to the point of execution and delivery feels like a death sentence with little hope of parole.

All the same, Sagittarians mean well. They just get so caught up in so many things, ideas, people, plans and private wishes that everything gets mixed up and backed up. Sagittarians are future-oriented, so much so that they sometimes fail to live in the present. All of the qualities that make this sign so refreshing, when taken to extremes, as Sagittarians are apt to take things, can prove to be a prime ingredient for pandemonium.

There is an impulse in Sagittarius that rebels against being a grownup. Sagittarius wants the world to bend to the waves of its own brain. When this fails to happen, there can be a carnival of complaints, protests, staged sit-ins, or freeze-outs. This sign has a remarkably difficult time accommodating itself to the boring, consuming world. The unevolved Sagittarian would rather bomb the encroaching territory than be controlled by its regulations and demands. Sagittarius' demands come first and fore-most on the agenda. Furthermore, they see their priorities as a form of truth and all truth as boundless and justi-fiable.

Sagittarians do not take kindly to anyone interfer-ing with their freedom and can verbally cut anyone dead who tries. This is a sign that can be stupefyingly blunt and tactless, leaving remarkably little floor beneath one's feet. Typical Sagittarian insight: "Well, it's a shame that you really have no friends. Maybe you should just lose all that weight that just keeps getting in the way of things."

This is someone you want to like, or someone you could like, or someone you do like, but not someone you can depend on. This type of Sagittarius in a male is notorious for the social standup. And his female counter-part can move from one "committed" relationship to an-other as quickly as she can change her jeans.

When lacking sufficient discipline, the Sagittarian mind is also lacking direction. Sagittarians can be the flightiest of dabblers, playing at their pursuits until the novelty wears thin and then turning their attention elsewhere. Procrastination is another pitfall that works against this talented sign. Sagittarians are not so much lazy as self-indulgent and inclined to obey slavishly the momentary demands of the child within.

Sagittarius

The scattered Sagittarian talks away her or his time. This is the proverbial armchair revolutionary and the boisterous barroom philosopher. However, the goal of bettering the system never gets beyond the big revelation. Immature Saggitarians can waste their brains, energy and money on pursuits, pastimes and ridiculous endeavors that, with time, keep them discontentedly in the same place.

A discontented Sagittarian is a sad sight. The invisible wings droop and usually there is just enough self-pity (even if humorously expressed) to prevent them from assuming any responsibility for their plight. When Sagittarians feel that there is no way for them to soar, they slide into a slump. This brings us to the Sagittarius in the shadow state.

Signs that live out their shadow selves exhibit the negative polar aspects of their sign and are mentally turned too far inward. The shadow state of Sagittarius is dark, gloomy, moody and contracted. This sort of Sagittarian feels cheated or abused by circumstance. Consequently, Sagittarians express this in their values or lack of values—which always affects how they deal with the issue of money. Sagittarians must do things *their* way, and when sufficiently self-contracted, their way appears to go out of the way to not include anybody else. These Sagittarians often have an attitude of superiority to others who, they strongly feel, are controlled by the system. These individuals take their ideas and their frustrations too seriously, feeling uniquely oppressed by the sorts of limitations the average person knows as "daily life."

There is a prodigal quality to the Sagittarian personality which manifests itself as a tendency to waste time, talent and opportunity. This sort of has-been-who-never-was always succeeds in seeing that things never work out as planned.

Fortunately, most Sagittarians do not fall into this swamp of self-sabotage. However, all can benefit from becoming more aware of their specific area of waste—and how this prevents them from receiving more from their life.

Truth and freedom are Sagittarian fixations, in the sense of seeing into the truth of things and not being bound by limitation. However, it is also important to be truthful with one's self—to be able to perceive one's limitations and areas of self-sabotage and to work in a committed, conscious manner to get beyond them. It is not following desires of the moment to the exclusion of everything else. It is a matter of having the courage of being committed to one's own possibility, and this requires discipline.

Sagittarian pitfalls limit freedom, growth and possibility. They shut doors on the experience of one's own potential by sacrificing time, dreams and ideals to self-indulgent illusions. Sagittarrians must have the courage and commitment to live in truth.

Power and Love: The Sagittarius Woman

The Sagittarian female loves love just as much as she loves her freedom. However, at all times she must feel free in her love.

Unlike her Sagittarian brother, this woman does not have to devote years to "the quest." Instead, she seeks comaraderie, comfort and meaning within love and can accommodate herself realistically to limitations.

The Sagittarian woman is vitally interested in the experience of living. A great deal of that has to do with the experience of love. She wants a life that is full and vital, with no substitutions. With her unusually open heart, she finds it.

This woman loves animals, ideas, children and uncharted lands. Following a stream or crusading for a significant cause sets her wheels in motion. When very young, she scintillates at someone who sparks her sense of adventure. When older and more seasoned, she yearns for someone she can respect who is her best friend.

The key to the Sagittarian woman is that she is suffocated by a lover who shows no respect for her freedom and individuality. She is also terribly bored by anyone who thinks on a scale much smaller than she. The Sagittarian woman loves the expansive feeling of love, and has to catch her breath at the petty details of living. Her nature is impatient and her personality not prone to wait for "the loved one's" proper moment. She likes men who get to the point quickly and grasp her attention with the sort of self-assurance that is warming without being pushy.

When immature, the Sagittarius female can be capricious and more preoccupied with playing than with experiencing the power of love. She is captured and perhaps blinded by surface presentation, sexual attractiveness, material power or its meretricious display. The wiser Sagittarian woman is able to put personal limitations in perspective for the sort of soul mate who shares a significant life view. She understands the power of love. She lives it. With her extraordinary, generous heart, she shares its light with all who surround her.

Power and Love: The Sagittarius Man

Ask a Sagittarian man if he remembers his first love and without missing a beat he'll reply Freedom. And this is no unrequited romance. It is an everlasting pursuit that many females may compete with—only to lose. Any woman who wins or at least captivates his soul, must share him with his primary love. Don Johnson, a classic Sagittarian, after publicly cavorting with a bevy of beauties, reacted to Taurean fiancée Barbra Streisand's incensed ultimatum by an innocent lack of understanding. "It's too bad," he concluded, strongly intimating that there was no way on earth that his behavior was ever going to change because of the wrong woman's demand.

The Sagittarian is always in serious pursuit of something. It can be women, adventure, dreams, goals, uprisings or shooting the rapids. But wherever his sense of adventure takes him in the moment, that is where he is going to go, and it is likely that there is no one love that will get in his way.

197

Love for the Sagittarian man can be for many things and for many people and does not have to be for anyone in particular for any length of time. In fact, this sign can still enjoy playing the field long after he's too old to even see it. Many Sagittarian men are playboys, who after settling down find a new flirtation soon after. However, when emotionally mature, and upon finding his ideal, the Sagittarian man can be the perfect mate who makes the most of every moment.

The ideal woman for a Sagittarian man is a friend who shares his ideals, dreams, and beliefs. Even then, despite the desires of his chosen, his sense of timing is such that he will want to do what he wants when he wants to do it. Therefore, the lady of his dreams must have a life of her own that makes its own loud demands.

Sagittarian men are independent, idiosyncratic and do not need the security of love as much as men in a lot of other signs. The Sagittarian man likes to roam and to experience a lot along the way. Having to account for himself to another person is not his favorite way of proceeding to the next point. He can be made to feel claustrophobic quite easily. When coerced, he can perform a memorable act of disappearing. Spontaniety is the timing of his spirit, a timing that cannot be controlled by even heaven above.

When feeling cornered, the Sagittarian man becomes brutally insensitive. His need to feel the air beneath his feet is the first and foremost law of his nature. This nature can also be highly self-serving.

However, when his natural generosity is inspired, the Sagittarian man can leap to the occasion with a remarkable élan. But, it *must* be inspired and not demanded on any sort of schedule. The banal, boring and predictable can break his spirit. And in that state, he is cranky and contracted.

The power of love for the mature Sagittarian man is the power of human possibility. Love catalyzes his own sense of inspiration and represents the person who shares his vision and verifies the potential of his dream. When evolved enough to be capable of the richness of a deep, loving exchange, this love becomes a lofty experience that is inspirational and expansive. This experience can inspire him to express himself in new, highly meaningful ways. Ultimately, it brings him back to himself at the same time that it takes him beyond himself. It could be the play that he has never written, the piece of music that he always knew was inside of himself to compose, the philosophy that he has never taken the time to truly formulate, the novel that he is now finally ready to begin.

For the evolved Sagittarian man, the power of love takes on transpersonal import. At his loftiest, he wants to share himself through his visions with the world, and in the process, to raise the workings of the world to his ideals so that all may be touched by that in him which is mysterious and sacred.

Power and Work: Sagittarius

In the area of work, Sagittarians tend to be lucky, and also a trifle spoiled. So often, they are the right person at the right time. In addition, their clever, versatile minds can maximize many work conditions.

However, Sagittarians have a limited amount of patience and this shows. They do what they want only when they want to, with no interference. Being forced to compromise, or still worse, give up and give in, can be fatal.

Because their love for liberty is so strong, many Sagittarians find the work niche that feels right. Among Sagittarians, it is not uncommon to find a factory worker who has a Ph.D. in philosophy, a used-car salesman who is a frustrated writer, a petstore owner who is a harpsichord musician, or a multimillionaire who travels all around the world, starting and selling businesses. Whatever the direction, the requisite work consideration that either contributes or gets in the way is the feeling, as Sagittarian Frank Sinatra sang it, "I did it my way."

To the Sagittarian personality, individuality is precious and ideally, work should reflect that. However, that is the ideal. In reality, in an impersonal, competitive and highly technological society, the demands of work often

199

diminish such an idealistic nature and make it difficult to stay sane and sanguine. Therefore, many brilliant and highly talented Sagittarians lose their power because they will not compromise their ideals for their goals.

There are many luminaries born under this sign who spend so many years "finding themselves" that the light begins to go out. Sagittarians do not want to pay dues or take the painstaking, plodding route between the dream and the deal. It often seems that many are, in fact, not serious when it comes to getting what they *say* they want most. That is quite often because what they *say* they want is a dream that will change as soon as a new idea pops into their head. The head of a typical Sagittarian is full of unformed ideas that swirl and collide and transform with time.

There is an extraordinary amount of talent and intelligence in the Sagittarian personality. When focused and properly channeled, the Sagittarian can create a plethora of thriving projects. However, a vital interest must be there to begin with. And after that, the spark must be maintained.

Sagittarians tend to take their talents for granted, and do not foster them with care or respect. Therein lies a great deal of Sagittarian foolishness. To be more powerful, that is, to enjoy the fruits of their gifts, they must consciously work with their inner reserves and stretch rather than scatter them. Whatever they bring a sense of joy to will bear its own reward in time. However, Sagittarians must cultivate patience—with themselves as well as others. They must develop a perspective that enables them to evaluate their creative input in time.

Sagittarians must not expect to be divinely inspired by their chosen direction. They must deal with restrictions through reason and with a sense of cultivated deliberation. Restrictions do not have to be a hindrance. Restrictions can *help* Sagittarians to see more than they originally conceived.

Sagittarius is the sign of wisdom, the sort of wisdom that comes from a higher power. Therefore, their special gifts are as precious as life, and should not be wasted through indolence and self-delusion.

At all times, Sagittarians must be conscious of what they do and say and the effect this has on other people. They must be prepared for the challenge of their choices and they will prosper through their expansive spirit that generates its own luck.

Powerful Sagittarius Psychology

> *The only thing which we all have in common is that we play tricks in order to force ourselves to abandon the quest. The counter-measure is to persist in spite of all the barriers and disappointments.*
>
> —Don Juan, in Carlos Castaneda's, *Tales of Power*

Yours is the most expansive sign, ever in search of adventure, ivory tower philosophies and the sort of experience that will bring you closer to the Source. Pettiness and small-minded people almost put you out of control. Their vision is large and flourishing, always favoring the future, frustrated to the soul by finite conditions impinging on freedom of expression.

In all sorts of ways you flee restrictions and thrust toward the tomorrows that will reward your ideals and further your dreams and creations. However, during the down times your own mind tends to become your enemy, and too easily it can put you out of control.

Sagittarians have a gifted intelligence, a creativity and a versatility that are unique to explore and enjoy in this lifetime. However, you must learn how to do that to make the most of your own potential, and this requires proper use of your freedom.

To thrive as a Sagittarian you must be impeccable. This requires awareness, conscious effort and a respect for timing. All of these things are not particularly in your nature to call upon easily. However, doing things the easy way is not going to help you access your own power. Diligence and discipline are necessary if you really want to grow and get the most out of your mental energies.

In order to experience yourself more powerfully, you must not allow self-indulgent desires to control you. This means learning when to say no to yourself and when to say yes. In essence, you must confront the impatient child within and take charge of it.

The petulant, impatient child will lead you to waste yourself. It will cause you to waste your energies, your talents and your time. These three elements, in proper working order, equal the realization of a dream. And you, especially, have so many dreams that you would love to see unfold.

Sagittarians have all sorts of vague excuses for their abandoned projects, procrastinations and prolonged delays. However, the reason that they believe is that the timing wasn't perfectly suitable.

You must make your own timing and then persevere, *despite* obstacles. Although you are often lucky, and used to things falling into place, you should not blindly depend on that. To many successful people, things are seldom ideally timely but they still make them workable with the proper entrepreneurial attitude toward their inner and outer resources.

Slow down, turn your dreams into goals and then give them realistic deadlines. Then take stock of exactly where you waste your own time. In many respects, timing is a Sagittarian pitfall. But it can also become a strength if you determine exactly how much time you have and how long it takes you to do things.

During the writing of this book, which turned out to be twice as long as I had originally anticipated, I had to become constantly conscious of what time I did have and how I could make the most of it. In addition to this book, I had other stringent work obligations and deadlines which also had to be met. Therefore, in order to accomplish everything well, I had to budget my time on a daily basis, and no matter what happened, regardless of any obstacles whatsoever, I had to live by it.

Being an impatient, freedom-loving fire sign myself, I would normally think of such a structured existence as suffocating. However, what I discovered was the opposite. This structure became like a support system that motivated me through the tired, uninspired moments. And what I came to find, writing my eighth book, was that I had never felt so inspired or creative. Discipline and strict organization became my constant companions. They enabled me to use my time powerfully, rather than time pitifully using me.

Discipline can be a joyful thing when you use it to multiply yourself, and you watch that growth as it accumulates weekly and monthly. On the other hand, there is no real joy in time-squandering, regardless of how you let it pass. This is because squandering is not playing or relaxing. It is letting time leak away without consciousness. Time-squandering is mindless and doesn't offer anything in the long run except anxiety.

To realize the power of your innate brilliance and creativity, you must learn the value of restriction. Restrict your focus. Restrict your time. Restrict your ambitions to what you can realistically accomplish. Restrict the number of times you say yes to yourself when you should be saying no. Restrict your impatience. Restrict your excuses. Restrict your attention to your goal.

Then as the fruit of all these restrictions grows, on a daily, weekly, monthly basis, watch your life expand and your accomplishments multiply.

Maximizing Your Sagittarius Power Potential

In order to make your expansive mind work creatively for you, you must treat yourself like a finely tuned instrument and use yourself with awareness and prudence.

In the morning, when you wake up, as your very first action, make a resolve. Greet the day with consciousness.

See it as a new beginning. Cleanse your mind of any problems or nagging worries of unfinished projects or uncompleted goals. Say to yourself, "I will create anew today and I will stay aware of all of my words, actions and feelings." Instead of feeling rushed or tired, look forward to the unfolding of your day as a new segment of your life.

A tremendously powerful technique for using yourself in a concentrated manner is the use of a mantra or mantras. Mantras are ancient syllables, usually in Sanskrit, that when repeated many many times, have a powerful effect on the mind. Each mantra is different, has a different purpose and a different vibration. When you become very skilled in mantra use, you are able to see the differences in vibrations immediately upon intoning them.

When you use a mantra repeatedly, you tune your mind into that vibration, and quite spontaneously it begins to work for you in daily life. Mantras aid concentration, heighten intuition, give you energy and a sense of well-being and internal strength that works in the most trying times. With disciplined, consistent use, it is possible to do mental work in half the time and to tap into your creative sources readily. Solutions to conflicts arise spontaneously, and as if by magic, you can find yourself doing some very constructive things without even thinking about them. In addition, with *proper use,* there is a quality of freshness to life, as if you were on vacation and you actually feel cleansed from within.

The following mantra that I offer is *om muni muni mahamuniye svâhâ.* It means "control, control, greatest control," and for that reason I feel it would be a good introduction for the restless and often self-indulgent and undisciplined Sagittarian mind.

The words are pronounced thus: ohm moonee moonee ma-ha-mooneeyay svâhâ. At first, repeating these unusual sounds may feel awkward. However, the rewards are so great that if you manage to get beyond your initial resistances, to reap results, the repetition can become an obsession.

It is best to begin your day with twenty minutes and try to work up to an hour. It is most desirable to change the mantra aloud, vibrating the syllables from deep within your diaphragm. The experience of a mantra is cumulative. Therefore, the more you use it, the greater and the faster will be your reward. Of course, mantras do not have to be restricted to the morning. You can also use them in the evening before beginning a taxing mental task. You can use them during those empty times of cleaning the house, taking a shower, taking a walk, going to work. I have used mantras during all of these times and have gained many rewarding results, including extraordinary mental energy on very little sleep, extraordinary concentration and intuitive power.

Two factors matter a great deal in mantra use: attitude and consistency. When you are intoning or mentally repeating a mantra, do nothing else mentally. Of course, all kinds of thoughts will come up; however, give the mantra your full attention as you would a movie that you are engrossed in, all the while keeping in mind that this act is for your great benefit.

Secondly, consistency is absolutely essential. If you do it for ten minutes one day and then for twenty four days later, you will not reap the benefit that is the potential of this practice.

In the end, you are either going to cheat yourself or aid yourself. It is your life and this choice is up to you. Mantras work. They bring results. All you have to do is do them properly and the rest is like magic.

One attorney I successfully worked with does her mantras every morning, and also while jogging and working out at the health club. "It's like money in the bank," she says.

It's much more than money in the bank. It's the power of your own mind.

X

CAPRICORN
(December 22–January 20)

Capricorn Nature

"I am therefore I am" might be the best way to sum up the Capricorn nature. Capricorns are terribly serious about everything they seriously undertake and that is because they take themselves so seriously.

A born executive with sky-high goals, Capricorn is the classic accomplishmentarian. Driven beyond high ambition, this is a sign that doesn't believe in giving up. Patient, enduring and steadfast in the face of all obstacles, Capricorn instinctively understands the value of time. This is a sign that can outwait all opposition and then confidently move in for the kill. Invariably, Capricorn gets what it wants because it goes about it in all the right ways. Hardworking, highly organized, diligent, down to earth and quietly determined, Capricorns make great tycoons, business chieftains, politicians, presidents and entrepreneurs.

The Capricorn mind is intrinsically materialistic. It knows the value of a dollar in several different countries and the most recent fluctuation in the price of gold. Capricorns value their possessions like some people value their children, and they look at life through the prism of appearance—what you see is what you get.

The average Capricorn does not dig any further. Surface impressions stick. And from this they form a base that is discriminating and judgemental.

Capricorn is most comfortable in a position of authority and assumes it whenever possible. Strongly believing in clear distinctions of "right" and "wrong," it sees things in black and white and sticks to this stamp regardless of new information. Finding comfort in emotional certainty, Capricorn remains rigid in subjective perspectives as well as in the selection of its personal imperatives. "This is good and everything else is bad because that's how I see it" is the classic Capricornian method of arriving at truth.

Capricorn is seriously concerned with the face that it shows the world. And needing to be seen in a light of distinction, it will drive to any extremes to achieve its reward. Displaying an indomatable will and a superhuman tenacity, the classic Capricorn wears down any opposition, be it human, the gods, the weather or a war.

Taking great pride in their ability to function effectively, Capricorns have little tolerance for people who don't. Capricorn is the sign of the self-made man/woman with the smart business mind and the stiff upper lip. In the Capricorn's climb to success everything unfolds according to plan, and the plan makes the person. There is no magic and there are no exceptions. Therefore, according to classic Capricorn thinking, anyone who fails is doing something wrong.

The archetypal Capricorn does not delve into psychological factors or emotional complexities. Sticking to the facts and getting to the point, they ascertain quite simply that something either works or it doesn't. And that is as deep as they care to go.

Capricorns are born climbers who make it to the top and eventually own it. And once securely positioned in place, attest that there is no other way to go. Like everything else, Capricorns take their status very seriously and never tire of their material rewards. The material to Capricorn is *worth*. And, it is *their* worth. Having an eye for fine quality, they fully enjoy the luxury of owning the best. To the Capricorn mind, excellence is always its own reward.

Underlying the Capricornian drive to the top is a desire for mastery, and often material power. Inherent within this plan is a sense of one's self as one's own creation. In the Capricorn scheme of things it is not enough to simply make it to the top, one must become the top in all its glory. Such is the drive of many politicians and Capricorn Richard Nixon in particular. His extraordinary tenacity, despite all obstacles, during the course of his political career is emblematic of the characteristic drive and endurance so often seen in this sign.

However, it is not merely material power which motivates the Capricorn nature to succeed. It is ego, pure and simple. Anyone bold enough to challenge the personal credo of an unevolved Capricorn will be most icily dismissed. To the very end, Richard Nixon believed in the self that he created, and not even a shattering, self-created crisis could bring him a sense of humility.

It is this kind of hubris which can make Capricorn a tyrant like beauty tycoons Elizabeth Arden and Charles Revson (the latter the founder of Revlon). When Capricorns mature, and some rare members are born that way, they have no need of self-aggrandizing displays to define their identity. Having evolved toward their polar sign, Cancer, they transcend the small ego-driven self to incorporate qualities of nurturance, sensitivity and care. While the first kind of Capricorn is trapped in the material, the more highly developed has extended its boundaries to the emotional and personal. The essential difference here is one of depth and depth perception, as well as wealth—the inner versus the outer, the full person versus the facade.

When Capricorn is dominated by position, persona and possessions at the expense of the inner world and the emotional life, then the result is compulsion, emptiness and intrinsic meaninglessness. Capricornian ambition and discipline achieve ends. However, it is the heart that opens the boundaries and sets one free. Living through compassion rather than ego, one is freer to enjoy material benefits without the fear of loss. Coming from a place of feeling rather than fearing, one is likewise free to experience oneself in a full range of spontaneous expressions rather than merely one imprisoning persona. The highly developed Capricorn senses when to yield and when to use force, when to let one's self go and when to assert positive self-control. The blending of the yin and the yang forces is a delicate balance which is reflected in the well-being. This is not a person stressed out from taking himself or herself too seriously. It is a person who is truthful, humble, reflective and wise. Mature Capricorns know themselves, know their depths and filter all of experience through the prism of their depths for greater compassion and understanding. And that is its own light of power.

Capricorn Strengths

When Capricorns transcend their superficial ego orientation, there is a core of a person who is real, substantial and potentially deep. They are strong and disciplined, serious and dependable. They remain steadfast in the face of obstacles, and their confidence comes from that.

Capricorn achievements are born from a highly concentrated focus and a tenacious involvement. They are enormously hardworking, highly organized, and methodical. In addition, they possess a keen business sense and are the most able decision makers.

Fueled by a fierce ambition, Capricorns are powerful initiators who prevail upon circumstance for their own purposes. Making the most of the situation, Capricorns know how best to lend substance to their dreams. They translate their visions into the most efficient, concentrated action that eventually sees its own rewards—even if there are sacrifices along the way.

Highly disciplined in anything they set out to do, from executing their business goals to following a regime of diet and exercise, Capricorns are always in control of their lives and live to create their own destiny.

As friends, they are loyal and devoted. As lovers, they are serious and substantial. In every personal interaction, Capricorns are people you can count on—in crisis, on a bad day or in the middle of the night.

Often spartan by nature, there is also a cornucopia in Capricorn that abounds with luxury. Capricorns love beautiful things, have excellent taste and an impeccable eye for intrinsic worth and detail. The designer Diane Von Furstenburg is a Capricorn and an excellent example of business tycoon, style judge, fashion force, caring friend and devoted mother.

Capricorns can have it all because they make it *work*. Whatever it is that Capricorns choose to embrace, their own substance brings weight and meaning. Capricorn's gifts give form to the world. Over time, Capricorns inspire others to realize the power of working hard for one's dreams.

Capricorn is the power of becoming one's own creation, a testimony of determination at its purest potential, the potential of each person to own a greater part of their life from which they gain value.

Capricorn Pitfalls

Capricorns have a way of beginning their sentences with "You should" and ending them with "really!" Concerned with "helping" other people find and remedy their flaws, they can be enormously tactless and insensitive people, dense as to their effect on their audience and damaging to other's feelings.

The undeveloped Capricorn dwells in the superficial—what a person is, is how they look. Period. Perception does not go beyond that and neither does the conversation. Everything sticks so conspicuously to the surface that it can be easily scraped off.

Capricorns have a feeling for things, not for people or their feelings. Nevertheless, they desperately want to be liked and held in high esteem.

Capricorns tend to judge quality from the perspective

213

of physical perfection. Therefore, Capricorn women are the first to run to a plastic surgeon at the appearance of a wrinkle, or to remove "fat" that exists only in their mind's eye.

There is a great deal of neurotic compulsion in this sign. Capricorns are perfectionists, but often about insignificant details that are not important to anyone except themselves.

Driven often to a ridiculous degree, Capricorn makes work for itself and turns pleasant circumstances into arduous experiences. All consciousness begins and ends in the outer mask. Consequently, communication is geared to form and not to content.

Undeveloped Capricorns speak without thinking, and when they do think, it is often to judge and to criticize. However, it must be said that they are not consciously cruel people. They are simply so caught up in their personal values and vocabulary that they are completely unaware.

This unthinkingness is a common trait among Capricorn men who often act as if divinely ordained to demonstrate their control. Many ruthless politicians are born under the sign of Capricorn, Richard Nixon being the classic. Capricorn men tend to be authoritarian in outlook and usually operate from assumptions rather than fact. The archetype of the unblinking tycoon who sees every situation as a potential business deal is the essence of this person. In the underdeveloped Capricorn's scheme of things no one else has an agenda or a life. It is a characteristic Capricorn problem to suffer from short-sightedness and to impose this on other people.

Capricorns fully subscribe to society's conventions and conditioning and care terribly that they have a visible place in the scheme of things. Money and position are their values. Desperately, they desire to be on top and to look down upon the scene as a flawless person who is reverentially respected. Capricorns are fueled by the demands of their ego and further driven by their fears.

When Capricorns are undeveloped, there is a blind, social-climber quality to all their interactions. Concern for reputation, status, and image make them remarkably limited in perspective and shallow in their ability to relate. Personal boundaries must be pushed outward to incorporate diversities in people and experience. Part of this comes in learning to value people in their complexity and growing from greater openness to these differences.

Expanding boundaries is difficult for emotionally blocked Capricorns. However, there are great psychological rewards in being able to experience the wealth of the inner as well as the outer worlds. Ultimately the prize is great wisdom. However, this implies a depth that can only be earned after a great deal of time.

When there is inner wisdom and psychological wealth, persistent, underlying fears around aging, loneliness, death and depression disappear to be replaced by a deeper understanding and more inspiring outlook. Furthermore, there is a sense of a ripening or accrual with time, a sense of becoming that is meaningful and metaphorical. The more that one is able to perceive, the more the individual boundaries are extended outward and the greater the experience of life. It is all a matter of personal evolution, which should be a conscious issue in each adult's experience. When the eyes become slowly unbandaged and the person becomes able to see—*beyond* fears, limitations and ego-bound restrictions to the potential in every moment, person and life experience, then one has the ability to affirm one's own possibility. At that moment, experience is no longer static and bound. It has richness, a sense of becoming and a boundlessness that enlarges with age. It all begins in a simple place: when nothing "out there" is any longer enough and the deepest part within oneself yearns to see.

Power and Love: The Capricorn Woman

Underneath the poised, self-confident facade, the Capricorn woman fears not finding the "right" relationship. Serious, insecure and substantial as a person, she deeply desires the perfect connection. The problem is that she often doesn't have it with herself.

Capricorn women tend to be hard on themselves and soft on the men they fall in love with. Along the way, a great deal of pride permits her enough poise to pretend that she is totally above pain. However, in truth, she sees her flaws long before her strong points. This motivates her all the more to exercise greater self-control.

Capricorn women keep plastic surgeons in Cadillacs and fitness centers thriving. Deep inside, this woman does not feel desirable unless she has won a war with her imperfections. Given this strategy, the imperfections don't stand a chance. For fully armed and prepared for combat, she enters fighting. Capricorn women work twice as hard when they want something. With this philosophy, though, they often confuse love with work.

In the initial stages of a serious involvement the Capricorn woman is overly alert to rejection signals and not secure enough to see beyond potential pain. Because of such a highly developed fear factor, the Capricorn woman tends to be a late bloomer with regard to love.

That does not mean that she lacks attention, popularity or sufficient suitors. Far from it. However, *her* choice for the casting of the central character can be quite another thing. And frequently it is problematic, since she tends to snub men who are very nice people and tends to zero in on desperados. Successful as always, she thus brings to bear a self-fulfilling prophecy of pain. Therefore, for many Capricorn women, love before thirty is a learning experience that they would very much prefer to forget.

No fool, the Capricorn woman never repeats her basic life lessons. These often have to do with the power of her choice. Her greatest challenge comes in staying open. For the hurt that can arise from surrendering to the wrong person can be substantial enough to make her close the door to feeling forever.

When mature, she is less superficially self-conscious and more aware of herself as a person of depth and dimension. At this point, she lives less from defense and more from pure feeling. This honesty, which is honorable, is also powerful in its effect on the course of a sane connection.

After achieving self-acceptance, the Capricorn woman is calmer and more capable of generating love. At this point, her relationship with a man will reflect the positive way in which she relates to herself. For the Capricorn womwn who is wise, love is a power that increases with age as it permits her to flower. Freed from fear, defense, anger and insecurity, love adds a luster to the Capricorn woman's normal patina. Living through affirmation rather than compensation, she comes alive to her own emotional potential, powerful as that is. And in so doing, she is transformed into the person she always knew that she could be, a woman rich from within and beautiful beyond the imagination of Beverly Hills, New York, Paris, Rome and the banalities of material perfection.

Power and Love: The Capricorn Man

A powerhouse in the boardroom, a towering monolith in business, when it comes to love, the classic Capricorn man is an insensitive moron. And not always a moron who is the most well-meaning.

Tyrannical control being the battery behind his vocabulary, he tends to run his relationships like a criminal courtroom. At a very early age, the Capricorn man overidentified with authority-type figures, and since then has assigned himself the power to proclaim.

On a very base level, the Capricorn male doesn't understand the premise of relating—that it takes *two* people. But that doesn't bother him because all he needs to know is what he wants and then its merely a matter of time.

He is logical, methodical and ruthlessly pragmatic. He is also highly ambitious and careful to nurture each and every goal. Life is his ball game and it just so happens that he is the pitcher, the guy at bat, the outfield and the umpire. And with all that's going on inside the big circle, it's easy to see that it can become a very hectic place.

Love for the Capricorn man is like a Howard Johnson's motel after fourteen hours on the road selling

217

vacuum cleaners. It provides relief and a certain measure of comfort. But, after all that, it's back to business and figuring out how best to market electric brooms.

So many serious goals and long hours can easily interfere with the needs of a stable relationship. However, the Capricorn man also has his personal needs and a big one is a sound supportive family base. So sooner or later, he'll find the time to find a wife.

Capricorn men win, they don't make namby-pamby compromises. Likewise, they don't expect to be challenged on their authoritative status. Nor do they have the inclination to negotiate. Nor do they have the patience to put up with some woman who demands give and take. Capricorn's patience is for what is "serious" and "important." And while women are wonderful necessities they should *be* women! and maintaining their proper place!

The Capricorn man upholds the sort of social convention that was characteristic of 1957. So, when it comes to love and power, he has the power and he'll love the women who promotes that.

There is truly nothing conciliatory to be said about this classic Capricorn nature. Is the moon green, does the night light up the day, will the Capricorn man ever change?

Why should he? He is a born dominator in search of the respectful submissive. He always succeeds in finding her and his setup always succeeds in working for him. As long as women abound who don't mind serving in the unarmed forces of their husband's ego, the Capricorn's system will continue its tradition and his love of power will over power his love.

Power and Work: Capricorn

Work is the doorway to power for the classic Capricorn mind and achievement goals are like precepts for their mental health.

A Capricorn man will tell you with a smile that he's just worked twenty-six hours without sleep or food. He smiles because he owns his own business and he can see the money in the bank. Or he smiles because he's been uniquely productive and has just distinguished himself in the company.

A Capricorn woman is on earth to teach women that they can be tycoons. Out to own the bedroom and the boardroom, success just seems to fall into their lap—after years of planning, paying dues, being anxious, getting frustrated and getting their hands dirty. Then one day that smiling face on the cover of a business magazine makes it all seem so easy.

Not so. The trick is that Capricorns don't expect things to be easy. The word isn't in their vocabulary. Cardinal earth signs, with an enormous amount of time capsule energy, they enjoy the feeling of driving themselves beyond belief. However, unlike Virgo, they are nobody's servant. At the end of the tunnel, an absent-minded pat on the back won't do. As they come around the bend after outdistancing all opponents they want the touch and feel of the reward.

Classic Capricorns are burning up with ambition. The thought of seeing their goals materialize is like wind in their face. Capricorns are exhilarated by the challenge and energy expended in the drive to the top. They love the climb. It is so natural that they do it in confidence. When the time comes when all the doors open and the goodies arrive, Capricorn is reborn. Gazing around at the huge office with its skyscraper view and designer furniture that looks like sculpture, wearing the designer clothes that demonstrate arresting taste and style, and knowing their chauffeur is waiting, one thing happens. The climb is almost forgotten. And these possessions have become the substance of themselves, interconnected and un-distinguishable. It is from this *identity* that Capricorn feels its power. This is who they *are* and who they were always meant to be.

To another person's eyes, *another* Maserti in the driveway does seem a bit excessive. To the Capricorn, it was *earned* and therefore has *self*-value. Capricorns *become* their attachments and in the process become self-elevated.

The problem comes when they stay at this level and project their values onto other people. In addition these values may *work* for them quite successfully, but being complete illusions, could one day also blow them apart. The stockmarket crashes, their business goes bankrupt, they hit a streak of luck that they outlive. And then there is sickness, old age and death. Who are they then? The fallen automotive tycoon John De Lorean is the classic capsized Capricorn. And what did he do sitting in a courtroom, bankrupt and facing prison? He found God.

Of course, one must smile. However, in talking of turning to the Bible, he was reaching inside of himself because, at that point, that's all there was. Eventually even his wife left him. Who was he then as a man stripped, abandoned and alone with himself? Well, he was what he always was and was *only*. John. And that could mean something that might not go away.

Until Capricorns get to this step, hopefully without loss and devastation, they are not only unaware of this answer, they don't even know the question. But the question exists all the same.

Truly powerful Capricorns enjoys their attachments but they are not owned by them. They have transcended their material identity to experience a place from within that is deeply self-sustaining. They dwell in the power of their own Source from which they have come to grow in understanding.

Powerful Capricorn Psychology

. . . the inner man continues to raise his claim, and this can be satisfied by no outward possessions. And the less this voice is heard in the chase after the brilliant things of the world, the more the inner man becomes the source of inexplicable misfortune and uncomprehended unhappiness in the midst of living conditions whose outcome was expected to be entirely different.

—Carl Jung

220

Capricorn

The Capricorn-Cancer axis has to do with the experience of boundaries and the experiences that our self-imposed boundaries bring us.

Classic Capricornian boundaries tend to be attitudes and values that are psychologically circumscribed and rigidly defined. Capricorn is ruled by Saturn, the planet of restriction and limitation, and on a higher level, wisdom and depth perception. The restrictive quality of Saturn enables the Capricorn mind to focus and succeed in the outer world. However, it is also necessary to be able to go deeper and move beyond old, limiting structures and perspectives in order to grow.

Deep within the Capricorn psyche, Saturn often functions like an austere parent who is overly critical of the child within. All Capricorns, both men and women, tend to become father figures to themselves. Consequently, they become self-determined, self-dependent and self-motivated. This combination creates rewards in the material world. Yet that internalized father never goes away, restricting the freedom, sensibility and spontaneity of the whole person. It can seriously narrow the outlook, perspectives and expectations. Eventually this becomes the quality of life.

In order to be freer and fuller, you must work from the best of Saturn's influence, but also you must be able to approach things from an emotional place that has depth, wisdom and understanding. Using the Capricorn symbol of the goat, the challenge is to climb *inwardly* as well as outwardly. Once a certain amount of satisfaction is attained in the material realm, be free to explore the riches of the internal. Explore and expand the inner person who has been dwarfed by the rule of the tyrannical inner parent.

On the most basic level, the lessons of Saturn have to do with survival in a cold, competitive and frequently ruthless world. However, life is far more than that. It is a boundless experience from which we are able to benefit in multifarious ways. The wisest way of living is not getting stuck in the cracks, but being free at all times to move on—to the next experience, person, or life cycle. When failing to view yourself from a more conscious, expansive perspective, your rigid and limiting Capricornian patterns stifle the breath of your entire being as well as the potentialities of those closest to you.

In order to be the best of who we are, every part of us has to breathe—our intellect, our emotions, our sexuality and our spirituality. When we grow, we grow through this inner person, and when life becomes deeply meaningful, it is from the inner world that images rise intuitively and interconnect to form meanings that are unique to each person.

Capricorns need to cultivate the garden within, to spend time with themselves in ways that can open the potential of the inner world. The depth that is evoked will enrich all experience and interpersonal contacts, and will provide a door for continuous growth.

The more that we are able to extend our boundaries, the richer and the more varied the life becomes. As a basic first step, Capricorns must be able to let go of ego attachments that they think they require for self-definition and go deeper into the place of truth within themselves. Psychologist Sheldon Kopp says, "This second look at his personal history can transform a man from a creature trapped in his past to one who is freed by it." Far more than other signs, Capricorns must free themselves by becoming deeply aware of themselves and their boundaries.

Observe yourself. Hear yourself. Watch your thoughts. Become conscious of where you are emotionally—and how you could become more compassionate to yourself and others. It is wonderful to be assertive. However, there are also times when you should be quiet and yielding for your ultimate benefit. As the psychoanalyst June Singer puts it, "One does not need to ride the rapids, one can *become* the rapids. The hidden river that has risen to the surface finds his or her own level and makes an impression on the world without any special effort to do so."

This is real power. In order to experience it, one must know one's self and one's limitations and flow with them but not be contained by them. This demands a delicate balance of action and awareness. When the consciousness is awake, the smallest acts bear their own significance. And in one apparently insignificant moment, the world can come ablaze with the power of one's own mind.

Maximizing Your Capricorn Power Potential

When the mind is tight and rigid, it is more liable to break from outside force. This rigidity is the weakness of the Capricorn mind. It is what holds the person back from growing into a deeper, wiser, human being.

Saturn, the ruler of Capricorn, has to do with the experience of restriction, limitation, and rigidity in the mundane sense. However, the more evolved experience has to do with wisdom, depth and understanding. This is the potential of Capricorn which must be earned through the spirit of inquiry and emotional openness. If you bring this openness to all encounters, the ability to stand back from your own judgements, you will be able to lose your boundaries in the experience. It will become you and you will grow.

The challenge of the Capricorn individuality is to rise to the experience of Uranus: freedom, insight, higher understanding, brilliancè, boundlessness. The lessons of Uranus say, "life is essentially joyous." It is only our own limitations which make it sad, lonely, painful or difficult. This is because we look at things in the wrong way, from perspectives that are limited.

However, when you rid yourself of prejudice, ignorance and distorted emotions, and begin to perceive in a manner that is pure and open, you begin to transcend your own personal boundaries, you are then capable of becoming a person who has personal power which comes from a source deep within. That source, brought into all experience, is a generative factor. It enlarges experience. It makes it both magical and meaningful.

In their highly focused drive to success Capricorns

overlook magic. Yet they are capable of it when they get out from under the dominant rule of the authoritarian inner parent. Experiencing magic in every day life means experiencing possibility in every situation and being open to that. However, in order to accomplish that, your mind must open up to perceive beyond the framework of self-conscious containment.

Capricorn's unique way of becoming more powerful is to see, feel and experience beyond boundaries. The average Capricorn mind is a highly conditioned one in which the values of society are deeply inculcated and the expression of the individuality is dwarfed by convention. Therefore, Capricorns have to be awakened and they have to stretch their minds.

There are a number of ways in which one can accomplish this. To begin, you must expand your sense of play. Capricorns tend to take themselves and their goals and possessions too seriously. However, the more you are able to see yourself through a sense of play, the more you will be able to expand your boundaries of perception. The most natural way is through being creative.

Painting, sculpture, and even finger painting, which is so abstract and boundless, coming straight from your primordial depths, are excellent ways in which to become more fluid and tap into your higher, intuitive faculties on the right side of the brain.

Keeping a journal is another. Here, you record not only your thoughts and feelings, but also creative, inspiring ideas that may lead to future involvements in which you can enjoy more of yourself. Reading over your journal in time, you will become fascinated by seeing a deeper, richer aspect of yourself unfold.

Finally, a technique that is of infinite value is meditation. There are many, many different meditation techniques that are effective in unfolding consciousness in different ways. For Capricorn, I suggest the following.

In a quiet room, sitting in a comfortable position, breathing evenly, focus your attention on the tip of your nose and count your breaths from one to ten. When you reach ten, start over. Repeat this process about nine times.

At this point, you should be relaxed. Visualize a paved path through an enchanted wood. The leaves on the trees are dappled with sunlight. Pastel wildflowers grow along the path and sway slightly in a gentle breeze. As you walk, and as you take in the beauty surrounding you, you smell the air. It is sweet. Except for the chirping of the birds, there is a hushed stillness. The quiet is mesmerizing and mysterious. Inside, you feel your mind stilled. A radiant feeling of joy uplifts you.

You come to a small clearing defined by a crystalline pond. Sunlight makes the water shimmer slightly. Lotus blossoms sit on the surface. The scene is so radiant that you forget yourself and merge with its beauty.

A figure, like an apparition, begins to appear in front of you in a blue robe. However, you are not afraid. Instead, you feel a sense of warmth and love that is like an unbearable joy. It flows upward inside of your depths until you feel tears leak around the edges of your eyes.

The figure is a very old, wise woman with a breathtakingly beautiful face defined by her large, luminous eyes, like amber jewels. She is there for you. You feel like you have gone home, to a place that you have long forgotten.

Ask her questions. She is there to give you the answers. Ask her such questions as, How am I holding myself back from growing into a richer person? What do I do to let go of my fear? What do I have to do to become freer? How am I holding myself back from experiencing the love that I'm deeply capable of? What do I have to do to be serene? And so on.

All of these answers will come. They may not come at the moment of meditation. They may come through a dream or unexpectedly in a quiet moment, words may arise from the unconscious that have great meaning and that bring things together, almost miraculously. They will allow you to see what was always there but what you could never see before.

In such a way, it is possible to experience revelations. Revelations mean that more of the self is being revealed, the deepest aspects of the self that holds all the power of wisdom and understanding that you will ever need.

Psychologist Nathaniel Branden talks about the *art* of being. This is opposed to the mechanical, unconscious experience of life. He says in his book, *Honoring the Self*, "As we continually extend the boundaries of what we experience as the self, we encompass more and more of what we had previously overlooked."

In order to experience greater power as an individual, Capricorn has to extend its own boundaries from within and begin to look *from there*. Learning how to go within is the key to this expansion. The second part comes in looking at others from this perspective and relating to their complexity and depth with understanding and compassion. It is the quality of relatedness that bears a wealth of meaning. It issues from the power of the heart rather than the shallow, foolish ego. It generates life and positive feeling that is enlightening and uplifting. The breath of this inner Source is both resplendent and limitless in its power to unfold possibility.

XI

AQUARIUS
(January 21–February 19)

Aquarius Nature

Authentic airheads, Aquarian minds are airborne and aglow with ideals that often have to do with utopian empires and progressive, inventive lifestyle alternatives. In astrology, the element air has to do with the cerebral realm and all that this implies, such as mental creations and concoctions, communications and intellectual vistas contained by the frameworks of the mind. Aquarians are often brainy people, full of brilliance and visionary explosions, seeing so far ahead that they leave the present behind.

The characteristic Aquarian is far more mental than emotional. Aquarians, in fact, have feelings about their mental constructs and intellectual aspirations. Their most beautific love experience passes straight through the brain.

The craving for a sense of possibility is a pervasive one in the Aquarian's scheme of things. It is the motivational force behind the humanitarian involvements and the strongly cherished dreams and ideals. The classic

Aquarian longs for a world of "brotherly" love and peace, uncontaminated by cruelty and ruthless power plays. Freedom of expression, lack of fear of domination and the feeling of pure, far-reaching connections with others is the deep, underlying Aquarian desire. Aquarians do not deal with life as it is day to day, but only as they would most ideally like it. This often poses problems, when, untempered by reason, it becomes the sole means of making a decision.

Aquarius is the sign of liberty and impersonal love, the *agape* that certain ancient Greek cults espoused but that has a difficult time existing in this complicated, competitive world. Likewise, Aquarius has a difficult time existing on its own terms, and its own terms are the only rules by which an Aquarian wishes to play. This is a sign that can be intellectually uncompromising, possessing a fixed, rigid mind set that creates means of maintaining its own path, regardless. The paradox of these people is that they always appear intellectually open. However, in truth, this can prove to be very far from the fact. Aquarians remain fixed in their ideas, and once commited to a direction, they have a remarkably difficult time changing course.

The end of the sixties, which sang of the "Age of Aquarius," epitomized the spirit of blind ideas put forth as truth, without any deeper understanding of the comprehensive whole, or the complicated timing of social change. The Aquarian mind, rolling on a track, does not take detours. Nor, is it intellectually open to their possibility. This is a sign associated with a great deal of fanaticism and willful rebellion.

Aquarians are often heedless and reckless, throwing caution to the wind and creating situations that are self-destructive. It is this blind which brings them their share of heartache and trouble. However, when they are able to evolve beyond the idiosyncratic, and work through their visions in painstaking, pragmatic ways, they are then able to climb those mountain peaks—without pain and conflict.

Pragmatism is the key to mastering Aquarian possibility. It is also often the hardest life lesson. However, when Aquarians are able to pragmatically implement their goals, they are then able to lend substance to idea and likewise, to embark realistically upon the path of progress.

Often, Aquarians are not realistic about expressing what is inside their heads. Consequently, their way of doing something is off. The timing is off. The approach is off. It may be way ahead of its time, or may be too forceful and overpowering as opposed to subtle, delicate, streamlined.

Like all air signs and Gemini especially, Aquarius has a lot of ego invested in its ideas. Whether this is Aquarians' version of reality or their insight into the "divine plan," it nevertheless functions as blinders which prevent Aquarians from seeing to the right or left. It is this encapsulated vision, when off the mark, that makes for so much of the personal chaos that Aquarians often find themselves in. They also often fail to go the next step in their thinking, which allows gestation and process to have just as much importance as the initiating idea. Lost in the clouds, Aquarians have a difficult time treading the earth. As a matter of fact, they loathe the idea of treading altogether and would much rather soar unencumbered to their mental destination. "*Why* does it *have* to be *this* way when it *could* be that way?" an Aquarian is apt to question, quite rhetorically. For it is never a question that truly demands an answer. First of all, Aquarians don't listen. Secondly, they are never content with reasonable answers anyway.

Eccentric, erratic and highly individualistic is the typical Aquarian business approach. Now there are of course Aquarian tycoons. However, they are not what I would call typically Aquarian. The typical Aquarian is the terribly honest, moral person who would never do anything wrong to hurt another person but despite all this wonderfulness, is wronged in return. Aquarians have never learned about playing in traffic. But, more to the point, they don't want to learn. It might restrict their freedom; their "I'm going to do exactly what I want to do exactly when I want to do it" might be somewhat compromised. There is a stubborn child in the Aquarian adult. And when this child takes over, life becomes a beautiful flower garden snuffed out with weeds.

The sign Aquarius is associated with the natural eleventh house, having to do with goals, aspirations and the group, as opposed to the individual. This lends lofty perspectives to the thinking process, which can be very exciting, inspiring and socially progressive. Trouble arises when other, equally important things are sacrificed to these lofty ideals. When something is at the expense of something else, there is a price to be paid. Often, in the Aquarian scheme of things, this price is very high on a personal level.

Aquarians tend to be emotionally detached, more caught up in the *idea* of doing good rather than simply feeling. Often, they are not aware of feelings—in themselves or others until it is too late. However, feelings always exist, whether or not you want to acknowledge them. Typical Aquarians often suppress feelings at the expense of a person or relationship. Sometimes that expended person is themselves, and you have the case of the "selfless" do-gooder who tries to make themselves invisible in order to please but not get in the way. This reminds me of one Aquarian woman whose Scorpio husband would not allow her to go out of the house and actually chained her to the bed despite her meek protests. Aquarians excel at protest; however, they have a hard time putting their foot down when it counts. In this manner, they can easily sabotage their own freedom, something that is ostensibly so important to them.

Until one is in touch and in control of the total picture, one cannot experience freedom. Real freedom issues from maturity, awareness and responsibility, not a solipsistic vision that transcends time. Great humanitarians were born under the sign Aquarius, but these people were not afraid to get their hands dirty. Such people as Frankling Delano Roosevelt, Abraham Lincoln and Charles Lindbergh acted with patience, persistence and thoroughness. Consequently, they brought about the change that they so desired. Aquarians must learn that it is not enough to be brilliant. Many hopeless eccentrics are brilliant. So are quite a number of people who are certifiably insane. However, to be powerful in the state of brilliance, to actually *take* the brilliance somewhere and make something from it, one must become grounded, centered and willing to compromise. To make the most of themselves, Aquarians must harness their will, direct it, and use it with awareness, all the time taking conscious responsibility for their choices.

The Aquarian who knows how to use her or his will consciously has great potential for expressing the power that is within. In the end, one must understand that the space between heaven and hell, called earth, is a place of limitation. We are here to work with that limitation and all it entails, not to work against it. Don't exhaust your energy trying to slay the demons. Make them your friends or render them impotent. Or learn what they are trying to teach you and use it wisely. But at all times be conscious of the whole and cut off from nothing. This is power, and this power can be the definition of your life.

Aquarian Strengths

Quite often brilliant, idealistic and possessing a futuristic brain, Aquarius is the sign of geniuses and lunatics, eccentrics and inventors.

Thomas Edison was one such mind. Humanitarian and having a strong sense of social justice, Aquarius has to do with transpersonal concerns and large-scale causes. Curious and on a quest of truth and beauty in its most abstract forms, Aquarius is theoretical and philosophical, alive to ideas with implications that are formidable and far-reaching.

Independent and individualistic, Aquarius is in love with liberty and alert to the plight of the underprivileged. Desiring to outthink timeworn traditions and to revolutionize the mundane humdrum, the Aquarian mind is a spectacle of visions spontaneously taking shape.

At their best, Aquarians are honest and noble, loyal to their values and possessing ideas that are ahead of their time. A friend to those in need, kind and generous to the core, they can be self-sacrificing and caring, eager to offer aid and reluctant to accept praise as their due reward.

Progressive in vision and pervasive in scope, the classic Aquarian dream is for utopian splendor, devoid of social ills, injustice and irrational wrongs perpetuated by the status quo. The virtue of the highly evolved Aquarian soul is righteousness and social indignation, the highest moral belief and the strongest convictions to carry things through.

The Aquarian mind is a prism for human potential and positive social change. Appreciative of purity and grace, courage and highly benevolent kindness, Aquarius longs to free the world and establish peace and fellowship for all.

Aquarius is the sign of the humanitarian embracing group values and goals that are far-reaching and filled with inspiration. Original and inventive, Aquarians are multi-talented and quite often artistic. Aquarians can be truly gifted people, ever expanding through involvement, keenly interested explorers defined by the need for contribution to each heartfelt involvement and cause.

Broad in outlook and often beyond their time, Aquarians seek a mode of self-expression that provides meaning and substance for their ideals. Often possessing stunning insights, Aquarians invite attention and intellectual exchange. Titillated by new ideas and turned on to new discoveries, Aquarians can live a life of the mind, with thought as the essential nourishment.

When it comes to relationships, they want someone they can respect and with whom they can share their values. Aquarians seek a friend in whom they trust. Detached, undemanding and understanding, Aquarians express love as an extension of their ideals. As this lofty state is so seldom satisfied, Aquarians are easily disillusioned and loving freedom, often live a great deal of their lives alone. Aspiring mentalities and inspiring conversationalists, Aquarians thirst for a connection with their own kind. Often aliens in a ruthless world rewarding selfish value, Aquarians are challenged to remain exemplars of the highest truths, rewarded only by glimpses of their visions coming to life with time.

Aquarian Pitfalls

The most fundamental problem Aquarians face lies in their failure to recognize the fallability of ideas for ideas' sake. This is a sign that gets easily lost in its own thinking patterns and that often experiences difficulty translating ideas and ideals into appropriate actions.

Aquarians are abstract thinkers who can perceive overall patterns from which they extrapolate truth. However, while such truths may be applicable to the life of the society as a whole, it is often off the beam in terms of the complexities of specific individuals. Aquarians tend to be blind to the feelings of their fellow man, especially when those feelings are problematic. Therefore, their ideals concerning the betterment of society often leave out the person.

Aquarians are often naive when it comes to people and this naiveté goes against them in all kinds of ways. People can beat them over the head with their own balloon and they emerge blinking and muttering about "trust."

Aquarians can take the do-gooder syndrome to such ridiculous extremes that they are capable of supporting a criminal population in the name of social justice. Words like "the system," "history," "social welfare" and "fate" creep into their conversation and keep them on a track that does not change with time, experience, misfortune, disaster or old age. The Aquarian brain plods on along its own course, regardless.

This reminds me of one Aquarian of my acquaintance, who upon seeing a homeless woman in the subway, disappeared to the nearest deli where she bought a huge ham-and-cheese sandwich. Returning with the sandwich and humbly offering it to the woman, she was firmly refused. "I don't want *food*," the woman informed her with great irritation. "I want money!"

Such Aquarians do not understand why the world does not work according to their ideals. Aquarians place a great deal of power in mental connections and fail to realize that perception is merely the first step in the life of a process.

These mental and emotional blinders often throw monkeywrenches into their personal relationships. The classic Aquarian often does not see the problems of the troubled son or daughter until it is too late and the person and the problem have become one. Denying and escaping they also do not see their own problems. In terms of love, they tend to treat their relationship like one long thought.

When Aquarians are cut off from the language of the heart, they hear only their own mental dialogue. Consequently, they can become a weird mixture of self-centered and self-sacrificing.

The self and how we see it, accept it or try to hide it, is the center of all emotional problems. With Aquarius, the sun, which symbolizes the self, is in detriment. This means that it is terribly weak in this sign. Therefore, the sense of boundaries is weak. Self-destructive behavior and bad emotional choices stem from this. Consequently, these are people who feel that they never fit in or who may choose to separate themselves in ways that are not healthy.

There are Aquarians who are narcissistic individualists, placing their desires above all other considerations. There are also Aquarians who are nice, bland people who never actually *do* anything with themselves. There are Aquarians who are militant revolutionaries, such as Angela Davis. There are Aquarians who luxuriate in their dreams and ideals, which never see the light of day. Finally, there are Aquarians who put their ideas into action and use their selfhood in all its glory to actualize a cause. Each of these Aquarian types has to deal with the issue of separation versus integration. Each must find its own meaning as a result of this conflict.

Aquarius

It is not easy for Aquarians to love on a personal level, because the very essence of their nature is impersonal, being the astrological sign of ideals and large groups. Therefore, they try to impose upon the tone of the intimate relationships a distant quality. Often the partner may be distant, physically or emotionally, or there may be problems in the relationship that create a space or sense of separation.

Whatever the pattern, it is very important to understand that the coldness or remoteness is the psyche's choice. This brings to mind one Aquarian woman who complained that her Virgo husband was so cold and controlling that he made her cry. Upon divorcing him and cavorting with an emotionally needy Libran, she complained about his constant desire for closeness and said laughingly, "Well, I guess Aquarians are supposed to be cold."

Her husband was a projection of her own psyche, which she could not begin to understand until she separated from him. This woman needed a great deal of distance. However, she was not responsible to herself in realizing that. Consequently, she suffered because of her choices.

Aquarians can conceive of the most bizarre relationship setups with the most bizarre people. However, as long as it works for the needs of both, something can be gained from the situation. One Aquarian woman I know lives in the basement of her ex-husband's house and continues a relationship with him that no one quite understands. Aquarian actress Cybill Shepherd's former husband lived in his own house, along with hers during the course of their marriage, while another Aquarian I know lived in a different state from her husband and commuted on weekends. Every Aquarian will confess that a significant factor affecting the success of their relationship is that they and their partner are frequently apart.

The fundamental Aquarian pitfall is the basic issue of responsibility. Aquarians can have lengthy, complicated and intricate reasons for why this does not apply to them.

However, the bottom line is that many Aquarians do not want to take responsibility for themselves, their choices or the problems that their choices have created. In such situations they will try to find a mommy or daddy figure to free the way for further denial and avoidance of their problems. And one significant denial is anger.

Being terribly nice, understanding people, Aquarians are often not in touch with their anger until days, months or years later, if ever. Deep within the psyche there is a disconnection that occurs between the cause of anger and the experience that it brought about. Like jealousy, anger to the lofty Aquarian mind is essentially loathsome and unacceptable. Aquarians will turn themselves inside out to suppress jealousy because its power over their rational thinking process terrifies them.

However, anger is a more complex experience because, the denial factor being so insidious, it is seldom an emotion that is conscious. At all times Aquarians want to be cool. So the mere thought of being transformed into a screaming banshee is hideous. When life finally opens the latch and all the moldy demons tumble out, it is not a pretty sight. For the classic Aquarian mind this is like temporary insanity. The shadow side of this perfection of human accommodation is rage. The longer the rage is allowed to fester, the more controlling the display will become.

Aquarian anger can be an extremely dominant emotion when consciously expressed. Many Aquarians are violent and irrational. When not unleashed, backed-up anger can come out through physical symptoms that interfere with the normal, unconscious functioning flow. In the end, to transcend one's demons and to become more powerful as a person, the first step is to become more conscious—of one's self, one's relationships, one's choices and how one creates his or her own karma. In everything we do not see, we lose control, we create bad karma and we create a blight on an area of our lives that could have otherwise offered possibility. Power has to do with being master of cause and effect, and of working from potential rather than self-created problems. Aquarius is a sign of enormous potential. The challenge for Aquarians is to realize it, grow into it with consciousness, and thrive, not merely survive in this chosen world.

Power and Love: The Aquarian Woman

On any given day, an Aquarius woman in a long-term relationship wonders what she's doing there. It is not necessarily that she *does*n't want to be there. She just doesn't feel completely fulfilled by love. Therefore, on some deep level something always feels missing. What that something is is a freer expression of self.

Aquarius might be the most difficult sign for a woman to be born in. This is because the transpersonal way of looking at life is far beyond the limited social conditioning of women. Aquarian women are not content with blandly accepting stereotypical role models. They question. They rebel. They seek greater freedom. They search for their ideals in a lot of different ways.

Nevertheless, they are still women. And as women, they have emotional and sexual needs that seek fulfillment. This is often problematic for a person defined by a great need for freedom and a desire to respect her lover as her friend.

What usually happens is that Aquarian women compromise. They hook up with a person who is powerful yet very far from perfect. Then they create their own space.

The ideal structure of an intimate relationship for an Aquarian woman is one in which she only occasionally sees the man. Existing as some sort of shadowy thing in the background, the Aquarian woman's husband goes about his business while she does her thing in life. Aquarian women thrive on being around a lot of different people and are easily suffocated by too much time alone.

Distant and emotionally detached, she can still be the friendliest of people. However, her desires are personal and not emotional. When the Aquarius woman becomes emotional, it is over someone or something that excites her mind.

Her mind is restless and overflowing with future projects and plans that promote a sense of greater possibility. Her desire is for love and partnership to become a part of that, not take her away from her pursuits. The feeling of being bound breaks up her energy flow and fills her with a sense of frustration. Consequently, it is not uncommon to find many unattached Aquarian women floating around, trying to sort out their relationship problems in their head.

It is the Aquarian woman's head which is both her blessing and the bane of her existence. Although frequently brilliant, this woman is also unbalanced in her essential beingness. The more unbalanced she is, the more lonely she can make herself through rigidly pursuing paths which make meaningful emotional connection impossible.

Aquarian women often embrace extremes and exhibit behavior which takes them away from their feelings. Caught up in group experiences and forming impersonal involvements with many people, their own personhood can get lost or submerged under the goals of the cause or the pressure of the project. Taken too far, in time, she can become cut off and alienated. At this point, it is very difficult for her to see how it all began.

I recall one Aquarian woman in severe suicidal depression, who in her manner of living drove herself to almost masochistic extremes. Upon encountering her by chance one day, in a terrible mental state, I suggested that she join me for a bite to eat. She fixated on the color of lipstick I was wearing and obsessively emphasized her feeling that I always look so pretty while she looked like nothing. In point of fact, this woman had at one time been a model. As we sat there, it seemed as if she felt that she didn't even have a face.

I took out my lipstick and gave it to her, but told her that she had to put it on and then go to the bathroom and look at her face in the mirror. Terrified, she protested that she couldn't. I persisted, telling her that the lipstick looked much better on her than it did on me and asked her if she would just go look in the mirror as a personal favor, appealing to her Aquarian desire to do for others. It worked. She left and came back and upon sitting down, wiped it off nervously. However, at that point, to my mind, it didn't matter. She had looked at her own face and it had started to ground her. That was the first step. The next step was that I reached in and related to the abused child within who I could practically see, huddled in terrifying loneliness. After dinner, I invited her back to my apartment, made her coffee and cared for that "child" like a tender parent. The next day she called to thank me, saying that she felt so much better that she couldn't believe it.

The brain of the Aquarian woman often abuses the child within, longing for love and emotionally undernourished by all the ideas it is fed. In this woman's case, she had to be on the verge of emotional breakdown before she would acknowledge the fact that she was lonely and starving for love. My aid to her that night was a quick fix, and she used it to stabilize herself for involvement on a new mental tangent. Aquarian women have a way of wearing out the pavement beneath them before they learn. Consequently they can be the most emotionally exhausting people to help or influence.

As long as we manage to stay alive, we all have heartbeats as well as brains. Those beats are to maintain our own aliveness. When we exhaust ourselves looking elsewhere, we can lose that vital thread, that middle ground that maintains our sanity. To experience the power of her own womanhood, the Aquarius woman must allow herself to be a woman, to go deeper than her own ideals to the truth of her own feelings which can freeze over in time. Love is a divine mystery. It does not have to be a trap from which you manipulate a clever escape. Emotional-sexual love has a deeper dimension than friendship. It is transformative and potentially very powerful. But first you must open a door within and dwell on the power of that mystery rather than denying its source. The source is one's own heart from which all is reflected. The wise Aquarian woman knows the power of her own heart. And she has learned to hear it above the sound of everything.

241

Power and Love: The Aquarius Man

When it comes to the subject of love and passion, the Aquarius man would rather read a book. Or see a good movie. Or make a good movie. Or explain how happy he is because after all these years, he has found a woman who is the perfect friend.

To the typical Aquarian man, anything *too* emotional is considered slightly offensive. In perfectly rational terms, he'll explain why. This may and probably does take up most of what was originally considered to be a perfect evening. Bedtime passes by in a blur of hot feverish announcements about historical imperatives and social betterment.

The Aquarian man is cold when it comes to anything *too* emotional. And any woman who is right there with him beat by beat, late-night critical debate after late-night critical debate, is sure to get straight to his soul. The Aquarian man's ideal woman is somebody who is brilliant, shares his ideals, and becomes his best friend.

And then there is his fantasy. The Aquarian man's problem is that he is compartmentalized. His heart is in the attic, his sexuality is in the basement and his brain is in the far beyond. Therefore, his feelings about women are often in conflict. Likewise, women are often frustrated concerning his behavior toward them.

There is a little of the old "goddess and the whore" thinking to the Aquarian male's orientation. It is not that he is asexual as he might appear. Rather, he is suppressed because he is devoured by a megawatt thinking process that prevails like a dominant parent. Therefore, if he is typical of his sign, he is not terribly turned on by the idea of sex on an ongoing basis, because for anything to have a vital place in his life, it must pass through his head. And usually, there is already so much in his head thta it's like a mass sitin to save the world.

Because of their compartmentalized makeup, Aquarian men can get caught up in pornography and/or sadomasochistic pursuits. They can also become severely alienated and waste years of their lives analyzing. Because their minds tend to be so fixed they are very slow to change or grow.

The realm of love is central to the core of human possibility because it requires an extension of our boundaries, an ability to get beyond our small ego self to incorporate "the other" into our existence. In so doing, we have the opportunity to grow and become more than we originally were. However, it is here that many Aquarian men have trouble. The head says one thing, the sexuality another, and the heart yet a third. However, all along the word that keeps popping up in conversation is "friend."

Aquarian men are often hopelessly confused without even knowing it. They are not in touch with their feelings and substitute their minds for their heart. Consequently, they can be cold, detached and insensitive to those subtleties that are warm and human. It is far easier, more natural and less messy just to be someone's friend. To the Aquarian man, it also feels a lot more elevated.

In their minds, Aquarian men can love a lot of people in a lot of ways, and the love is lofty and transpersonal. However, with a very heavy one on one, their sense of freedom is compromised, and their cherished ideals are challenged. This is not a happy feeling.

However, when an Aquarian man avoids personal love for too long, he becomes cut off and alienated. This deadness and fragmentation becomes a sickness in his soul that contaminates his entire life. His power comes from emotional integration and from being able to bridge the personal and transpersonal through his being. Then his edges are rounded out and he is not merely a brain but a force behind his own brilliance. Through love, his brain can meet his lower depths and give power to his heart and his sexuality. Love can vitalize his entire being by making him more aware of himself, as a being *and* a body. The Aquarian man, perpetually so other-oriented, needs to feel *himself* in a way that has meaning. This wisdom has great power, for it breathes of human possibility.

Unfortunately, many Aquarian men have to go through a serious crisis before they are able to emerge from their mental containment. Old ways of seeing, hearing and believing must die and their minds become a void through which mental illusions evaporate like phantoms. This is a terrifying process for such a fixed mind, but it clears the way for a new way of feeling. The mind has found its heart in all its simplicity. As the personal feelings begin to flow like a quiet hum of peace, so will the Aquarian man begin to know his own power.

Power and Work: Aquarius

Full of ideas, the Aquarian mind has to find its niche in the working world. Being a person who does not readily compromise, this is not always easy. Future-oriented, Aquarians are often frustrated with earth-bound limitations especially in the work place.

Believing in liberty as a spiritual truth, Aquarius does not readily settle for routine. Socially aware of the need for reform, the Aquarian brain is emblazoned with visions. Best suited for work that stimulates their curiosity while it simultaneously appeals to their sense of integrity, Aquarians are seldom happy in the work place. Even when working for themselves, Aquarians can become alienated and feel strongly out of place with the rest of the world. Theirs is the noble route, not the cheap ruthless path that diminishes people. Alas, this world is seriously lacking when it comes to the sort of choices of which an Aquarian would approve.

When it comes to ideals, Aquarius will never compromise. Instead, it will struggle to find a way in which to do something better. However, sticking to its own path often involves a great deal of sacrifice. There are times when this might become more than one can bear.

Unrealistic regarding limitation, it is a tendency for this sign to bite off far more than it can chew. Earthly matters have an insidious way of piling up while one's head is bobbing in the ionosphere. The Achilles heel of many Aquarians is the tendency to shut out the boring details while the brain is busy making life begin anew. Restrictions are considered useless and confining, while freedom becomes the self-propelling force that moves the

244

plan beyond the limitations of time.

Aquarians have a unique way of hearing and seeing only what they want to. They tend to be deaf to the suggestion that something won't work and will stay stuck to the wrong track if it appears that it is the only place to play from. Consequently, self-destructive patterns can pop up in the work place and will continue and escalate as long as the Aquarian mind remains rigid.

In the work sense, power to the Aquarian means successful self-expression and the ability to fulfill goals. However, to be more powerful, it is also necessary to be more flexible. Sometimes this requires a more diplomatic manner of dealing with problematic situations, which in turn requires consciousness and the ability to take in the entire picture.

Deep in the Aquarian psyche is the tendency to announce, "I'll do it *my* way or not at all." However, finding a delicate balance would better many lost situations, while maintaining realistic perspectives would serve as preparation for potential problems.

In the end, to be more powerful workwise, Aquarians must operate beyond both extremism and sacrifice and find a way in which their ideals work for them rather than against them. A continual awareness of the multifarious demands of each situation will keep them in touch with the earth, a hard resting place but a necessary one if one is to stay alive and thrive.

Powerful Aquarian Psychology

> A warrior takes everything in life to be
> a challenge. . . . What matters most to
> a warrior is impeccability in one's own
> eyes.
> —Joseph Goldstein, *The Experience of Insight*

To use yourself most powerfully, you must learn the proper use of freedom. Part of this means knowing yourself and your boundaries and becoming aware of the fact that there are sane boundaries in every situation.

An Aquarian out of control is like Icarus, who flew too close to the sun, melted his wings, and fell into the sea. There is tremendous self-destructive potential in this brilliant sign when it starts to burn itself up with ideas and energies that become chaotic.

What many Aquarians consider freedom more often has to do with compulsion and enslavement. When you are free, you are not fixed in any direction. You are flexible. At any time you can change course. Or you can turn back. Or stop altogether.

It is the fixed quality of the Aquarian mind that limits the expansion of ideas. At all times stay open. Perceive your attachments. Are they starting to pull you down? Should they be traded in for preferences?

When life begins to say no, Aquarians are often at a loss to understand what this has to do with their own behavior. Become more sensitive to the causes, the effects from which you are reaping. What is it that you are supposed to be learning? What is the fear that has kept you from finding the answers you need to go on?

Living from one's ideals may be laudable, but to be effective it is also necessary to be realistic. Do you deny whatever you do not wish to see? Facing disturbing truths can bring one much greater freedom. Where are you cutting off, mentally and emotionally, that is affecting your life in negative ways?

Concentrate on listening to what your life is telling you. Aquarians tend to suffer from selective hearing, shutting out what is painful, denying what arouses fear. The degree to which you disconnect is the degree to which you do not know yourself. Only when you know yoruself can you use yourself powerfully.

Using yourself powerfully means using your skills and awareness with a consciousness that is awake, alert and wise. Along the way, it is important to be realistic about your ideals and to be willing to alter the course of your actions if they are limiting you. Ask yourself, are your ideals an excuse for inactivity, for noninvolvement or lack of commitment? Or are they actually bettering your life and bringing it meaning?

Aquarius

Always question yourself, your responses and your actions and develop the ability to see yourself from the outside. In all attitudes, always challenge yourself to go deeper—deeper in understanding, deeper in compassion.

Aquarians often stay fixed on a superficial level of experience, and that level becomes the tone of life. Consequently, relationships can be shallow and lacking in meaning. When you are able to go deeper in terms of your relationship with yourself, you will then attract deeper and richer relationships into your life and they will become a source of great meaning.

Everything in your life should have meaning. Nothing should be stagnant. Your life should be a vital experience that changes, grows and deepens in dimension. However, you must take the responsibility for the content. You must treat your life as if it were your own personal creation. At all times, you are responsible for its form and for its content.

Focus on your life. Focus on yourself. Own your experience. Own your feelings. If your feelings are unacceptable, don't let them frighten you. Go deeper into yourself. Feel compassion for your own creatureliness. But at all times know who you are. Know all the fragments and inconsistencies. In your mind's eye, watch them as they arise.

Along the way, every day, there will be obstacles to your happiness. Use these obstacles. They are in your path to teach you and with the proper attitude, you can change them into opportunities.

Aquarians concentrate so much on others that they forget themselves and the complexities of their own life. Your existence means something. However, treating it with meaning is an art. Cultivate that art. Become conscious in every moment. Expand yourself and extend yourself forever. The journey is never finished. After reaching each mountain peak, there is a higher one that awaits you. Get on with it. And as you go, go with joy.

Maximizing Your Aquarius Power Potential

There are many different ways of perceiving. To be more powerful, you must perceive with your heart. When you perceive with your heart, you are at one with the object of your perception. You take it in and understand its essence intiutively. There is no subject-object distinction. There is only an even flow from you to the other person, without thought.

The classic Aquarian problem is one of disconnection. The head is disconnected from the heart, the thoughts are disconnected from the feelings, and the feelings are often distorted and suppressed. This tendency to live in the head, to perceive through the head, cuts you off from a deep, rich, expression of yourself and others.

When your heart expands and becomes your source of intelligence, you are then perceiving at a peak intuitive level. So often, Aquarians are confused concerning the behavior of others close to them. They do not understand how developments came to be and that is because of an inability to *feel* another person. Logic and analysis alone will not enable you to understand the depths of another person. Only your own depths, opened up and pulsing with life, will enable you to comprehend the inner life of another in all its complexity.

There is a Buddhist term for this experience: *karuna*, or "compassion." Compassion does not mean pity or sympathy for another. It means, instead, seeing your feelings in the feelings of another. Even if a person seems strange to you, and even if you don't particularly like that person, you can still see how he or she reflects you. In doing so, you will be bridging a gap. You will be seeing beyond the illusion of separateness.

There is an Aquarian acquaintance of mine who is remarkably intelligent. Yet emotionally she is seriously blocked, like so many Aquarian people. Incessantly she asks my opinion concerning people in her life whom I do not know. Do I think that they feel this way? Do I think that they feel that way? and on and on. This woman is so out of touch with her feelings that she cannot understand the feelings of those close to her. Instead, she relies on the emotional judgments of other people to tell her what she should know in her heart.

We all have very important lessons to learn through our opposing sign. In the case of Aquarius, this sign is Leo, the sign of the heart. Leos have huge hearts that the entire world passes through. Leos hear with their hearts and consequently, they tend to be happy people who are at home with strangers. There is a magic and vitality that Leos bring to experience through their heart that Aquarians can learn from. The heart is our vital center. Physically, it is the central power of the body. Our entire life depends on our heart. Likewise, emotionally, people who are cut off from their heart are very sick in their souls. They are strangled by their own thoughts which create a lonely, sterile experience of life. The heart brings richness and vitality. When you live through your heart, wherever you are, you are never alone.

There is a Buddhist meditation which is very simple, yet very powerful for developing the heart. It is called the Loving Kindness meditation, and it promotes a boundless feeling of warmth, kindness, understanding and lightness of being. Ultimately, it will eliminate the sense of separateness and promote a sense of unity which is a powerful feeling for the idealistic Aquarian mind. Done in the morning, this meditation will generate a feeling of well-being that can flood the day, when the mind remains conscious in its dealings with people.

Sitting comfortably and quietly upon arising, clear your mind of all worry, noise, and internal chatter. Ideally, this should be done by first reciting a mantra. A mantra is something like a prayer, but does not always have literal meaning. It is a number of syllables, usually of Sanskrit derivation, that when intoned properly, have a powerful vibrational effect. What is most important regarding a mantra is the perfection and consistency with which it is intoned, not the meaning of the syllables. Mantras are very powerful tools, that when used consistently, change the vibrational rate, promote a sense of well being, heighten intuition, eliminate negativity and elevate consciousness.

The mantra that I will offer here is one associated with Tibetan Buddhism. It is *om mani padme hum* (pronounced Ohm ma-nee pod-mee um). It loosely means "Hail to the jewel in the lotus," which can be interpreted otherwise as "Hail to one's own possibility, to one's own enlightened potential," the heart being the center of that experience.

After intoning these syllables aloud, deeply and from your center for about fifteen minutes, enter into the stillness. Let your mind be absorbed by the stillness around you. Then say,

> I send the energies of my heart out into the universe and ask that I be cleansed of the fears, worries and compulsions that are holding me back. I ask that I may be happy, peaceful and free of suffering.

Pause for some moments, then say,

> I now send love out into the universe to heal the sorrows of others, to give them light in their darkest moments and to aid them in peace and happiness that they may share with others.

(These words are a guide. You may use your own, but say them with feeling.)

Now, sit in stillness for a few moments and contemplate the feelings in your heart and mind. Your heart and mind should be one. And they should feel elevated.

The more you perceive your heart and mind as one, the more you will be ble to enter fully into the experience of others with loving compassion, seeing your heart in their heart, your suffering in their suffering, your joy and fears in their joy and fears.

Living through the center of your heart, you will

attain great wisdom. It is the wisdom that will eliminate much of your suffering and that will light the way to greater awareness and a more powerful experience of life. Do this meditation consistently each morning, and watch the circle of yourself stretch and light the way like a quiet force which always guides you.

XII

PISCES

(February 20–March 20)

Pisces Nature

Pisces is the sign of the psychic, the healer, the intuitive who is in tune with the synchronicities of the universe. Pisces nature is emotional, sensitive and subjective. Their imagination and intelligence are subtly insightful.

The Pisces soul is one of mystery and longing. Deep inside a slumbering divinity haunts a more conscious experience of life. There is an unearthly quality to the Piscean sensibility that is associated with the twelfth house. This is the place of monasteries and hidden meanings, astral experiences, dreams, drugs and superconscious states of mind.

Pisces is a sign that deeply reflects its ruler, Neptune, the planet of fantasy and illusion, romanticism and phantasmagoria, compassion, sympathy and the supernatural. Like the vibration of Neptune, the Pisces mind is changeable and fluid, fanciful and ready to flow in any direction.

Pisceans are secretive and hold a place inside themselves that they share with only a soul mate. Because they

255

are so psychic, subjective and idealistic, this soul experience is often unsatisfied. Instead, they will merge with and see themselves mirrored in their life supports and security blankets and the deeper need for unity will be sublimated by the experience of sharing. When this choice is made, the need for truth and meaning will be overshadowed by a fast-forward movement from emotion to emotion, person to person and place to place.

As in a funhouse, this sign can get lost in its own reflection and in the confluence of colors and psychological impressions. Therein lies the loss of attention, which is a classic Piscean trademark. Even a highly developed ability to focus can be diverted by a magic moment. Pisceans live for their perceptions, as subjective or incandescent as they may be. It is this supersensitivity that defines and contains a highly emotional inner world, imaginative and never without movement or color to capture and reflect the world from without.

Because of the strong pull of the subjective realm, Pisces is considered to be a highly idiosyncratic sign, associated with both sacrifice and selfishness. The ability to connect intuitively with and reflect everything around them can bring the purer Piscean to an experience of compassion that is simultaneously spiritual and a great source of truth. This is the selfless healer who merges with another's suffering, while being able to move that person into a lighter part of themselves. It is the Piscean genius to see the greater, boundless picture and to share that in a manner that is magical, imagistic and often nonverbal. The visionary quality to this sign is its key to the kingdom of the infinite and wise. However, when these panoramic perceptions are combined with a selfless caring in purely spontaneous solicitude, then this individual is a transpersonal example of the power of love.

This, of course, is an ideal only to be reached through the process of evolution. In the more mundane sense, the Neptunian influence functions as a source of inspiration, confusion or self-delusion. This lack of deeper self-awareness is always a paradox in a person who can see so clearly into the conundrums of another's mentality. However, there are a great many paradoxes in this sign, just as there are finite fluctuations in thoughts and feelings.

When Pisceans act unconsciously they are capable of falling in love in five minutes and out of love in about four. The reason for these changes is both arbitrary and generally incomprehensible. The unconscious Pisces may claim that the erstwhile love suddenly looks different, that they seemed weak, needy, overly emotional or psychologically suffocating. In point of fact, it may very well be the Piscean and not the person who is characteristic of these qualities. Pisceans operate a great deal from psychological projection. What they often see in another person is themselves. And when these qualities happen to be qualities that the Pisces does not want to own, then the projected person will get rejected in record time. On the lowest, most unconscious levels, there is a chillingly ruthless ability to dissociate from all people, circumstances or confining situations. It is as if there is a split of consciousness that separates a known person from a perplexing stranger.

With the Pisces personality there is always something more than meets the eye. Pisceans are born with the talent of acting and quite intuitively play roles. Of course, they may not always consciously realize this. In one moment one kind of behavior may seem most appropriate. However, the next day they may have to conjure up an entirely different character.

The key to the Piscean personality is that it gets caught up in whatever is in front of it that colors the moment. When emotionally captivated, there is an inability to perceive boundaries. A Pisces cannot stop once he or she has surrendered to an enthralling experience.

Pisces loves feeling. In the middle of this emotional expression is a confluence of external and internal sensations that vary in intensity and dictate the direction of consciousness. The more unconscious the less they are able to direct their focus. On this level the mind is turned so far inward that all peripheral impressions are simply censored at the pass.

Pisceans do not see themselves clearly. They see

their visions, their dreams, other people with whom they are not emotionally involved and perspectives and possibilities. In their mind's eye they can also see panoramas of light, color, fantasy, phantasmagoria and God. They make marvelous artists, painters, photographers, film directors, actors, writers, musicians, psychotherapists, healers, helpers and mystics. However, until they become more conscious of their own psyche, their personal power will be limited.

There is a profound need for escape in the Piscean personality. This is a mystical, unearthly sign that is receptive and reflective of its impinging surroundings. It is not a sign that is at home in a deadened world or in restrictive circumstances. Change, fluidity, freedom and possibility are essential ingredients to their sense of well-being. The desire for the ideal can drive Pisces to divorce itself from reality and take flight in a dream world inflated by drugs, alcohol, romance or far-fetched fantasy. The weak-willed Pisces will escape from truth to live among its own illusions. On the other hand, the consciously striving Pisces will know the value of sorrow and will sacrifice both pleasure and security for its ideals. A vaster reality defined by perfect love and perfect truth awaits the unconscious Pisces. All the Pisces must do is release the fear and listen to her or his own heart.

Pisces Strengths

The Pisces mind is like no other. Like the vast, swirling ocean, the Piscean inner world is a rich tapestry of impressions and sensations, some brilliantly intuitive, others fleeting flights of fancy. Yet all are unique in some way.

To walk down the street with a Pisces friend is like entering a magic realm. What the Pisces mind does not see, it will invent, quite naturally so. Rush-hour traffic turns into a floating opera, the entrance to a bank becomes the portal of an enchanted castle, strolling police become dragon keepers who guard a wizard who lives within.

Pisces

The Pisces mind is most comfortable with the open-ended and likewise, the number of possibilities it can invent to justify reality are limitless. Reality does tend to have an intrusive effect upon the Piscean imagination. To this degree, there are times when many Pisceans appear to be lying. In point of fact, however, their version of truth is highly subjective.

The Piscean mentality does well in the arts where it can create. They have the ability to see both what is there and what is not there.

When the Pisces heart is developed, the intuitive faculties are so keen that it is possible to enter fully into the experience of another as if it were one's own subjective reality. The power of intense emotional comprehension is of a superhuman magnitude. The acuteness of the impressions that crystallize in the imagination are magic to another, yet ordinary reality to the Pisces mind. For this reason, this is the most natural sign for emotional and psychological healing, and for physical healing through the powers of telepathy. Viewed from this lofty level, Piscean therapeutic interaction has the ability of taking on religious implications. It is possible in the presence of such a person to rise to the higher self and to experience the freedom and unity of all things. It is here that we have a person with the power to transform emotional suffering.

The genius inherent in the Pisces experience is the understanding that one does not have to be anything, yet can be everything. Each Pisces bears a stamp of uniqueness that can be the beginning of a legacy. This legacy has to do with joy and magic and perfect universal love. Along with this comes the wondrous Piscean sense of possibility in the midst of a sea of limitation. This is a mysterious, fluid, changeable sign that is never completely at home on the earth, always quietly yearning for an experience of exaltation or spiritual completion. It is this search for something more, for infinite possibility, that comes to define the Piscean individuality. When evolved, the light of the innocent child radiates outward and experience becomes illuminated with a sparkling vitality. Positive Pisceans celebrate life and passionately seek to share their spirit with those around them.

Pisces has a scintillating sense of humor that is magical, ascerbic, penetrating and always captivating. The trenchant Piscean wit is a function of the ability to see past the veil of circumstance into absurdity. To the Pisces mind not only is truth stranger than fiction, it is also a lot more interesting. Within the realm of truth lie miracles. To the positive Pisces mind miracles are perfectly normal happenings. In fact the Pisces mind has enough magic to create a universe. But first they must be willing to relinquish the security of their tiny cloud.

Pisces Pitfalls

The fundamental Piscean personality problem is escapism. This ranges from addictions to delusions, deceptions and simply blanking out on experiences that the mind does not want to deal with. The ancients used to call Pisces the sign of "sorrow from self-undoing." Indeed, it appears that the issue of self, either feelings of no self, self-inadequacy, or its converse, self inflation, is the core of this sign's emotional problems.

This brings to mind one Pisces female of my acquaintance. She is a woman with a brilliant mind and awesome musical talent, who has spent all of her adult life manipulating people and situations so that she could remain irresponsible.

Male or female, an undeveloped Pisces is extraordinarily parasitic, always found psychologically feeding off other people, never able to stand alone and face themselves. The sad truth about this sort of weakness is that it is characterological. The psychic energy is turned inward and is a very powerful emotional gyroscope—for undoing. This type of person rarely learns from the shattering effects of its own self-created experiences because it never looks outward. Those often startlingly beautiful eyes that appear to flicker and dance are, in reality, lowered into the demanding inner world where a part of the Pisces nature is kept secretly.

Communication with these Pisceans does not really do much to clear the focus of their vision, for theirs is a subjective world, highly emotional and strongly fantasy-oriented. I recall a Pisces I once knew who attested to the fact that he didn't have to go through actual experience because he could have any experience he wanted in his head. There are a great many glowing things to be said about the marvels of Piscean imagination. However, when the inner world works against participation in the outer world, there is definitely a problem. In this individual's case, the self-created problems were of epic proportion. I remember him once saying, "People say I'm selfish but the truth is I don't have a self." This one small statement summed it up.

Unevolved Pisces men are subtly haunted by their lack of center. While the highly developed members of this sign use this as a sort of genius to reflect the minds of others for emotional and physical healing as well as for all sorts of artistic endeavor, the immature members of this sign become problems unto themselves. Here we find the drug addicts and alcoholics that the ancients termed the "garbage pail of the zodiac." However, there is another version of the Pisces man who is far more deadly. This is the individual who has not risen enough above the gnawing space of self to be able to love. Trapped within his inner world, his mind is a whirl of confusion, apathy and anxiety that carries him forward in time. Focused inward, he floats through life unconsciously, buffeted by what is before him in the immediate moment. This type of Pisces man appears to be devoid of will and bound to the mysterious fluctuations of his own personality. On the surface, he may be thoroughly charming, witty and personally scintillating. In other words, he can be a perfectly dazzling individual—until, with remarkable detachment, he disappears.

It is the apparent lack of conscience or concern with which this man makes his moves that makes him a fascinating character to analyze—from afar. Indeed, it often seems that one is dealing with several different people simultaneously, all of whom possess a different vocabulary, which ranges from cool and witty, to warm and emotional, to cold, perfunctory and indifferent.

It is not what he actually says but what his behavior appears to be saying that defines the truth. Words are not the most important means of communication for Pisces. However, their meaning can be far more reflective of fantasy or wishful thinking than reality. Pisceans communicate most truthfully through their behavior. But even this can be extremely confusing because it fluctuates without any apparent signals to indicate the onset of some sort of change.

If troubled Pisceans are lucky, and many of them are, some devastating experience will force them out of their little psychic womb, and they will be forced to confront the world. This brings to mind a rather dramatic Pisces story which illustrates the transformative power inherent in such a critical experience.

This young man had lost years of his life to a pathetically and pathologically monotonous and banal existence in which he huddled and hid out in his inner world. On a daily basis, he used marijuana to help maintain the distance from the job and the loneliness that were intolerable. In his mid-thirties, driven by impulses inside himself which he did not understand, he broke through his existence as a hopeless loner by becoming obsessively involved with a girl.

The girl was a doomed vision, a former drug addict, an alcoholic, and an occasional prostitute. Mr. Pisces' involvement with this girl was a compulsive, masochistic one. Hating herself with the deepest revulsion, she likewise treated him with the same conspicuous lack of caring with which she treated herself. However, she broke through his frozen sexual fantasy life and made it come alive. She was a whore, and for once he felt no guilt. She was also young and her alcoholism was so advanced that she was dying. For that he felt sad and wanted to save her. For once in his life, he had gotten beyond himself. And that was *his* hope. For the first time in his life, he felt alive.

Down the road, the girl was found dead in a drug pusher's apartment with a needle in her arm. More than anything else, she had wanted to die, and life gave her the death she wanted.

The Piscean young man went off the deep end with alcohol, lost his job but was given one last chance. The condition was that he sign himself into a hospital to rehabilitate. He did, and once again, life forced him to communicate with people. The loneliness that he had known all his life like his own skin, began to disappear and he began to have feelings for his fellow inmates and to become involved in their problems. He also began to develop a self-esteem where none had existed before. Little by little, he became a new person, a person who could care. As a new person, he got a new job, a job that he liked in a place where he was treated like a valuable person. A miracle had taken place in his life and it all began the moment he got beyond himself.

Later, he was to say to me, "I remember you talked to me about Pisces compassion and I always thought that that was the one area in which you were wrong. I never had any compassion. I never knew what it was like until recently."

And I said to him, "It feels good, doesn't it? Even though sometimes it hurts."

In the Pisces experience, self is inextricably tied up with feeling. Through feeling, there is the potential for great power. There is no substitute for plunging in the waters, for surrendering, being engulfed and being reborn. However, within this realm of self-projected feeling, there is a delicate balance between the power of sacrifice and the pit of martyrdom. It is here that we encounter our final Pisces pitfall.

There are Pisceans who are confirmed caretakers and others who are effective enablers. The two types are escaping selfhood, through the oceanic immersion in the plight of another. As most Piscean pitfalls, this is not a conscious act, but rather one born from instinct and fluidity of feeling. That primordial sense of "no self" is surrendered to and the individual merges with the pain of another ultimately to experience the relief of separation. Where once separation was perceived as a threat, it now becomes a psychological reprieve. It is valid, rather than demonic, in that it eliminates the void of total aloneness.

What all of these pitfalls have in common is that the self has yet to be discovered and experienced in a conscious, life-affirming way. These emotional states fundamentally have to do with the negative, control aspect of power, rather than life-affirming love or self-love.

Power is a subtle issue in the Piscean personality. All Pisceans are aware of the issue of power and their relationship to it. However, ironically, the Piscean individuals who most consciously set up the power-love dichotomy completely miss a simple point: the power of the spontaneous power of love, wisdom and compassion within their own souls.

There can be great cruelty in the Piscean nature and a whiplash sarcasm that diminishes and defiles. There can also be great fear because of a larger-than-life, overactive imagination. Both are the result of excessive subjectivity—a mind turned too far inward and away from the sense of compassionate connectedness that is the Source of this nature.

To move beyond such pitfalls, one has to at least become conscious of the pain—if even to choose to bring about more pain. The new choice must be lived out while the life changes and the heart and mind change.

Power is to be found in the new consciousness. Power comes by awakening to the Source within and living it. To do this, a Pisces needs no education. It must only live through its own heart to meet the challenge of its own soul.

Power and Love: The Pisces Woman

The Pisces female was formed with her own set of rose-colored spectacles which fit snugly over her eyes. Quite magically, her vision can create little miracles that bear synchronistic meaning. The right person emerges at the most auspicious moment. She gets a "special feeling" and a phone call follows. She has decided to make a major life change only to encounter a new opportunity.

Alas, in the oceanic area called "love," she is not quite so serendipitous. The Pisces woman is the original romantic. Her pulse races at the thought of grand love, the more phantasmagorical the better. Even if some ingredients are missing, Pisces will fill them in. If truth be told, the result will very likely be so inordinately captivating that she doesn't really *need* the man. He plays his part as a sort of catalytic carryover of childhood fantasies of castles and kings and beautiful, gossamer fairy queens. Fairy tales have always seemed more real to her than the world at large. However, the problem with real life is that despite her greatest imaginings, in time, her fairy prince turns into a troll.

Pisces women are very often unlucky in love because they lose their minds to their illusions. A Pisces woman in love is like an airplane landing on a rainbow. There is a lot missing—such as the landing. But on the other hand, she doesn't mind. What the Pisces woman is most in love with is her preciously wrought dream and how this illumines her inner world.

Pisces women are strongly attracted to men in positions of power—material or otherwise. That is because they have a deep inner need to surrender to an almighty force that they sense is stronger. To the average Pisces woman's mind, great success and power is sexually seductive, since it fits into the script of princely provider who will allow her to luxuriate in her dreams.

While the Pisces woman prefers to see herself as very independent, she still dreams of a pair of strong arms that will support her on her emotional days, or better yet, a pair of hands that will pay the rent. The average Pisces woman scintillates at the thought of a male powermonger who makes her feel protected and cared for. Yet the irony is that it is these very men who make her feel most alone. When the truth dawns she is crushed. However, it is usually not for long. In time, she turns to encounter a new hero.

There is always an element of hyperbole in the female Pisces love plight. The essence of the story is as if it's all being directed by a divine plan. However, when the larger-than-life elements are missing, the Pisces is indifferent. Even if she answers the telephone, the Pisces woman is really not home. When some poor fool who is not a hero hungers for her, she can be as cool as air conditioning in the middle of December. If something cannot be a moment, her impulse is to swim away from it. That is because in her mind it's the moments that count even more than the man.

However, the problem with the pageantry of grand passion is that it always bears a price. It is that price that always implies a sacrifice of some kind.

Sacrifice is a key word to the experience of Pisces. In romantic love, there is the initial sacrifice of reason. Eventually, there is a sacrifice of the dream to the experience of the truth. However, the desire for the ideal is still all-encompassing and must be played out in life on some level until it is satisfied.

The martyr or self-deprecating enabler is another common theme in the female Pisces love scenario. This is the classic abused woman who will not leave the abuser, the self-despairing servant of the addictive personality, the woman who becomes victimized by a bad relationship. This sort of Pisces woman, who has no clearly defined conscious center, verifies her existence through the existence of another. Like the Pisces woman living through her romantic dreams, she perceives her world through the prism of her own suffering. However, this situation is more complicated than might appear, for this behavior is primordial empathy that is far stronger than reason will allow. At some point, a Pisces woman must progress through her own illusions, enchantments and negative attachments to encounter truth. With age, she has the potential of gaining great wisdom through the experience of love, and when she reaches this plateau she then has the potential of coming into her own power.

The power of Pisces is the capacity to perceive truth. The power of the Pisces woman is to live through truth, to gain meaning through her intuitive perceptions, to allow them to guide her for the deeper understanding which her soul demands.

When her consciousness is elevated and she is in tune with the goddess within, she will have the power to attract the love experiences that her soul requires. However, until she hears her own voice, until she moves beyond the tinsel and dazzle of the external world to the powerful voice of wisdom within, she will continue to experience dissatisfaction in her quest for love.

The Pisces woman must find her soul mate, and for this her mind must be empty and pure. She must be like a pool, crystalline, tranquil and beyond compulsion or confusion. Through her expanded heart, she is able to love and take pleasure in many things, people and experiences. Most of all, she is able to generate love and life from the center of her being. When cleansed of illusion, she is able to live in her own light, and this light will empower her along her path of love.

Power and Love: The Pisces Man

As one experienced woman I know put it, "There is a Pisces man in every woman's past." That is because Pisces men are the most beguiling. Artists, psychics, psychologists or psychotics, there is always a deadly sort of charm that chills out all feminine reason and resistance.

The Piscean personality pulls one in and evokes simultaneous supplication. However, in the middle of total feminine surrender it is not unlikely that the Piscean attention will drift elsewhere, and he will continue to swim on.

Although Scorpio men are claimed to be kings of the sexual sphere, Piscean men are the great seducers. The key to the Pisces man's success is that he goes straight to the source: the soul.

What the Pisces man is capable of engendering in a woman is total surrender. His danger comes from the fact that he doesn't really know what to do with the body afterwards. Often he's not sure if he wants to do anything at all.

Piscean men are like addictive drugs that start out as harmless as vitamin C. Typically, the Pisces man is an

unassuming sort of fellow who nonchalantly lets loose a
larger-than-life personality spiced by an arresting sense of
humor. That's the beginning. Without even wanting to, Mr.
Pisces beguiles the gods. He can't help it. He doesn't
know how it happens and he doesn't know where it's
going to go. He just is who he is and in the area of love,
that is unconscious, confused and hopelessly charming.

All charm and no soul is a terrifying combination.
However, the truth is that Pisces is trying to find his soul
through the love connection. The problem is that every
time he becomes connected his self also disappears.

Deep down, Pisces men want to experience their own
fluid, mystical soul in the soul of another woman. Few
accomplish this, so they settle instead for security. Others
never love but live through drugs, dreams and sexual
encounter. Still others abandon the quest altogether, become celibate and seek God.

Opening one's eyes under water is something like the
experience of a Pisces male in love. It's all very vague and
cloudy and kaleidoscopic. This perception of change is
something with which Pisces is particularly comfortable.
Pisces men operate on the premise of change being the
only verifiable stability. Too much routine terrifies him, as
does the feeling of being responsible for the expectations
of another person. In the love situation, Pisces' feelings
must be fluidly evoked. Ultimatums and demands have a
demonic effect on his sensibilities. Essentially, the Pisces
man is not controllable or confinable. While *appearing*
totally entrenched, he is also capable of swimming in a
completely different direction should there seem to be too
much sand up ahead. To stay on course, he must be fueled
by longing.

In the realm of love, longing is a profound Piscean
experience. Quite commonly, Pisceans love from afar.
Unrequited love, distant or doomed, long-lost loves like
preserved flowers, fatal attractions that consume their
control—these are the most seductive Piscean situations.
The Pisces male has a characterological weakness for
forbidden fruit—even if he is frightened and disturbed by
his own impulses. This brings us back to a paradox in the

male Piscean personality. While these men are sexually attracted to danger, emotionally they seek security and a relationship in which they have some control. However, let no faithful Piscean partner find out that any Piscean man who is really in control, is not really in love.

That is why it is futile to pursue a Pisces man to attain romantic splendor. The most one might attain is marriage with a man who is physically present while his fantasies take him elsewhere. Damsels driven to please will never be the ideal love, although they may very well make it to the altar. That is because in the deepest part of him, the Pisces man is most deeply moved by what he can't actually possess.

The Pisces man is a mystery unto himself and is capable of a vast number of connections. Because of his need for love and his deep psychological insecurity, one of the connections will be marital. However, what happens after that point can be predicted only by one factor—the quality of the emotional content.

Pisces is an idealist with a great deal of emotional needs. However, these needs are for the most part inexpressible. They exist as a swirl of impressions that are seldom fully examined. On the conscious level he has the practical need for emotional and usually material security. Within this realm, it is common to see a Pisces man married to a financially solvent woman, an older, socially established woman, or a strong, dominant woman who displays power and control. This bastion of security does a great deal to make the Pisces man feel safe, for under the surface he is a fearful man fueled by an overactive imagination.

This kind of connubial comfort can quietly contain him. Alas, it is not enough for the yearnings of his soul. Many Pisces men never heed the cry of their own soul. Some drown it through alcohol or drugs. Others surrender through art, music or mysticism. However, the most powerful acknowledgement is through the mystery of love.

Pisces men can love a lot of people in a lot of different ways. It is not that they necessarily cease to love

269

their earthly wives. But rather it is when they fall upon and completely lose themselves to an unearthly love that they *find* a portion of themselves. They find their souls and are made vitally alive through their own nature.

The rare Pisces man who is capable of unconsciously attracting this experience to complete that "missing" part will lose his reason and die, in a sense, to the undefinable. To the degree that he allows himself to die, that he allows his own conscious reasoning to surrender, is to the degree that he experiences his own divinity. In this respect, love, the unearthly, transcendental gesture, is reflective of the ancient religious rites of Bacchus.

The participants of the Bacchus rites reacted against prudence which, it was felt, denied divine possibility or illumination. Through their sexual and drug-induced rites they sought intoxication as a means of merging psychologically and spiritually and in the process, lighting the inner world with the beauty of God.

To become one with God, to merge and rise with one's own divinity through love, is the apogee of the Piscean experience. This is the power that love potentially holds for this sign, though of course this ideal state is seldom realized.

One sees the Piscean man taking his intoxication in more earthly ways—through drugs, alcohol, sexual fantasy, and then settling with age, into a security nest to endure divine discontent.

To arouse "divine" love in a Piscean man, a woman must be a goddess in the deepest psychological sense: that is, she must have the power to evoke relatedness on all levels: experiential, emotional, sexual, spiritual. And as in mythology, she should be somewhat removed and not looking for love. Any woman *looking* for love from a Pisces man will never really find it. That is because, just as this man longs for his own godhead, he must likewise long for the woman in whose reflection he sees it mirrored. This woman is never totally within reach, yet through the power of her soul, she totally connects to him.

The Pisces nature is a mystical one, whether or not it finds any type of earthly expression. It appears that the experience of living on earth brings the Pisces man to a crossroads of conflict: intoxication and inevitability of encroaching death amid a world that is increasingly meaningless in any deep personal sense. This is not the easiest of conflicts, especially with an individual who is deeply driven by both. Somewhere along the way a resting place comes, called confusion.

It is now easy to see why for a normal, well-intentioned woman, falling in love with a Pisces man, can be like someone coming down with the first signs of the plague. What Pisces needs is not what he wants, and most of the time he doesn't even know what he wants until he knows he can't have it.

Love is a very potent power that the Pisces man does not really know how to handle. That is precisely because he cannot "handle" love. He can only "handle" security, hence the Pisces man's struggle between the two worlds.

This is one paradox which defines him. Another is a highly emotional nature which can also turn curiously cold. This man is a chameleon who changes like sunlight flickering on the surface of the sea. Because he is so changeable, it is possible for the Pisces man to escape from conflicts. Besides having an escapist's mentality, he is easily diverted, and for that reason, he has a tendency to repress his own deeply disturbing feelings.

It might also be said that love comes quite easily to the Pisces man. He is used to things "happening" quite magically. It must also be added that he does not want to take responsibility for how he reached this state or how he will end up. What he really wants to do is float and feel exhilarated by his own feelings.

Unlike men in many other sun signs, this is a man who needs love as a vital expression of self. Again, unlike other signs, this expression can be totally transpersonal as in the healer, the therapist, the mystic. To attain compassion and a transpersonal level of love is the spiritual challenge of most individuals. However, for the Pisces archetype the challenge is to come back down to the personal plane to learn about self through the conflicts of love.

The most powerful function of love is its ability to transform frogs into princes, to create miracles of heart and mind and to enable us to transcend ourselves. This is also the power inherent within the Pisces man. To encounter it, he must first be willing to encounter his divine discontent. For there is truth deep inside him that will guide him through his personality to the soulful experiences that he must have. There are Pisces men who pass through life forever searching. There are others who lose a sense of time and lead a somnolent existence. There are still others who must encounter their own soul through the experiences of the transpersonal. Whatever the direction, once his quest has begun, he will not be an easy man to love.

A great Pisces possessed by the quest, Albert Einstein, said,

> I am truly a lone traveler and have never belonged to my country, my home, my friends, or even my immediate family, with my whole heart; in the face of all these ties, I have never lost a sense of distance and a need for solitude.

For the archetypal Pisces man, love is a power at once fated and transformative. Like his own soul, it is a mystery that bears its own divinity, yet is also curiously essential. I suspect that Einstein intuitively understood the power of love but had a different quest and encountered the sacred through the transpersonal. He once said, "I know little about nature and hardly anything about men."

The power of Piscean love is the power of knowing, knowing the unknowable through the heart and understanding the power of the heart to know all.

Power and Work: Pisces

Work must be an activity in which one invests one's self emotionally—or else it is meaningless. The Pisces mind that is merely passing time to make a living is a deadened one, unable to access the luminosity of its most powerful gifts.

Pisces are at their most powerful workwise when they are able to lose themselves in work. Within this context, they are less ambitious than emotionally motivated. Pisceans do exist who are moguls in the business world. However, for the most part, this is not their milieu. When their imagination is activated or when their spiritual-mystical nature is highly motivated, they are successful in every sense of the word.

Typical Piscean areas of powerful endeavor are all areas of the arts, psychology, psychism, mysticism and medicine. Because Pisces is a mutable, multifaceted sign, many of these areas can be combined to create a totally new career.

As every sign expresses its shadow side (opposite), there are those Pisceans who repress their intuitive nature to try to tune into a strongly structured Virgo-type profession such as banking, business, corporate law. However, this direction is so strongly inimical to the Piscean personality that it can create a serious mental and emotional strain.

Such is the case of one Pisces executive who was also editor of a very conservative, establishment-oriented business magazine. When circumstance caused him to leave his endeavor, he began to discover his own openended, mystical nature and became dumbfounded. His comment was, "The person I've been thinking I was my whole life is another person. Now I know why I've felt so depressed without even knowing I was depressed."

A Piscean who is misdirected to the point of losing his own soul, along with years of his life, is indeed a powerless person. For a Piscean to be most powerful in relationship to his work, he must be able to experience it in terms of its intrinsic value to his own uniqueness. This is the sign of higher truth, compassion and universal love. Essentially, Pisces represents all of the values upon which formal religion is based. These qualities, repressed and converted into a rigid, ego-oriented structure, ultimately bring frustration rather than fulfillment to the sensitive Pisces nature.

However, many lower, power-possessed Pisceans also exist. These individuals are always profoundly self-deluded. Because there is no core to speak of in the Piscean personality, there are many individuals in this sign who, deep down, feel like nothing. Psychologically speaking, they cannot touch bottom. Because they exist in a highly competitive world to which they are emotionally receptive, the natural inclination is to want to fill themselves up with the fruits of values antithetical to their own authenticity. This type of Pisces, feeling like nothing distinctive, will go to great lengths to try to become "someone." He will color himself with the "right" achievements, the "right" people, the "right" connections to the "right" experience when he will become *someone*. All along the way the anxiety is building. The need to compare and compete is increasing. Jealousy and resentment are waiting in the wings for that day when the dream falls apart.

This is a heavy load to assume volitionally, and being around this type of Pisces one has a tendency to feel weighed down. This highly creative mind, which at its best does not function in a linear fashion, is obsessed and possessed to use everything in sight to aggrandize selfhood. This brings to mind one very sad woman in both the print and television media who compulsively "worked the room" to make contact with anyone who would be important enough to put in her people roster. Her "friends" were chosen for their name, since their name was a door to the many doors they might be able to open. Through the years, the minor triumphs mixed with the disappointments, the fear, the feeling of being "passed over" by people she thought she knew, finally to end up alone, loveless, lost, friendless and with nothing to fall back on except the memory of her own illusions. The cruelest lesson for this woman was that for so many years her true self, the self that could have risen up and given her richness, was repressed in the mindless striving after what appeared to be the glitter of this world. Only with the tragic death of her mother did she start to look at her own life that had been dying all along.

In work, just as in love, Pisces cannot go against its own nature if it is to experience authentic power, the power that quietly breathes but is never stated. For Pisces to be most powerful it must maintain its intrinsic purity and not be corrupted by the appearances of this world. The Pisces who transcends immature, extraneous, self-inflated tactics and who is pure of heart and mind will become powerful. Whatever direction this power takes, it will dictate the future, and from there a unique, joy-filled pathway will unfold.

Powerful Pisces Psychology

Let my soul smile through my heart and let my heart smile through my eyes.

—Paramahansa Yogananda

At your best, your mind is like a beautiful garden in bloom. There is great abundance to the Pisces nature. It pulses with inspiration, possibility and transcendence. Through your vision and purified heart, you are capable of creating miracles.

But first you must fly. Fly above your small persona into your divine self. Soar above the clouds and look all around you. You are the one with the space and the space is limitless. This is your soul and you breathe its divine light.

In everything you do, let your mind feed the God within you. In every act you perform, perform it for the God within. Let laughter and joy ignite the energy of your own divinity. Reach out with your heart and heal the darkness of all who surround you. As you face each day, give thanks for the beatific powers of your own soul.

Your soul is your guide and your light. Listen to its voice and allow it to lead you to the experiences you must have to grow into your own light. At your most elevated, you are the power of divine love. Through this, you are a vehicle of the highest Source and your legacy is joy, magic, love and deep inner freedom.

Go within to touch the Source. Contemplate it. Dwell on it. Let it begin your day and let each day be a fresh encounter with the mystery and power of the divine.

Maximizing Your Pisces Power Potential

There is a place deep inside of you that will always remain mysterious. It longs for a transcendent connection to take hold and guide you to those experiences that are ablaze with higher meaning and import. These experiences, in which you see your soul reflected back, verify your existence and your sense of possibility. At once, there is the throbbing sense of unity and elevation. From this perspective, life reveals its color and its magic. Likewise, the feeling of love, urgent and overpowering, swells from your depths like the chords of a majestic hymn as you feel yourself rising and expanding in the beauty of the moment, connected to a vast, limitless beyond. This vision is your power and your legacy to claim. You can create a space within that brings you there.

Your mind must be in a state of receiving, and this can be done through meditation. Meditation allows you to enter the realm of the superconscious, a vast and limitless source of meaning and the locus of power, wisdom and understanding. With regular meditation, you will begin to notice changes in yourself that will lighten your mind and heart. Negative people and experiences will drop away to be replaced by people of a higher vibration, a vibration that reflects your own. The quality of your connections will deepen and become enriched, and you will have a positive sense of the unexpected, a sense of magic, synchronicity and metaphor coming to bear upon your life. Change will herald possibility. Endings will offer their own meaning. And more and more, you will have a subtle, wordless sense of connection to all things.

Meditation cleanses your mind like a cloth wiping

away film. There are layers of film within each of us based on our negative attitudes, illusions and delusions. On these, we base our reality, our choices, our desires. So often, these melt into our needs—so many of our needs are based on illusions. They bring us unhappiness. They bring us away from the higher, more radiant aspects of ourselves. In order to find true well-being, in order to discover the power and glory of ourselves, we must return to ourselves and begin the journey within. We must discover and unfold through the light of consciousness. Only the light of consciousness will bring the experience of unity and love that is all-pervasive.

There are many different kinds of meditation. Meditation is a technique, and therefore the specific kind employed is less important than the consistency of use. However, I include one meditation here which I find to be particularly inspiring.

In a quiet room in which you feel an emotional affinity, begin by concentrating on your breaths. In and out, rhythmically rising and falling, bring your consciousness to the tip of your nose and allow all of your worries, concerns and preoccupations to flow out through your nostrils. Once you have attained a state of relaxation, say the following words:

> **I direct my thoughts to my inner being and I ask for the grace to experience my true nature, the God within me, the Source of joy and love. I am a being of love. I am light. I am one with the great Source referred to as God. Deep within myself, I know this peace and feel the unity of creation as it extends all around me. I enter the silence deep within as I utter God's name to elevate my mind.**

With eyes closed, mentally repeat the name of God, whether it be Jesus, Jehovah, Buddha, Om, Rama, or any other. Use a word with which you feel comfortable, and for about ten or fifteen minutes, invest your entire being in the sound of the word.

Now say:

With awe and love for the divine within me, I now take a moment to visualize myself happy and in a state of peace and love. On a daily basis I will have the power to love myself and others more. I will be less critical and self-critical. I will use my heart to look and I will see, more and more, the beauty in others, and as I grow stronger through wisdom, I will find joy in bringing out their strengths. May I perceive, dear God, this sense of unity with you and with others, regardless of their differences, and may I use this power of well-being in all that I do.

This meditation, done daily, will bring you to the Source of power which will guide you, aid you and elevate you to the most powerful experience of yourself, freed from yearning, fully aware of that which you can become.

Notes

INTRODUCTION

1. Carlos Casteneda, Tales of Power (New York: Simon and Schuster, 1974), p. 8.

ARIES

1. Goethe, Faust Part One (England: Penguin, 1949 ed.), p. 82.

TAURUS

1. J. C. Cooper, Taoism (England: The Aquarian Press, 1972), p. 48, 49.

CANCER

1. Nathaniel Branden, Honoring the Self (New York: Bantam, 1985), p. 123.
2. Walt Anderson, Open Secrets (New York: Penguin, 1980), p. 65.

SCORPIO

1. Bhagwan Shree Rajneesh, Tantra: The Supreme Understanding (Oregon: The Rajneesh Foundation International, 1975), p. 145.
2. Carlos Casteneda, Tales of Power (New York: Simon and Schuster, 1974), p. 8.

SAGITTARIUS

1. Op. Cit., p. 23.

CAPRICORN

1. Carl Jung, Psychology and the East (Princeton: XX, the Bollingen Series, 1978), p. 185.